THE
TRUTH ABOUT
ORGANIC
FOODS

ALEX A. AVERY

Published by Henderson Communications L.L.C.
1422 Elbridge Payne Road, #250
Chesterfield, MO 63017

ISBN-13 978-0-9788952-0-4
ISBN-10 0-9788952-0-7

For more information, or to order, go to:
www.TheTruthAboutOrganicFoods.org

Printed in the United States of America.

About the Cover
Cover photo by Steve Brotzman
Cover design by Alex, Jakki, Sharon and Cheryl

Acknowledgements

First and foremost, I thank my father, Dennis Avery, for nurturing my inquisitive nature and encouraging me from an early age to pursue my love of science and the truth. He is the reason I have followed this career path and had so much fun in the process. I also thank my wife for her unflagging support and patience throughout the writing process, as well as her tough and wonderfully honest opinions as the manuscript progressed. I owe Anne and Alice for their editorial advice and administrative support. And finally, for all the wonderful farmers and farm families that I have met and gotten to know over the past 12 years, thank you for sharing your lives with me.

Table of Contents

Foreword

In the last few decades, there has been a growing mistrust of science and technology in the United States. This mistrust is exemplified by parents avoiding proven technologies like vaccinations, and a turn away from mainstream medicine to embrace supposedly "alternative" types of treatment that are "more natural." Nowhere is this rejection more apparent than in the realm of food and nutrition.

Organic foods are hot now — they constitute the fastest growing segment of the food industry — and food purveyors from Whole Foods to Wal-Mart are trying to capture part of this burgeoning market. Why the increased popularity? It seems to be a given in many people's minds that organic foods are somehow "better" than the conventional variety.

Consumers buy organic foods for many reasons—they may consider that organic foods are a) more nutritious, b) safer because no pesticides are used on them, c) safer because no hormones, antibiotics or biotechnology are used in their production, d) "more natural" because they can't be irradiated, e) better for the environment, and/or f) organic agriculture will save the family farm. Any one of these reasons will suffice for the organic food adherent — but as Alex Avery convincingly demonstrates in "The Truth About Organic Foods," none of these supposed benefits are real.

As he explains, much of the impetus behind the whole food/organic food movement derives from the myth that in the past, when most of American society was agrarian, our children were healthy, our lives and health were better and longer than they are today, our food was more nutritious, and our soils were chock full of all the nutrients required for healthy agriculture. And supposedly the major reason for these benefits was that our food was produced naturally — without synthetic fertilizers or pesticides — and consumed with minimal, if any, processing. But none of these assumptions are true—expected lifespan is much longer today than during the early 20th century, for example, and our food supply is more diverse, abundant and safer than it has ever been. Further, in spite of their supposedly idyllic rural existence, many young men were excluded from the military during the early years of World War II because of nutritional deficiencies and related illnesses. These were so widespread that the government set up the first national nutritional guidelines (now known as the RDAs or Recommended Dietary Allowances) to help improve Americans' nutritional status.

Mr. Avery traces the roots of the organic movement back to the early days of modern agriculture, to a time when there was no other choice, and shows how modern technology — beginning with the first successful industrial production of ammonia-based fertilizers — transfigured the agricultural landscape, and improved the food supply as well as farmers' lives. But there were always nay-sayers—people like Rudolf Steiner who claimed that some foods could transmit benefits to specific parts of the body — that fruits, for example, were important because of the protein they provided to the gastrointestinal tract. Today, of course, we know that fruits are poor sources of protein for any part of the body. They provide many other nutrients, but proteins are better derived from other classes of food. Still, Rudolf Steiner had and has his followers, and although modern chemistry and technology have vastly changed the agricultural landscape, old myths die hard, and new ones are constantly arising.

The great contribution that "The Truth About Organic Foods" makes to the literature is not just that it exposes organic industry marketing myths, but that Mr. Avery explains in clear and non-technical prose why these myths are not, indeed cannot, be true. Most of us, in our modern urban and suburban enclaves, know next to nothing about how our food is produced or where it comes from. This ignorance makes us easy marks for activists who claim to have special insights into the right and proper way to farm, to eat, and to live. Most chapters of "The Truth About Organic Food" begin with statements by organic food proponents, and follows with rational statements from scientists who have the expertise to know better. Further, Mr. Avery explains why the organic proponents' statements are misleading or just plain wrong — not as a matter of opinion, but as a matter of scientific fact.

Organic fruits and vegetables have lower pesticide residues — according to the Organic Trade Association, for example. Well, yes, some of them do have lower levels of synthetic pesticides than their conventionally grown counterparts. However, as Mr. Avery points out, since the levels of these pesticide residues are typically on the order of parts per billion (think one second in 32 years), they do not really threaten consumers' health. Further, those are just the synthetic pesticides — no one is talking about (or measuring, apparently) those pesticides that are approved for organic agriculture (yes, even organic gardeners must fight off plant predators somehow). Some of these, such as the fish poison rotenone, are indeed not healthy for human consumption, or compounds you'd want to have leaching into the groundwater.

In spite of his insistence on telling the truth about organic foods and agriculture, Mr. Avery is not trying to discourage consumers from buying or eating organic foods. His point is that consumers have the right to know what the truth is about these products, and the right to make an informed decision. A very pleasant and enlightening means of obtaining the necessary information is to read "The Truth About Organic Food." It just may make you think twice before spending more to buy foods that are really no better than conventional ones.

Ruth Kava, Ph.D., R.D.
Director of Nutrition
The American Council on Science and Health
New York, NY

The Myth of the Organic Utopia

What is the "organic utopia"? Is it just a caricature that I've created so that I can easily debunk it? No, it really exists. The leaders and followers of the organic movement truly believe there is a wondrous organic utopia waiting for us, complete with perfect children and frolicking deer and antelope, if we will be "wise" enough to farm the way they say we should.

I've heard speakers at organic farming conferences discuss the waiting organic utopia. I've read about it in numerous organic publications. One of the best examples appeared in the August 2004 edition of *Acres USA*, a monthly publication that bills itself as "a voice for eco-agriculture." It contained an article adapted from the keynote address to the 2003 *Acres USA* conference by Sally Fallon, president of the Weston A. Price Foundation, an activist group that promotes raw (unpasteurized) milk consumption and organic farming. This is Ms. Fallon's vision of the organic utopia:

> ***Raw-Milk Economics.*** *You have two cows, not genetically manipulated and produced through natural breeding, who feed on fertile green pastures and produce delicious high-fat milk. They are*

cheerfully milked by your round-faced children with naturally straight teeth and wearing pure cotton clothes, colored with natural dyes and produced in the nearby town. The cows give birth to calves every year, and soon you have a herd of 30 cows, all producing delicious, healthy milk.

Out-of-work orthodontists gather up the manure in the milking shed and distribute it on your pasture, in which happy chickens run around, turning over cow paddies and eating bugs to produce nutrient-rich eggs.

You make naturally yellow butter and delicious cheese. You feed the whey and skim milk to your small herd of hogs, which they thoughtfully turn into bacon and lard for cooking.

Reformed FDA officials help you make lacto-fermented juice from the fruit grown in your orchards and pickles and chutneys from your garden produce. All these products you provide in your on-farm store to farm shareholders, many of whom are grateful survivors from the low-fat era. You make more money than you can possibly spend on your family and so donate to local schools, theaters, symphony orchestras or opera companies. You also build a nice house on another part of your farm where another family lives, and you pay this family handsomely to help with the work. That in turn allows you to take a big vacation twice a year and learn how people live in other parts of the world. Missionary groups teach raw-milk economics to people living in other countries, and every year two foreign exchange students come to help out on the farm.

Soon we have 200,000 farms, all producing raw-milk products and providing them in on-farm stores or by home delivery. These farms create an explosion of prosperity at the local level. Small towns revive, and along with them, small businesses. Every town produces a distinctive lacto-fermented soft drink, and every town supports several great restaurants. Fast food places transfer into local hands; new owners cook french fries in tallow or lard. Unemployment disappears, and everybody makes a decent wage. No one uses pesticides on their farms, so the chemical companies close down that part of their operation. Many corporate employees are freed from the system and find better pay and more fulfilling work with local businesses or on farms.

It becomes more profitable to put land just outside cities and towns into dairy farms rather than houses. Towns and cities grow, while urban sprawl gives way to green spaces. Wealthy farmers and wealthy small businessmen put their money in local credit unions; the power of international banks wanes, and so does their influence in Washington.

This new wealth is real, so there is no longer any need to wage war to keep the economy afloat. The health care crisis resolves, and inner-city hospitals are torn down and replaced with inner-city dairy farms, supplying fresh milk to resident families. School lunch programs feature raw milk and products of local farms. Because children are now eating real food, their brains get wired properly; they are filled with curiosity and learn easily; teaching becomes a joyous profession once again. Happy, well-nourished children contribute to an artistic flowering — music, painting, literature, dance, and dramatic arts flourish.

Eventually, there are 200 million people drinking raw milk. And all of them live happily ever after.

Ms. Fallon's organic utopia fittingly ends with the words "happily ever after," because the whole thing is truly a fairy tale. It's a romanticized glorification of the agrarian economy of 1840 that bears no resemblance to historical reality. For all the talk of round-faced children cheerfully milking the cows, farming with or without modern inputs requires long hours of hard, monotonous work. Dairy farming demands milking cows two or three times per day, seven days per week, 365 days a year. Crop farming involves spending hours on a tractor in the hot sun or stoop labor weeding vegetable crops by hand or with a hoe. Cows, crops, pests, and weeds don't take vacations.

Farming is also dangerous. Each year, roughly 100 children and adolescents die from farm injuries, with another 22,000 injured in the U.S. alone!

The inherently hard and risky work of farming is a major reason why so many people left the farm and moved to cities as soon as mechanization reduced the necessity for hand labor at the start of the 20th century. Unlike farmers, most "city workers" leave work at 5 p.m. They get their weekends off. They have broader cultural opportunities. And organic farming is inherently harder than conventional farming because of the restrictions on the technologies allowed.

While this particular organic utopian fantasy centers around raw organic milk, it is the same basic organic utopia I've heard before: the rebirth of small farms and their associated small communities, the return of incredible natural health, the ending of animal cruelty, the demise of multinational corporations, the flourishing of local small businesses and local manufacturing, the rebirth of rural communities, the end to urban sprawl and blight, renewed societal happiness, and new-found individual fulfillment from work and a simpler life, with full employment and living wages for all.

Nor is Ms. Fallon the first to predict an end to war as a result of an "organic restructuring" of global society.

But it's a pipe-dream to think we could enrich our nation and society by returning to an agrarian, rural-centered economy a la 1840. Ms. Fallon's utopia is dependent on people paying exorbitant farm-gate prices for milk, butter, and cream. By my calculations of her vision in the United States, Ms. Fallon expects consumers to spend $1.5 trillion per year — 8% of the annual U.S. Gross Domestic Product — on dairy foods alone. How does overspending on one food category increase the wealth and wellbeing of anyone other than the farmer?

Then there is the fantasy that eating organic foods would resolve "the health crisis" and our children's brains would be "wired properly," resulting in smart, easily teachable children who would excel in the performing arts.

In fact, while organic activists such as Ms. Fallon and the W. A. Price Foundation are claiming that raw organic milk is "critical for health," the FDA says drinking raw milk is "like playing Russian roulette with your health." Those are the agency's words, not mine. Raw milk can harbor a menagerie of disease-causing organisms, which is why mandatory pasteurization of milk was instituted in the U.S. starting in Chicago in 1908. Pasteurization of milk prevents the spread of tuberculosis, listeriosis, diphtheria, polio, salmonellosis, strep throat, scarlet fever, and typhoid fever.

Instead of acknowledging these dangerous realities, Ms. Fallon blusters right on past them, saying, "The day is coming when no conscientious couple will dream of starting a family until they have found a source of pure and healthy raw milk for their children … when no doctor will omit raw milk as part of his treatment; and when no government official will dare to impede access in any way to raw milk and other pure foods, which will come from small, local farms." In other words, more blind organic utopian fantasy.

Of course, most organic utopian thinking is less radical or transparent. Instead you'll find it scattered about in your everyday life as subtle suggestions that organic food is simply healthier, safer, more nutritious, and far better for the environment. Hardly ever are these rosy assessments questioned rigorously, nor is much evidence ever offered to support them.

As a result of the constant organic mantra and an uncritical, fawning press, I have watched increasing numbers of consumers come to believe in the organic utopia — at least in part. Perhaps they believe that organic foods are more nutritious (they're not), or are safer (they're not). Or they believe that organic farming is better for the earth or involves less cruelty to farm animals (wrong there too).

This increasing belief in "natural goodness" has moved beyond food and farming politics into many realms of our society, from medicine to manufacturing. As a result, the organic utopia has become a significant impediment to the further advancement of our society. It is now unfortunately blocking societal acceptance of better, more environmentally friendly, less costly alternative technologies such as agricultural biotechnology. Ag biotech has drastically cut farm use of pesticides and soil erosion, just as a start, yet organic utopianism and selfishness are serious impediments to the wider adoption of biotech crops.

Even worse, developing countries have adopted policies directly leading to the deaths of thousands of people based in large part on the activism and false vision of the organic utopians.

In 2002, organic activists convinced the president of the African nation of Zambia to reject shipments of U.S.-donated corn for famine relief based on claims that it was poisonous because some of the corn was from biotech-improved corn varieties. While Americans had been safely eating this corn for years, it was locked up and shipped out of the country. Thousands died from starvation and malnutrition, especially young children and infants.

The point is that the organic utopia is a myth, yet it is having real and serious impacts on people and society. In response, The Center for Global Food Issues decided several years ago that consumers deserve to hear the other, less flattering, and more scientifically grounded side of the organic food debate. We started writing articles debunking the exaggerated claims of organic proponents. We began highlighting critical shortcomings of organic farming methods. We pointed out to reporters that none of the professional food science organizations endorsed specifically eating organic foods or using only organic farming methods and that scientific studies have found no superiority in organic foods or farming methods.

The Center for Global Food Issues is not anti-organic. It is pro-human and pro-wildlife. We're pro-improvement and pro-ingenuity. Call us the world's best-informed non-believers in the organic religion. We don't buy into the rhetoric and hype surrounding organic and we think an objective look at the evidence indicates that extended beyond a small, niche clientele, organic farming would be worse for overall societal health and worse for wildlife habitat conservation because it takes significantly more land to produce each ton of food.

But that's different than being anti-organic. If people want to spend the money to buy organic food, that's fine. If farmers want to work harder and longer to produce food without the modern technologies that are now available, that's fine. That is what is so great about living in a free democracy; live and let live.

Organic farmers and activists unfortunately don't have the same live and let live philosophy. They promote themselves and their products by directly impugning the safety of non-organic foods and the ecological impacts of non-organic farming practices. Rather than simply saying, "Buy our products! They're great, you'll love them, and they're a good value," organic activists and marketers are constantly saying, "Buy our products because they won't kill you and your children and our farming methods won't trash the planet like those other guys'."

Marketing through product disparagement has long been part of the seamy underbelly of capitalism, but the organic industry has taken the art to new lows. And while some in the organic movement are motivated by belief, many are motivated by money. Take note of how many of the opening quotes in each chapter of this book are made by those with a financial stake in promoting organic foods. This profit motive is denoted by a ($) next to their identification throughout this book.

The media, always on the lookout for a good scare story, have found a steady fountain of fear among organic activists and like-minded environmental groups. These groups are often supported with donations from for-profit organic and "natural" product companies. In fact, environmental activists have made an entire industry out of demonizing modern agricultural practices and chemicals. The advice for consumers is always to "buy organic." The press and the average consumer rarely examine organic foods and farming practices with the same critical eye as they do non-organic. This is likely due to the automatic virtues assumed for organic because of its "pure and natural" aura. But natural isn't always better. After all, poison ivy, cholera, arsenic, and botulism are all natural.

All of this negative spin on non-organic farming and food has grown into a general societal unease about new agricultural developments and technologies as well as ever-tightening regulations on existing farming practices. The incredible promise of agricultural biotechnology — to produce safer, healthier food using less pesticides, less land, and less water, and in a more environmentally friendly way — has almost been stymied by the efforts of organic farming activists. Almost, but not quite, and as a result of biotech crops, U.S. farm pesticide use has declined by hundreds of thousands of pounds per year.

As a strong believer in these new farm technologies, I want to balance the debate. This book is an attempt at that balance. This book is NOT an anti-organic rant or a call for the banning of organic farming. Bans are the mechanism of choice for the organic movement — bans against synthetic fertilizers, synthetic pesticides, biotechnology, and anything else the organic community deems unnatural.

This book IS a look at some of the unflattering realities of organic food and farming that all too often never make it into magazine and newspaper articles. I also examine the differences between organic and non-organic farming methods and why it is that non-organic farmers choose to use the inputs and technologies that they do.

I use peer-reviewed scientific literature and other respected sources, such as the United Nations Food and Agriculture Organization, where appropriate and available to support my conclusions. However this book is not meant to be an exhaustive compilation of the scientific research in any given area. It has been written primarily for the average consumer, not Ph.D. students. I hope that all, however, including academics and scientists, find it interesting, educational, and sometimes even entertaining.

Alex A. Avery

Chapter 1:

The Strange, Romantic History of Organic Agriculture

How did the "organic movement" get started? Who started it, where and when? The answers are interesting and illuminate the somewhat absurd foundation for the entire organic philosophy.

It could be argued that organic farming is the default farming system of mankind and that food was "organic" for most of human history. After all, prior to the 20th century synthetic fertilizers and synthetic chemical pesticides simply didn't exist. But today's organic farming movement goes far beyond simply farming without the use of modern inputs; it's a belief system and a world view that crystallized at the dawn of the 20th century as a backlash against modern science.

Moreover, the roots of this anti-science backlash extend into the early 19th century, when arguments nearly identical to the current debate over "natural" versus "chemical" were raging within the scientific community.

In the 18th and early 19th centuries, it was thought that certain biologically associated chemicals couldn't be made in the laboratory. These biochemicals, such as the urea found in animal urine, were called "organic" because they were made by living organisms. In contrast, chemical compounds such as sodium chloride (table salt) that could be created in a lab by combining other chemicals were referred to as "inorganic."

The notion that certain chemicals could only be made by living creatures was at the core of "vitalism" — a scientific theory of life that was held by many scientists prior to the 20th century. Vitalism held that life arises from and involves special "life forces" that are apart from the purely physical/chemical realm. But the theory of vitalism was dealt a major blow in 1828 when a young scientist named Friedrich Wohler informed his teacher that he had made "urea without requiring a kidney of an animal, either man or dog." Wohler had accidentally made urea in the laboratory by heating inorganic salts together in a dish. As Wohler wrote, he had witnessed "the great tragedy of science, the slaying of a beautiful hypothesis by an ugly fact."

A fierce debate between vitalist and non-vitalist scientists ensued for the next 75 years. By the turn of the 20th century, vitalism was dead within the mainstream scientific community, having been replaced by our modern understanding of chemistry and biology.

The final nail in the coffin of vitalism was the successful synthesis of ammonia utilized for fertilizer on an industrial scale in 1909. This critically important technological feat was the spark that ignited the modern organic farming movement.

The man that would eventually fan that spark into a fire was an Austrian spiritualist/mystic named Rudolf Steiner (1861-1925). Steiner was a devoted vitalist who claimed that unseen "ethereal" and "astral" forces permeated the universe and were intimately tied to living creatures. Steiner taught his followers in the early 1920s that synthetic nitrogen fertilizers were "dead." Synthetic fertilizers did not possess critical "vital" forces, thus yielding "dead" food. Steiner recommended using only animal manures and crop rotation to fertilize fields. He taught his followers that the "new" food from synthetic fertilizers was spiritually and physically deficient and resulted in poor health. From Steiner's teachings in the early 1920s arose the modern organic farming movement.

Before we delve more deeply into the teachings of Steiner and how he inspired others to launch the modern organic movement, let's briefly trace the steps of agriculture from its beginnings roughly 10,000 years ago to the 20th century so you understand just how critically important synthetic nitrogen fertilizers are in feeding and clothing the modern world.

Farming is believed to have begun with the domestication of wild animals around 12,000 years ago — animals such as dogs, sheep, and goats. This process of animal domestication began the shift of mankind from being primarily hunter/gatherers to pastoralists, and eventually to farmers who tended crops as well. While these early animal keepers continued to hunt and gather, they were also looking for suitable pastures/foods for their animals and this restricted their travels to smaller regions. The more settled life of the pastoralists led to a shift from harvesting wild edible plants to the planting and cultivation of these plants near human settlements.

Over time, these man-collected and nurtured plants evolved to have characteristics more suitable for life among/with humans than to life in the wild. For example, they developed seeds that didn't drop off at the end of the season, staying on the plants so humans could pick them. Eventually, some of these plants became our modern crop varieties such as wheat (first domesticated in the Middle East and Europe), rice (in Asia), and corn, squash, and potatoes (in the Americas).

By 5,000 years ago, man had developed fairly sophisticated agronomic practices to grow and fertilize crops. Fertilization is important because without regular additions of nutrients to the soil, fields will quickly be depleted as nutrients are taken up by crops and removed with their harvest. The most important soil nutrient is nitrogen, but phosphorus, potassium, and more than a dozen other micronutrients like selenium and iron are also vital.

Early farmers dealt with the need to renew soil nutrients in a variety of ways. For example, the Egyptians farmed the frequently flooded lowlands along the Nile River and its extensive delta, where nutrient-rich silts from upstream were deposited on the fields during the annual floods. Other cultures raised grazing animals extensively on grasslands and pasture and collected the animal manure to fertilize grain and vegetable crops.

Where does the nitrogen in the upland silt and animal manure come from? Ultimately, it comes from the air we all breathe, which is 78% nitrogen. But the nitrogen in our air is chemically unavailable to all creatures except bacteria because it is in a di-nitrogen (N_2) form. Converting di-nitrogen into compounds usable by plants and animals is called "nitrogen fixation."

Bacteria are the only life forms naturally able to "fix" nitrogen. In fact, only 200 such types of bacteria have been identified. Some of these bacteria live in special root structures of a class of plants called legumes, which includes clover, alfalfa, soybeans, and about 20,000 other species, including some trees and shrubs. Nitrogen fixing bacteria live in root nodules, where they make nitrate (NO_3) from atmospheric nitrogen (N_2). The bacteria in the root nodules then exchange the nitrate they make for sugars manufactured by the plant. It's a classic symbiotic relationship between plant and bacteria.

In the Americas, native farmers developed cropping systems based on planting legumes such as beans alongside non-legume crops to fertilize them. The "three sisters" of Native American agriculture were corn, squash, and beans. The fixed nitrogen produced by the beans helped fertilize the corn and the squash.

History of Fertilizer

Since the beginning of agriculture, the most common organic fertilizer methods have been (1) recycling of animal manure, (2) growing legume crops alongside or in rotation with non-legumes — techniques recommended as early as 200 B.C. by the Romans, and (3) simply abandoning a field once it had been "exhausted," also known as letting a field "lie fallow."

Fallowing a field allows native wild legume plants to return and grow. Over time the legumes — via the symbiotic bacteria in their roots — will slowly rebuild fixed nitrogen levels in the soil that were depleted during the years that non-legume crops were grown. This is also the same basic concept behind the "slash-and-burn" agriculture practiced in parts of Africa, South America, and other tropical regions by landless peasants. The farmers "slash" down the vegetation in a section of tropical forest, the plant residues are then burned, and the nitrogen-rich ashes fertilize the nutrient-poor soils of the tropics. The farmers then get two to five years of crops before the soil nutrients (mostly nitrogen) are depleted. Then the farmers abandon the field and clear a new section of forest or bush land.[1]

Two hundred years ago, as human populations grew larger and farm land became scarcer, farmers found another way around the inherent limits on legume-based fertilization (i.e., the need for more land and animals): They began to borrow from the past instead of taking additional land from nature.

Starting in the early 1800s, farmers tapped into the huge deposits of nitrogen-rich bird droppings (guano) found on remote and coastal islands. Over

---

[1] In Africa, huge amounts of land have been brought into bush-fallow rotations at the expense of wildlife habitat because of population pressures brought on by the extension of modern medicine and basic hygiene during the 20th century. The population pressures have also caused fallow periods between crops to become shorter because of a shortage of arable land. The short fallow periods do not allow for full restoration of the soil's fertility, resulting in lower crop yields. In turn, the low crop yields mean less crop residues, and other organic materials that are important for soil quality are returned to the soil, further degrading yields and sustainability. It has become a vicious downward spiral of lower crop yields, reduced soil fertility, and further degraded soil structure.

many centuries, seabird guano had accumulated on these uninhabited, rocky islands into massive deposits; some more than a hundred feet thick. Seabird guano is rich in nitrogen and also phosphorus due to the bird's steady diet of fish. These are the two most-needed plant nutrients, making seabird guano a very effective fertilizer.

Guano mining took off in the 1830s and principally served European and American farmers. Guano was dug by hand, often by convicts and native peoples. In Peru, where the richest and largest guano deposits were found (due to the very dry conditions along Peru's coast that preserved the guano for as long as 2,500 years), the industry has a notorious history. As Brian Fagan describes it in his book on the history of El Niño, while few Peruvians visited the guano islands off the coast, "They could not have avoided hearing stories of the horrors or seeing foreign laborers herded into crowded boats for a short voyage from which few returned. Across the water, hundreds of indentured laborers, convicts, army deserters, and coolies were worked to death, laboring twenty hours a day without respite under the eyes of ruthless supervisors and fierce dogs. They dug deep trenches into the hardened guano with picks and shovels, earning a few pesos for each ton they extracted. Dilapidated ships were moored alongside the precipitous cliffs. Gaunt, exhausted men tipped wheelbarrow loads of cemented bird droppings into filthy canvas chutes into the holds below. Mainlanders could see lung-clogging dust hovering over the island on still days as the toxic smell of ammonia filled the air. Blistered hands and cut legs turned septic. The sick and injured became wheelbarrow hands, coughing from chronic respiratory ailments or bent over with gastrointestinal disorders. Each morning a burial detail carried off the dead and interred them in shallow graves, where ravenous dogs dug up the corpses and gorged themselves on fresh meat. No one bothered to rebury the rotting bodies."[2]

Commercial mining of guano for fertilizer accelerated until the mid 19th century. During that time, there was a fierce rivalry between American and European interests. In 1856, the U.S. passed the Guano Island Act, which allowed businessmen to claim guano-rich islands as U.S. territories in an effort to keep down fertilizer prices for American farmers. Some 60 islands in the Pacific and Caribbean were claimed under the act, including the strategically important Midway and Johnston Atolls, which played key roles during the U.S. island-hopping campaign against Japan in WWII.

---

[2] Fagan, B. *Floods, Famines, and Emperors: El Niño and the Fate of Civilizations*, Basic Books, New York, NY, 1999.

By the late 1880s the once seemingly abundant guano fertilizer resource was running out. Peru alone had exported over 12 million tons of guano fertilizer to Europe and had extracted some 20 million tons in all.[3] The coastal islands had been exhausted and few new undiscovered islands remained.

With the depletion of the ancient guano deposits, humanity turned to the few known natural deposits of the mineral sodium nitrate, or Chile saltpeter ($NaNO_3$), in Chile's remote Atacama Desert. These natural nitrate deposits are limited, and their extraction and processing generate undesirable wastes. Their use on the farm also entails considerable risk of salt accumulating in the fields, thereby harming future crop growth. Chile saltpeter is still allowed for use by some organic farming groups, but the industry as a whole strongly discourages its use.

Given all of these technical and geopolitical problems with natural nitrogen fertilizers, the global search for a cheaper, more plentiful, and more sustainable source of nitrogen fertilizer became intense.

The First Synthetic Nitrogen Fertilizer

At the start of the 20th century, scientists knew that the air contained vast amounts of nitrogen and began searching for an industrial method of converting it to plant-usable fertilizer compounds.

The search ended in 1909 when German chemist Fritz Haber worked out the basics of an industrial method to "fix" atmospheric nitrogen chemically using heat and pressure.

With the help of his brother-in-law, chemist Carl Bosch at BASF Corporation, he developed a relatively cost-effective and efficient industrial process for turning atmospheric di-nitrogen into ammonia-based fertilizers. The method was dubbed the Haber-Bosch process and is still the basis for synthetic nitrogen fertilizer production today. The first industrial ammonia production factory was built in 1910. After WWI, the method was adopted extensively in Europe and North America to make "synthetic" nitrogen fertilizer.

The Haber-Bosch process is conceptually simple: Hydrogen (H), most often obtained from methane (CH_4) and water (H_2O), is purified and reacted with nitrogen from the air (N_2) to produce ammonia (NH_3). The carbon (C) from the methane is reacted with the remaining oxygen to form carbon monoxide (CO),

---

[3] Hudson, RA. *Peru: a country study*, 4th edition. Federal Research Division, Library of Congress, 1993.

thereby completing the reaction. In practice, it took considerable work to develop the right methods for efficient ammonia production, namely the right metal catalyst to encourage the reactions and the right temperatures and pressures. The process remains one of the most important scientific advances in human history.

Both Haber and Bosch were eventually awarded separate Nobel prizes for their work on this process, but the awards were highly controversial. This was because synthetic nitrogen is important not only for fertilizer. Fixed nitrogen compounds are also critical in the manufacture of explosives. The massive 7,000-pound fertilizer bomb used by Timothy McVeigh in 1995 to blow up the Federal Building in Oklahoma City was a mixture of ammonium nitrate fertilizer and diesel fuel.

Until the advent of the Haber-Bosch process, whoever controlled the distant mineral nitrate deposits controlled both the means to grow food and the materials with which to produce explosives and munitions. Without the Haber-Bosch process to synthesize ammonia, Germany would probably have run out of munitions by 1916, thereby ending World War I two years earlier than actually occurred. Nor would Germany have been able to produce the food and munitions needed to wage WWII.

We need to mention that Fritz Haber was also a major force behind the development of mustard and other poison gas weapons used in the first World War. He was the driving force behind the development of Zyclon B, the cyanide gas pellets used in German concentration camps to kill Jews, Russians, and other "undesirables" during WWII. This is an especially ironic turn, as Haber was a Jew and several of his own relatives eventually became victims of Zyclon B.

The development of the Haber-Bosch process rapidly changed fertilizer and farming economics. In 1913, Chile supplied an estimated 56% of the world's industrial nitrogen from its sodium nitrate deposits in the Atacama Desert. Synthetic nitrogen, in contrast, accounted for only 2% of the world's nitrogen needs. By 1934, however, sea bird guano and sodium nitrate minerals together supplied only 7% of the world's industrial nitrogen while synthetics accounted for 65%.

At last, humanity had found an inexhaustible and sustainable supply of fixed nitrogen for fertilizer. How inexhaustible? There are approximately 2 million tons of nitrogen in the atmosphere over every square mile of the earth's surface, totaling nearly 4 quadrillion tons of nitrogen in our atmosphere. And because the nitrogen that is synthetically converted into ammonia- and nitrate-based fertilizer eventually returns to the atmosphere as N_2 gas, it is literally an inexhaustible supply.

While much of the hydrogen for ammonia synthesis currently is obtained from methane (a.k.a. natural gas), it could theoretically come from any number of cheap and sustainable sources, such as water, sea water, or coal. The process can be driven with energy from virtually any source, including solar, wind, nuclear, geothermal, etc.

Today, synthetic nitrogen fertilizers supply more than half of all nitrogen used in agriculture — more than is supplied by nitrogen-fixing legume crops and manure combined.

Dr. Vaclav Smil, an agronomist at the University of Manitoba and an expert on nitrogen fertilizer production and the history of the Haber-Bosch process, writes:

"Only about half of the population of the late 1990s could be fed at the generally inadequate per capita level of 1900 diets without [synthetic nitrogen] fertilizer. And if we were to provide the average 1995 per capita food supply with the 1900 level of agricultural productivity, we could feed only about 2.4 billion people, or just 40% of today's total."[4]

Thus, 60% of all humans alive today owe their existence and survival to synthetic nitrogen fertilizer. In turn, a significant amount of the world's remaining wildlife habitat also owes its existence and survival to synthetic nitrogen. Without it, far more land would have been cleared for animal forage or legume crops to make up the fixed nitrogen shortfall. The two go hand in hand.

Organic Origins in Synthetic Fertilizer

As mentioned, the invention of synthetic nitrogen fertilizer (and modern chemistry in general) created a backlash among "vitalist" thinkers and romantics. The manufacture of ammonia via synthetic chemistry was the exclamation point on discrediting vitalist beliefs and theories, much as Galileo had overturned the earth-centric view of the universe in the 15th century. Some were simply unable to accept the new reality.

One of the most ardent vitalists — and the man whose teachings ultimately launched the modern organic farming movement — was Rudolf Steiner. Born in Croatia in 1861, Steiner grew up in Austria as the son of a railway sta-

---

[4] Smil, V. *Enriching the Earth: Fritz Haber, Carl Bosch, and the Transformation of World Food Production.* Cambridge, MA: MIT Press, 2001.

tion manager. As a child, Steiner, a good student who excelled academically, professed to be clairvoyant and to be able to follow the "further journeys" of those who had died.

Steiner studied the work of Goethe in college, the German playwright, romantic philosopher, and amateur scientist who has often been called the "father of vitalism." Goethe believed that all that is physically seen and sensed in the world is a mere reflection of the spiritual world. Steiner endeavored to extend Goethe's "experiential" science and created his own philosophy, which he called anthroposophy — literally "man-body-knowledge." Anthroposophy holds that, through training, one can be taught to "see" and "sense" the non-physical, spiritual world that surrounds us and that this world is at least as important to our health and wellbeing as the world revealed through conventional science.

Steiner was incredibly arrogant, but he was also extremely prolific and charismatic. Before his death in 1925, Steiner gave over 6,000 lectures on topics ranging from nutrition, medicine, and homeopathy to the arts and theology. He edited numerous respected intellectual magazines, wrote several plays, and was an avid architect. He even created a new type of school for the children of the Waldorf Astoria company's factory workers that emphasized hands-on learning, art, music, and physical activities (eurhythmy). Even today there are hundreds of "Waldorf Schools" throughout the world that continue to follow Steiner's teaching philosophy.

Steiner claimed that certain foods transmitted their "forces" to specific parts of the body. For example, root crops such as carrots were supposed to be particularly good for the head.

Steiner stated that "the human being starts to be an earth-man in the womb; he has at first almost nothing but a head. He begins with his head. ... And the head particularly needs minerals. For it is from the head that the forces go out that fill the human body with bones, for instance. Everything that makes a human being solid is a result of the way the head has been formed. ... You can see from this that we need roots. They are related to the earth and contain minerals. We need the minerals for bone-building. Bones consist of calcium carbonate, calcium phosphate; those are minerals. So you can see that the human being needs roots in order to strengthen his head."

According to Steiner, leafy greens were good for the heart and lungs — important primarily for their "forces" rather than their nutritional content. Steiner taught that fruit was critical for the protein it provided to nourish the digestive organs. As Steiner put it, "When I eat roots, their minerals go up into my head. When I eat salad greens, their forces go to my chest, lungs, and heart — not their fats, but the forces from their fats. When I eat fruit, the protein from the fruit stays in the intestines. And the protein from animal substances goes beyond the intestines into the body; animal protein spreads out."

Steiner's beliefs about nutrition relate directly to his agricultural beliefs. In an early-1924 lecture on human nutrition, Steiner hinted at his farming beliefs (and his belief that synthetic nitrogen fertilizers produced nutritionally inferior food):

> You can see that it is also a question of giving proper nourishment to the plants themselves. And that means we must realize that plants are living things; they are not minerals, they are something alive. A plant comes to us out of the seed we put in the ground. The plant cannot flourish unless the soil itself is to some degree alive. And how do we make the soil alive? By manuring it properly. Yes, proper manuring is what will give us really good plant protein.
>
> We must remember that for long, long ages men have known that the right manure is what comes out of the horses' stalls, out of the cow-barn and so on; the right manure is what comes off the farm itself. In recent times when everything has become materialistic, people have been saying: Look here! We can do it much more easily by finding out what substances are in the manure and then taking them out of the mineral kingdom: mineral fertilizer!
>
> And you can see, gentlemen, when one uses mineral fertilizer, it is as if one just put minerals into the ground; then only the root becomes strong. Then we get from the plants the substance that helps to build up our bones. But we don't get a proper protein from the plants. And the plants, our field grains, have suffered from the lack of protein for a long time. And the lack will become greater and greater unless people return to proper manuring.
>
> There have already been agricultural conferences in which the farmers have said: Yes, the fruit gets worse and worse! And it is true. But naturally the farmers haven't known the reason. Every older person knows that when he was a young fellow, everything that came out of the fields was really better. It's no use thinking that one can make fertilizer simply by combining substances that are present in cow manure. One must see clearly that cow manure does not come out of a chemist's laboratory but out of a laboratory that is far more scien-

tific — it comes from the far, far more scientific laboratory inside the cow. And for this reason cow manure is the stuff that not only makes the roots of plants strong, but that works up powerfully into the fruits and produces good, proper protein in the plants which makes man vigorous.

If there is to be nothing but the mineral fertilizer that has now become so popular, or just nitrogen from the air — well, gentlemen, your children, more particularly your grandchildren, will have very pale faces. You will no longer see a difference between their faces and their white hands. Human beings have a lively, healthy color when the farmlands are properly manured.

This, in a nutshell, was the New Age spark that lit the organic farming movement. Synthetic "mineral" fertilizers produced food that lacked the "vital" forces imparted to them from animal manure. The resulting food lacked "proper protein."

Steiner's first lectures specifically on farming, in which he laid the foundations for what would become "biodynamic" farming, were given in June of 1924. Though he died in 1925, just nine months after this series of lectures, his followers took his claims as gospel and ran with them. His farming lectures were published posthumously in 1929 under the title "Spiritual Basis for the Improvement of Agriculture."[5]

Here are just a few of Steiner's agricultural teachings.

According to Steiner, the earth contains "forces which come not from the Earth but from the so-called distant planets, the planets beyond the sun — Mars, Jupiter and Saturn." These forces influence "the life of plants ... and awakens the senses of the plant-being in such a way as to receive from all quarters of the Universe the forces which are molded by these distant planets."

"Have you ever thought why cows have *horns*, or why certain animals have *antlers*? ... The cow has horns in order to send into itself the astral-ethereal formative powers, which, pressing inward, are meant to penetrate right into the digestive organism. ... Thus in the horn you have something well adapted by its inherent nature to ray back the living and astral properties into the inner life."

According to Steiner, manure has special cosmic properties as well. "What is farm-yard-manure? ... it has been inside the organism and has thus been

[5] Steiner, R. *Geisteswissenschaftliche Grundlagen zum Gedeihen der Landwirtschaft.* R. Steiner-Nachlassverwaltung, Dornach, 1929.

permeated with an astral and ethereal content. In the dung, therefore, we have before us something ethereal and astral. For this reason it has a life-giving and also astralising influence upon the soil."

Steiner claims that the best way to improve a farm is to add more "living forces" to manure. "The living forces are far more important for the plant than the mere substance-forces or substances."

How do you do that? By burying a handful of manure inside a cow's horn for a year. "You see, by burying the horn with its filling of manure, we preserve in the horn the forces it was accustomed to exert within the cow itself ... all the radiations that tend to etherealize and astralise are poured into the inner hollow of the horn. And the manure inside the horn is inwardly quickened with these forces, which thus gather up and attract from the surrounding earth all that is ethereal and life-giving."

Steiner also suggests taking the "same part of the [yarrow plant] that is medicinally used ... and sew it up in the bladder of a stag. ... Now hang it up throughout the summer in a place exposed as far as possible to the sunshine. When autumn comes, take it down again and bury it not very deep in the earth throughout the winter." Steiner claims that by adding this to a pile of manure, you will "re-endow the manure with the power, so to quicken the earth that the more distant cosmic substances ... are caught up and received."

Got problems with plant diseases? Bury oak bark in an animal skull, "the skull of any of our domestic animals will do, it makes little or no difference. We put the chopped-up oak bark in the skull, close it up again ... and lower it into the earth, but not too deep." After a year, it's ready. "What you add to your manuring matter from the resulting mass will lend it the forces, prophylactically to combat or to arrest any harmful plant diseases."

Are field mice eating your harvest? "Catch a young mouse and skin it ... at the time when Venus is in Scorpio, you obtain the skin of the mouse and burn it. Carefully collect the ash and other constituents ... and sprinkle it over your fields ... you will find this an excellent remedy. Henceforth, your mice will avoid the field."

Steiner's cosmic fantasies almost seem like a caricature. After magical fertility potions brewed using cow horns, stag bladders, and intestines, all that seems to be missing is eye of newt and tongue of frog for the fairytale cartoon to be complete.

Steiner admits how absurd this sounds. "I know perfectly well, all this may seem utterly mad. I only ask you to remember how many things have seemed utterly mad, which have nonetheless been introduced a few years later."

Steiner then offers Swiss mountain railways as an example of something "mad" that was later successfully introduced. But engineering a railroad in the Swiss Alps is hardly the same as believing in invisible cosmic forces concentrated by animal skulls and entrails.

For those who would like to read more of Steiner's farming advice and concoctions, an expanded appendix at the back of the book containing lengthy excerpts from Steiner's lectures is included. It is a thoroughly amusing read.

Amazingly, Steiner's "unusual" theories and potions are dutifully adhered to by a surprising number of followers. Today they call themselves "biodynamic" farmers and have grower associations, certification bodies, and devoted customers around the world. There is even a line of "biodynamic" cosmetics. You're likely to find them in most upscale supermarkets in any major city in the Western world. Just look for anything with the "Demeter" or "biodynamic" label.

Sadly, most people who buy "biodynamic" or "Demeter-certified" foods have no idea about the radically weird notions and philosophy behind the label. They simply accept without question the claims that biodynamic farming works "with the health-giving forces of nature" and that it is a so-called "ecological" farming system.

Not long after Steiner's followers published his lectures and began spreading his gospel, another anti-synthetic fertilizer advocate came onto the scene. Sir Albert Howard, a British botanist who worked with farmers in rural India — at the time a British colony — observed and refined farm waste composting techniques for maintaining soil fertility. Howard eventually wrote a book on the topic, published in 1940 under the title *An Agricultural Testament.*[6]

Howard considered crop diseases as symptoms of poor crop nutrition and, hence, poor soil stewardship. Like Steiner, Howard believed that synthetic nitrogen fertilizers — or as he called them, "artificial manures" — produced only illusory increases in yield and resulted in nutritionally deficient food. He claimed the crop and livestock diseases and human health problems increased rapidly after the advent of "artificial manures." Howard couched all of these claims as hypotheses for future study, but most of his readers took them as verified facts rather than theory.

For example, Howard claimed that the people of northern India were far healthier than those in the South, East, and West and that this was due not to their diet so much as to their excellent farming that produced healthier food. As Howard stated, "the very remarkable health and physique enjoyed by the Hunza

---

[6] Howard, A. *An Agricultural Testament.* Oxford University Press, London UK, 1940.

hillmen appears to be due to the efficiency of their ancient system of farming."

He disdained the simple-minded thinking of "laboratory hermits" (his name for chemists and other scientists) and extolled the virtues of "natural" farming. He firmly believed that farmland could not be maintained indefinitely through synthetic nitrogen fertilizers. As he states in his chapter on soil fertility and national health, "when the natural produce of sea and soil has escaped the attention of agricultural science and the various food preservation processes, it would seem that health results and that there is a marked absence of disease. ... With the introduction of [synthetic fertilizers] there has been a continuous increase in disease, both in crops and in livestock."

Howard concluded one chapter of his 1940 book with this passage, which could be easily confused with the writing of any of a number of today's organic activist groups:

> *In allowing science to be used to wring the last ounce from the soil by new varieties of crops, cheaper and more stimulating manures, deeper and more thorough cultivating machines, hens which lay themselves to death, and cows which perish in an ocean of milk, something more than a want of judgment on the part of the organization is involved. Agricultural research has been misused to make the farmer, not a better producer of food, but a more expert bandit. He has been taught how to profiteer at the expense of posterity — how to transfer capital in the shape of soil fertility and the reserves of his livestock to his profit and loss account. In business, such practices end in bankruptcy; in agricultural research they lead to temporary success. All goes well as long as the soil can be made to yield a crop. But soil fertility does not last forever; eventually the land is worn out; real farming dies.*

Howard followed his first book with another in 1945, *Farming and Gardening for Health or Disease.*[7]

Sir Howard's books, especially his claims that human health declined after the widespread use of synthetic fertilizers (citing a "Medical Testament" from a group of doctors published in 1939), were a major factor in the rise of a dedicated organic farming/food movement. Howard's books and writings greatly influenced two other organic pioneers: Lady Eve Balfour in England and J. I. Rodale in the U.S. Both of these individuals would propel organic farming to

---

[7] Howard, A. *Farming and Gardening for Health or Disease* (The Soil and Health). Faber and Faber, London, 1945.

the next level following WWII.

Lady Eve Balfour was the wealthy niece of a former British prime minister and a boutique farmer. She studied agriculture at the University of Reading and began farming after inheriting her father's estate at Haughley in 1919. Her interest in an "ecological" approach to farming began in the 1930s, after she heard others extol the virtues of natural food. This was a very fashionable topic among the intellectual elite of the day. No doubt, this was the result of the previous advocacy work of Steiner and Howard, along with other vitalist romantics. In fact, Sir Howard's book from 1940 (and the "research" it was based upon) formed the essential foundation of Lady Balfour's beliefs. In 1939 she started an experiment on her farm and a neighboring farm, which she purchased to form the now-larger "Haughley Estate." The purpose of the research was, as she later put it, to "fill the gap in the evidence on which the claims for the benefits of organic husbandry were based."

The "Haughley Experiment" compared the products of "organic" farming on half of the farm with "conventional" products grown on the other half. The "Haughley Experiment" continued from 1940 through the early 1970s. However, Lady Balfour didn't wait for results before claiming she had "proof" of organic food's nutritional superiority. In 1943 she published *The Living Soil and the Haughley Experiment*.[8]

From WWII through the 1970s, Balfour was a leader of the British and European organic movements. She continued to host long-running "experiments" on her farm in an effort to prove that organic foods were more nutritious. She helped found the Soil Association, today the largest organic trade and certification group in the UK. She also helped start the International Federation of Organic Agriculture Movements (IFOAM), the main international organic lobby group.

Despite her early claims and the expressed purpose of the Haughley Experiment, Balfour admitted in 1977 at an IFOAM conference that after more than 30 years of research she could find no nutritional differences between organic and conventional products. As she put it, "The many different chemical analyses, carried out on crops and livestock products, revealed no consistent or significant differences between the sections." She nonetheless claimed victory, saying "this lack of difference was in itself significant in that on the organic section, receiving no added minerals, the analysis of soil

---

[8] Balfour, E. *The Living Soil and the Haughley Experiment.* Faber and Faber, London, 1943.

and crops showed a nutrient status that remained consistently as high as that of the others."

Balfour's address to the 1977 IFOAM conference also reveals that Steiner's beliefs were still at the core of the organic farming movement 50 years later. Balfour reassured her audience that just because they couldn't find any nutritional differences between organic and conventional foods, that didn't mean that organic wasn't still superior. She told them, "Inorganic chemicals are inert. A food-chain is not only a material circuit, but also an energy circuit. Soil fertility has been defined as the capacity of soil to receive, store, and transmit energy. A substance may be the same chemically but very different as a conductor of living energy. The hypothesis is that the energy manifesting in birth, growth, reproduction, death, decay, and rebirth can only flow through channels composed of living cells, and that when the flow is interrupted by inert matter it can be short-circuited with consequent damage to some part of the food-chain, not necessarily where the block occurred. The [Steiner-founded Anthroposophical Society's] Research establishment at Dornach in [Switzerland] has provided some evidence in support of such a view."

At the same time that Lady Balfour was championing organic farming in the UK, J.I. Rodale began championing organic farming in the U.S. In fact, Rodale was the first person to actually use the term "organic" when describing food grown without synthetic fertilizers. He launched *Organic Farming and Gardening* magazine in 1942 and also published *Pay Dirt*, a book with an Introduction written by Sir Howard. In 1946, Rodale published *The Organic Front,* further attacking chemical fertilizers and to respond to a growing number of scientist critics. One chapter was, in fact, titled "The Dangers of Chemical Fertilizers."

What is most remarkable about the work of both Balfour and Rodale is the unquestioned acceptance of Howard's claims that the nutritional content of food had markedly declined with the advent of synthetic fertilizer and that crops and livestock were mostly free of disease and nutritional ailments prior to the widespread use of synthetic fertilizers. It's a revisionist history that is simply amazing in its audacity. In fact, this is the same romantic lens through which Steiner viewed traditional farming.

For example, Rodale writes in *Pay Dirt*: "Old farmers who remember how their grandfathers grew crops often speak of their method of preserving all organic residues which originated on the farm. They will tell you of the fine crops and of the very little plant and animal disease and insect depredation."

Howard, Balfour, Rodale, and, of course, Steiner, all claimed without evidence that foods grown in manure are more healthful and/or nutritious than foods grown with synthetic fertilizer. This debate reached a high level as early as 1946, as illustrated by an editorial in the preeminent British medical journal *The Lancet* in June of that year. *The Lancet's* editors were responding to the unsubstantiated (and therefore unscientific) claims of organic farming promoters that their food was nutritionally superior. *The Lancet* editorial refers to the "somewhat emotional reaction against modern agricultural methods, particularly against the use of artificial fertilizers, which are supposed to ruin the land and the crops grown on it. Lately a number of societies have sprung up to advocate the wider use of compost, in place of artificial manures. All will sympathize with the desire of the reformers to achieve a stable agriculture and adequate health and nutrition for mankind, but it must be admitted that many of the statements made in preaching this new gospel are unacceptable both to the scientist and to the practical farmer."

And so it is today. Despite having the support of some of society's wealthiest patrons (Lady Balfour, Prince Charles, liberal foundations with billions of dollars in assets) and despite having researched the issue for over 60 years without successfully documenting any nutritional benefits, organic activists insist that today evidence is finally "emerging" that organic foods are more nutritious. This evidence has been "emerging" for nearly a century, yet it hasn't emerged enough to convince even a fraction of professional nutritionists. But that is the subject of Chapter 2.

Chapter 2:

Nutrition Notions

Organic Faithful Say:

"Organic food IS more nutritious, especially if fresh, and eating it is vital to good health; let those who claim otherwise try to prove their case! ... [According to physicians S. Davies and A. Stewart] 'the quality of (regular commercial) food is often so poor that the actual nutrient intake in terms of vitamins and minerals is inadequate and can produce disease.' ... The proof IS there! The odds favoring your having a long healthy life depend upon your following the organic food pathway."

Robert F. Heltman, Organic Food Is More Nutritious!
Townsend Letter for Doctors and Patients #172, p.12–13

"Petrochemical-based fertilizers supply only nitrogen, phosphorus, and potassium to the soil. Foods grown by organic methods, on the other hand, come from soil that has been replenished by the addition of organic materials rich in the full spectrum of minerals. Organically grown food is more healthful, not only because it is grown without poisons, but because it provides a complete range of minerals and other micronutrients."

John Robbins, author of Diet for a New America
May All Be Fed, p. 169

"Aside from pesticide contamination, conventional produce tends to have fewer nutrients than organic produce. On average, conventional produce has only 83% of the nutrients of organic produce. Studies have found significantly higher levels of nutrients such as vitamin C, iron, magnesium and phosphorus, and significantly less nitrates (a toxin) in organic crops."

Dr. Joseph Mercola with Rachel Droege, in Why Do You Need Organic Food?
http://www.mercola.com/2003/jul/23/organic_food.htm

Reality Says:

John Stossel: "Is [organic food] more nutritious?"
Katherine DiMatteo, director, Organic Trade Association: "It's as nutritious as any other product."
Stossel: "Is it more nutritious?"
DiMatteo: "It is as nutritious as any other product on the market."
Stossel: "There's a sales campaign to dream about."

Excerpt of interview between reporter John Stossel and Katherine DiMatteo,
executive director of the Organic Trade Association,
on ABC TV's 20/20, February 4, 2000

"I wish I could tell you that there is a clear, consistent nutritional difference between organic and conventional foods. Even better, I wish I could tell you that the difference is in favor of organic. Unfortunately, though, from my reading of the scientific literature, I do not believe such a claim can be responsibly made."

Dr. William Lockeretz, professor, School of Nutrition Science and Policy, Tufts University
Proceedings of the 5th International Federation of Organic Agriculture Movements
Conference on Trade in Organic Products, p. 49, 1997

"If people want to believe that the organic food has better nutritive value, it's up to them to make that foolish decision. But there's absolutely no research that shows that organic foods provide better nutrition."

Dr. Norman Borlaug, agronomist and 1970 Nobel Peace Prize laureate
Reason Magazine, April 2000
http://reason.com/0004/fe.rb.billions.shtml

"The [U.K.] Food Standards Agency considers that there is not enough information available at present to be able to say that organic foods are significantly different in terms of their safety and nutritional content to those produced by conventional farming. … From a nutritional point of view, the composition of individual foods is relatively unimportant. What matters is the nutrient content and overall balance of the diet as a whole. A varied and balanced diet which includes plenty of fruit, vegetables, and starchy foods should provide all of the nutrients that a healthy individual requires, regardless of whether the individual components are produced by organic or conventional methods."

UK Food Standards Agency
Food Standards Agency View on Organic Foods, April 2001
http://www.foodstandards.gov.uk/pdf_files/organicview.pdf

T he notion that organic food is more nutritious or healthful than "conventional" foods is the oldest of organic myths. While modern-day organic activists claim that organic is about "the environment" and curbing the environmental damage from "industrial" farming, the movement got its start largely on claims of greater nutrition, healthfulness, and wholesomeness. Remember from Chapter 1 that German mystic Rudolf Steiner inadvertently launched the organic farming movement when he lamented that crops grown with synthetic nitrogen fertilizer lack "vital energies." Nutrition remains one of the primary motivations of organic food buyers.

Fortunately, a considerable amount of research has been conducted on the nutrient content of organic vs. conventional foods over the last century and the bottom line is that there are no significant, consistent, or meaningful nutritional differences between organic and non-organic foods.

This fact is reflected in the "reality" statements above. Note that two of the three reality quotes come from dyed-in-the-wool organic supporters — the executive director of the Organic Trade Association and an unabashedly pro-organic nutrition professor speaking at an organic industry conference.

The official statement above is from the Food Standards Agency in the U.K., an agency chock full of highly trained government scientists. It is also echoed by official statements of the U.S. Department of Agriculture, also chock full of highly trained scientists. In 2000, USDA Secretary Dan Glickman said the following at the unveiling ceremony for the USDA's "Certified Organic" seal held at an upscale, organic supermarket in northern Virginia:

> *"Let me be clear about one other thing. The organic label is a marketing tool. It is not a statement about food safety. Nor is 'organic' a value judgment about nutrition or quality. Organic is about how it is produced. Just because something is labeled as organic does not mean it is superior, safer, or more healthy than conventional food. All foods in this country must meet the same high standards of safety regardless of their classification. For nutrition information, look at*

the nutrition label. And, as for quality, that's a matter of personal preference."

The Agricultural Marketing Service (AMS) within USDA is in charge of the National Organic Program, not the USDA's Food Safety Inspection Service or its Food and Nutrition Service.

Should Nutritional Differences Be Expected?

Since one of the major differences between organic and non-organic is the choice of pesticides used, it is reasonable to ask whether differences in pesticide residues on organic and non-organic foods are of nutritional consequence. Although much is made of organic farmers' rejection of synthetic pesticides, it is important to remember that organic standards allow the use of an array of chemical pesticides. However, residues of pesticides, either conventional or organic, are nutritionally inconsequential. For more on pesticides, see Chapters 5 and 6.

NUTRITIONAL ADVANTAGE TO NON-ORGANIC

There may be significant nutritional differences in organic and non-organic processed foods. Apparently, fewer organic processed foods are fortified with vitamins and minerals during processing than their non-organic counterparts. There are two examples of this, both relating to children's food.

Organic rules around the world essentially prohibit the fortification of foods with vitamins and minerals. As such, parents who feed their babies or children on an exclusively organic diet may be putting their kids at a significant nutritional disadvantage.

A good example is iron in baby food. Most baby foods are fortified with iron, which is essential for growth and development. Judy More, a U.K. pediatric dietician and former chair of the Pediatric Group of the British Dietetic Association, warns that babies eating exclusively organic baby food could get 20% less iron than babies eating non-organic, fortified baby food.[1]

An even better example of this can be found by comparing a common children's cereal with an organic version.

Nature's Path Foods makes EnviroKidz™ Organic GorillaMunch™ cereal. The organic GorillaMunch cereal is very similar to Kellogg's Corn Pops™. As you can see from the list of ingredients, both cereals are made from corn, sugar, and

---

[1] Martin, N. "Organic Baby Food 'Lacking in Nutrients'" *Daily Telegraph*, London, March 2, 2006.

What is important in nutrition is the content and bioavailability of nutrients in our food — i.e., carbohydrates, proteins, fats, vitamins, minerals, etc. The biggest factor affecting the amounts and quality of these food nutrients is adequate plant nutrients in the soil for healthy crops. Thus, how a crop is fertilized can play a role in the nutritional content of the food and many studies comparing conventional and organic foods have focused on fertilization and soil fertility properties.

First, there is a major misconception over so-called "synthetic fertilizers" when it comes to nutrition. John Robbins, author of *Diet for a New America* and *May All Be Fed*, illustrates this misconception perfectly in the quote at the start of this chapter. Robbins misstated that "petroleum-based fertilizers supply only nitrogen, phosphorus, and potassium" to crops and no micronutri-

salt. The organic cereal lists "organic corn meal, organic evaporated cane juice, sea salt."

The organic cereal cleverly tries to disguise the sugar under the euphemism "evaporated cane juice." But that's how sugar is obtained. In Kellogg's Corn Pops, they are listed simply as, "milled corn, sugar, corn syrup, molasses, salt. ..."

The base nutrition of the two cereals is very similar. Both provide 110 to 120 calories and 26 to 28 grams of carbohydrates. The organic

ents. In fact, the only "petroleum-based" fertilizer of the three is nitrogen, and using the term "petroleum-based" is a stretch. As explained in Chapter 1, the "base" of synthetic nitrogen fertilizers is nitrogen extracted from our atmosphere (which is 78% nitrogen). The only thing that fossil fuels provide is energy and hydrogen for the transformation of di-nitrogen to ammonia. Thus, a more accurate term would be "air-based" synthetic fertilizer.

As for phosphorus and potassium, these minerals are obtained from exactly the same source as organic fertilizers of these plant nutrients: rock ores. There is no such thing as "petroleum-based" phosphorus or potassium fertilizer.

Consumers need to understand that farmers are keenly aware of fertilizing their soils with more than just the Big Three soil nutrients of N, P, and K (the abbreviations for nitrogen, phosphorus, and potassium). All farmers, both organic and so-called "conventional" (a term which I think misleadingly implies a lack of willingness to adapt and improve), monitor their soils to ensure adequate levels of the 26 key micronutrients necessary for healthy plant growth. The difference is that conventional farmers have a wider array of inputs to supply these micronutrients and ensure that their crops are fully fertilized. Organic farmers are far more limited in their choice of soil amendments and as a result their crops are theoretically more likely to suffer nutrient deficiencies.

GorillaMunch cereal provides nearly twice as much sodium as the non-organic, whereas the Corn Pops provide more carbohydrates in the form of sugar than the organic.

But only the Corn Pops is fortified to provide between 10% and 25% of the recommended daily allowance (RDA) of 11 important vitamins and minerals. In comparison, the organic cereal provides none except for a measly 4% of the RDA for iron.

All of the vitamin and mineral fortifications are aimed at preventing serious diseases of malnutrition in children: vitamin A (retinol) to prevent blindness and death, vitamin C (ascorbic acid) to prevent scurvy (internal bleeding, loss of teeth, weakness), iron to prevent anemia (lack of sufficient red blood cells), vitamin D to prevent rickets (weak, uncalcified bones), thiamin (vitamin B_1) to prevent the nerve disease beriberi, riboflavin (B_2) to prevent ariboflavinosis, niacin (B_3) to prevent pellagra (a disease that causes severe nerve dysfunction), vitamins B_6 (pyridoxine) and B_{12} (cobalamin) to prevent anemia, folic acid to prevent birth defects like spina bifida in infants, and zinc for a healthy immune system and proper growth.

The non-organic Corn Pops clearly offers a significant nutritional advantage compared to the organic cereal. Which one would you feed to your child?

In addition, there is no known advantage to organic sources of nitrogen. Contrary to the beliefs of Steiner, Howard, Balfour, and Rodale, we now know that the chemical compounds taken in by plants from manure and other "organic" sources are no different than those taken in from synthetic nitrogen fertilizers. Plants can only take up nitrogen compounds in their inorganic, chemical ion forms. Nitrogen in its organic (biological) forms, such as in proteins, DNA, and RNA, is simply inaccessible to plants. Feeding plants biological nitrogen is like feeding steak to newborn infants; they simply can't eat or digest it.

Plants must wait until the organic materials (manure, bits of plants, etc.) are degraded and decomposed, releasing the nutrients into their inorganic, chemical forms, before the nutrients can be physically taken up by a plant's roots in any appreciable quantities. In fact, one reason why organic farmers generally achieve lower average crop yields is the naturally slow degradation rate of organic matter in the soil. This slows the release of chemical (ion) nitrogen forms available for uptake by the crop.

Steiner's claims about declining protein levels in food after the advent of synthetic nitrogen fertilizers were simply wrong. Organic crops fertilized only with animal manures tend to have lower protein content compared to crops

---

Amazingly, in the summer of 2004, Kellogg's was prohibited from selling vitamin and mineral-fortified breakfast cereals in Denmark by the Danish Veterinary and Food Administration for fear that consumers could exceed safe levels of the nutrients in their diet — this despite any evidence that children and adults are being overexposed to vitamins and minerals via fortified foods.

The agency is apparently worried about consumers who may eat excessive amounts of some fortified foods or take too many dietary supplements and that not enough studies have been conducted on the potential toxicity of vitamins and minerals in children.

The spokeswoman for the Danish food agency said that "the knowledge on toxicity of vitamins and minerals is very limited and practically non-existent for children." She acknowledges that deficiency for certain nutrients does exist, "but only in small groups like immigrants who aren't getting enough vitamin D or pregnant women who need folic acid. We need to take care of all of the groups in our population."

While the health and food authorities of dozens of countries around the world have strongly encouraged fortification of basic foods consumed by children, Denmark has become so paranoid over "toxicity" that it is literally taking the vitamins from the mouths of babes.

fertilized with synthetic nitrogen fertilizer because protein requires significant amounts of nitrogen for its creation.[2]

These facts demonstrate that fertilizers can at least modestly impact a food's nutritional content. So with this background, we can now consider the various studies that have searched for nutritional differences between organically and conventionally produced foods.

The Studies: Valid or Invalid?

When fertilizer science moved into the modern age in the early 20th century, many studies were conducted comparing the nutrient and mineral content of foods grown using traditional animal manures and plant composts to crops grown using the then-new synthetic nitrogen fertilizers. Several of these studies have been contemporarily misconstrued as "proving" that organic farming methods (manure) produce nutritionally superior foods. The most infamous of these is a 1949 study by Dr. Firman Bear at Rutgers University.[3] The Internet is full of pro-organic Web pages citing this report as "conclusive evidence" that organic foods are more nutritious.

Unfortunately, Dr. Bear never tested organic foods. His research merely proved that crops grown on soils deficient in minerals tend to have lower amounts of those minerals than foods grown in soils with adequate mineral levels. This basic tenet — that growing crops in mineral-poor soils will result in mineral-poor crops/foods — is true for all types of farming. That is exactly why farmers fertilize their fields with 26 trace minerals in addition to the three major plant nutrients, nitrogen, phosphorus, and potassium (NPK).

Because Dr. Bear's research did not examine differences between adequately fertilized organic and conventional crops, no serious organic groups cite Dr. Bear's work. In fact, several organic Web sites admirably debunk the use of Dr. Bear's research to support higher nutrition claims by competing organic marketers.

But there are still plenty of unsupported nutrition claims made. The U.S. Organic Trade Association's (OTA) Web site includes a "Nutritional Considerations" page that states, "There is mounting evidence that organically grown fruits, vegetables, and grains may offer more of some nutrients."

---

[2] Woese K, et al. A Comparison of Organically and Conventionally Grown Foods — Results of a Review of the Relevant Literature. *Journal of the Science of Food and Agriculture* 74:281-293, 1997.

[3] Bear FE. Variations in Mineral Composition of Vegetables. *Proceedings of the Soil Science Society* 13:380-384, 1948.

What is the "mounting evidence"? The first study the OTA cites is a meta-analysis (a statistical analysis of the combined data from multiple, separate research studies) by then-graduate student Virginia Worthington. This paper was published in *The Journal of Alternative and Complementary Medicine* (JACM), which is hardly a mainstream scientific journal.[4]

Meta-analysis is relatively new in science and is highly prone to error and bias. Therefore, it must be done carefully for the results to have any validity. As an emeritus professor at the University of Iowa Hospitals and Clinics wrote in 1999:

> *"Doing a meta-analysis requires the collaboration of clinicians and experienced statisticians to search databases, review bibliographies,* and locate unpublished work, particularly studies with negative results, *which tend not to be published. Winnowing the data that must meet strict meta-analysis requirements may reduce the reports to 10% of the original number. Control populations have to be similar."* (Emphasis added.)

Worthington reviewed data from 41 previously published studies (dating back to the 1940s) that had ostensibly examined nutrient content differences between organic and non-organic crops and foods. She then lumped all of the data from these studies together and conducted rudimentary statistical analysis to look for any statistically significant differences between organic and non-organic foods.

The term "garbage in, garbage out" applies perfectly to doing a meta-analysis, and in this case it appears a fair amount of garbage went into Worthington's review. Perhaps this was due to her clear bias in favor of organic foods. For over 15 years, since well before she became a graduate student, Worthington has run a "naturopathic" clinic in the Washington, DC, area. Naturopathy is a form of "alternative medicine" where disease and illness are treated using herbs, diet, massage, and other "alternative" methods, rather than science-based medicine.

Worthington claims to have found statistically significant differences in four nutrients — vitamin C, iron, magnesium, and phosphorus. (See Figure 1, page 42). According to Worthington, the average difference in these four nutrients ranged from 13% to 30% higher in organic. For all the other param-

---

[4] Worthington V. Nutritional Quality of Organic Versus Conventional Fruits, Vegetables, and Grains. *Journal of Alternative and Complementary Medicine* 7(2):161-173, 2001.

eters, either there wasn't any significant difference found or there were too few data to make any statistically valid conclusions.

But there are strong reasons to doubt even these modest conclusions because of the selection of research studies included in the meta-analysis. Twenty-three of the 41 "studies" were published in openly pro-organic publications of little scientific rigor. For example, four papers were published in *Biodynamics*, a niche journal devoted entirely to promoting an extreme form of organic farming developed by followers of Rudolf Steiner (he was the "vital cosmic forces" guy). Five were merely presentations given at international organic farming conferences, where organic activists go to rekindle each others' enthusiasm.

One so-called "study" heavily skewed Worthington's overall end results. It was a commentary article (not a research report) written by Bob Smith and published in the *Journal of Applied Nutrition*.[5] The commentary was based on very crude and highly unorthodox testing of a tiny sample of foods. It was published as a commentary rather than a peer-reviewed research report because it clearly didn't measure up to even minimal scientific research standards.

WARNING: Any analysis, Web site, or group that includes the Smith commentary as evidence of organic food superiority should be dismissed out of hand. Most erroneously refer to Smith's commentary article as a "study."

This so-called study has been commented upon and its results have been repeated on so many Web sites it's unavoidable. Literally thousands of organic Web pages refer to this "study." For example, a 1995 article published in the *Organic Gardening Almanac* and "reprinted" on dozens of organic Web sites cites it as evidence of organic food's nutritional superiority.

In an article titled "Are Organic Foods Really Healthier for You?" Naturopathic Physician (whatever that is) Walter Crinnion writes:

> In addition to the mental and emotional benefits of growing and eating organic food, there are also the physical benefits. These physical benefits can be boiled down to nutrients present in organic foods that are not in commercial foods and toxins not in organic foods that are present in commercial foods. A recent article in the Journal of Applied Nutrition *gave credence to the notion that organic foods have higher nutrient levels than non-organic food. In this study the*

---

[5] Smith B. Organic Foods vs Supermarket Foods: Element Levels. *Journal of Applied Nutrition* 45(1):35-39, 1993.

mineral content of organic apples, pear, potatoes, wheat, and sweet corn were compared to commercial varieties. Overall the organic foods showed much higher levels of nutrient minerals and much lower levels of heavy metals.

Here are a few of the nutrients that were found in higher levels in the organic foods:

- *Chromium is a micronutrient that is low in Western diets. Its deficiency is associated with the onset of adult diabetes and atherosclerosis (hardening of the arteries). Chromium was found to be higher in organic foods by an average of 78%.*

- *Selenium is one of the antioxidant nutrients that protects us from damage by environmental chemicals. It is protective against cancers and heart disease. It was found to be an average of 390% higher in organic foods.*

- *Calcium, needed for strong bones, averaged 63% higher in organics.*

- *Boron, which has been shown to help prevent osteoporosis (along with calcium), averaged 70% more.*

- *Lithium, which is used to treat certain types of depression, was 188% higher.*

- *Magnesium, which reduces mortality from heart attacks, keeps muscles from spasming, and eases the symptoms of PMS, averaged 138% more.*

In short, many of the minerals that I most often prescribe to my patients are found in much higher levels in organic foods.

The continued and repeated reference to Smith's commentary article requires that we examine its huge scientific shortcomings in detail.

Smith ostensibly examined six foods (apples, pears, potatoes, wheat, sweet corn, and prepackaged baby foods bought at local Chicago stores) for their mineral/elemental content (iron, magnesium, etc.). But he only examined four to 15 samples of each food. This is far too small a sample size to obtain scientifically valid results, especially considering the large natural variation in mineral levels in crops. Moreover, Smith provided no experimental data, no details about the sample size (in weight) for each different food (all he says is "4-15 samples"), and no information on the range of mineral concentrations observed in the mystery sample size. Instead, he reports only average percentage differences found between organic and conventional.

The biggest problem, however, is that Smith analyzed undried food samples, breaking a cardinal rule of mineral content analysis. Most scientists conduct mineral content analysis only on carefully weighed samples of freeze-dried food. Fruits and vegetables can lose considerable weight through water loss during storage and transport, and this can dramatically change the apparent concentrations of minerals. This large variation in water content swamps out other differences and makes the analysis completely unreliable. That is why the USDA's Food Chemistry Laboratory and other conscientious food chemists test only freeze-dried food samples — i.e., with the water variable taken out of the equation.

Smith found no differences in mineral concentrations in prepackaged baby foods. These are vacuum-sealed in glass jars and are not subject to fluctuating water content as are unprocessed fruits and vegetables. Smith noted the baby food results in passing, stating only that "there were minor differences and these differences were inconsistent."

Smith's conclusions for the whole foods he tested, however, are dramatic, heavily skewing Worthington's "average percent difference" results for magnesium, phosphorus, and iron.

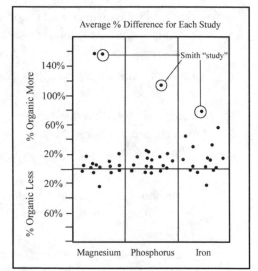

Fig. 1. Distribution of results from 16-18 studies.

(Smith did not examine vitamin C or nitrate levels, as these cannot be studied through the method used by Smith.) For these three elements, Smith's results showed the largest differences of all the studies Worthington examined (See highlighted data points in Fig. 1). The fact that Smith's results were so much different from those of the other studies should have been a major clue that his results were not valid.

Without the inclusion of the bogus Smith data, it is doubtful the differences Worthington found would have been statistically significant for magnesium and phosphorus (and perhaps even iron, given the extremely small sample size tested by Smith).

As with Dr. Worthington, it is also worth looking at Mr. Smith's background. At the time he wrote his commentary, Bob Smith was the president of Doctor's Data Labs, Inc. (DDL), in Chicago, Illinois. After leaving DDL, Smith became vice president of Great Smokies Diagnostic Labs in Ashville, North Carolina. Both labs hawk various elemental hair, blood, and urine analysis services to people who believe they may suffer from nutrient deficiencies or heavy metals and toxin exposure. (See "Misleading Mercury Poisioning" lab reports for more on the medical quackery peddled by Doctor's Data Labs, Inc., Great Smokies Diagnostic, and other such labs.)

One way to sell more of these lab services is to write articles convincing people (and naive or greedy doctors) that nutrient deficiency is common and that "special foods" and testing are required to find and correct the problem. There is extensive controversy in the medical profession over the tests that these labs conduct and the "cleansing" treatments that physicians and "alternative practitioners" sell to people after receiving test results from these labs. Both labs are extensively linked via Web sites and industry associations to

---

"MISLEADING MERCURY POISONING" LAB REPORTS, WEB POSTING BY DR. JOHN SEHMER, A PHYSICIAN WITH DUKE UNIVERSITY MEDICAL CENTER:

From: John Sehmer, M.D., M.Sc.
To: OCC-ENV-MED-L-request@LIST.MC.DUKE.EDU =
<OCC-ENV-MED-L-request@LIST.MC.DUKE.EDU>
Date: June 11, 1999, 8:57 a.m.
Subject: "Misleading mercury poisoning" reports Doctor's Data, Inc. labs

"I have now seen three patients convinced they have mercury poisoning based on visiting a physician who specializes in [chelation therapy] and brandishing reports from mercury urinalysis performed by Doctor's Data Lab, Inc., that graphically shows their mercury levels to be off the scale. Normal value is listed as less than three micrograms/gram creatinine and one patient's level was 45. One report did not make sense as despite the creatinine level being 20% of the lab's "reference range" the mercury level was once again so high as to be shown as being off the scale. Attempts to contact the lab by myself and

organic food activist groups and natural healing groups.

The second "study" listed on the OTA's nutrition Web page was an examination of previously published research commissioned by the U.K.'s largest organic farming group, the Soil Association. This literature review was carried out by Shane Heaton, a completely unqualified individual with a financial stake in the results.[6]

The Soil Association paid for and trotted out Heaton's so-called "study" after the head of the U.K.'s Food Standards Agency publicly stated that organic foods were no more nutritious than any other foods and were mostly a waste of money. In the face of a stinging dismissal by the country's top food expert authority, the organic lobby group was trying desperately to prop up its 40 years of unsupported claims that organic food is more nutritious with a biased review of a cherry-picked set of studies comparing organic with conventionally grown foods.

The Organic Trade Association says the Soil Association report shows that organic foods are "higher in vitamin C, essential minerals, and phytonutri-

the family physician have been ignored. Naturally these lab reports cause great concern in the patient and are very good for the chelating physician's business. I could not convince one individual who subsequently had all his mercury fillings removed."

The quackwatch.org Web site contained some interesting information about Doctor's Data, Inc.:

In 1986, Doctor's Data, a Chicago-based laboratory, agreed to stop accepting human hair specimens from New York State unless it can obtain a permit from the New York State Department of Health. The company also agreed to pay $25,000 in costs and penalties. Action was taken because a bogus "nutrition consultant" had been using the test as a basis for prescribing vitamins, minerals, and other supplements.

Yet Doctor's Data is still peddling these hair tests. In fact, in 2001 the *Journal of the American Medical Association* published a study by physician scientists at the California Department of Health Services, Environmental Health Investigations Branch, indicating this type of elemental analysis was seriously flawed and should not be relied upon.[7] Doctor's Data, Inc., simply claimed

---

[6] Heaton, S. Organic Farming, Food Quality and Human Health: A Review of the Evidence. Soil Association, U.K., 2003. ISBN 0 905200 80 2.
[7] Seidel S, et al. Assessment of Commercial Laboratories Performing Hair Mineral Analysis. *Journal of the American Medical Association* 285(1)67-72, 2001.

ents." In contrast, even the director of the Soil Association says only that the report provides "indicative evidence suggesting nutritional differences" between organic and non-organic foods. The Soil Association recommends further testing to determine if there really are any differences.

A look at the report itself, however, indicates that further research is unlikely to find any differences.

A large number of existing research reports had to be dismissed as "invalid" to arrive at the feeble conclusion of "indicative evidence suggesting" differences. Of the 99 reports ostensibly reviewed by Mr. Heaton, 70 were disqualified as being "invalid." In fact, Heaton dismissed any studies that compared mineral levels using freeze-dried sample analysis — the type of mineral content analysis relied upon by the USDA and other scientifically respected food analysis labs. The fact that the only studies deemed valid were the ones that examined nutrient levels on a wet-sample basis is reason enough to dismiss the entire Soil Association review as fundamentally flawed.

Interestingly, 24 of the 41 studies in Worthington's review were deemed "invalid" in the Soil Association review. And like Worthington, Heaton's livelihood depends on consumers believing that organic foods are superior. He runs both a retail organic food company and an "organic nutrition counseling" service in Australia.

that it was unfairly lumped in with labs that "do a poor job — employing outdated methodologies."

The quackwatch Web site also has a well-written article by Dr. Robert Baratz, M.D., D.D.S., and Ph.D., on bogus mercury testing by companies like Doctor's Data, Inc. Dr. Baratz says:

> Mercury poisoning is very rare and requires considerable exposure, usually at work. People don't get dangerous amounts from tooth fillings (no matter how many they have), chewing, or eating a normal diet. Thus, routine mercury testing of persons who are not industrially exposed should be regarded as a scam. … If a health professional advises you that mercury amalgam ("silver") fillings cause disease or should be removed as a "preventive measure," head for the nearest exit and report your experience to the practitioner's state licensing board.

Dr. Baratz has extensive training and practical experience in internal medicine, emergency medicine, oral medicine, dentistry, material science, and research methodology. In addition to practicing medicine, he serves as a medical and dental consultant to many state licensing boards, federal agencies, insurance companies, and the legal profession.

Heaton's only true academic degree is in business management and marketing. Heaton's only nutrition training is a couple dozen weekend seminars on how to be a nutritional therapist from the "Institute for Optimum Nutrition (ION)," a New Age business that trains "nutritional therapists" in return for hefty tuition and accreditation fees. A typical nutritional therapist "certificate" from the ION costs about $15,000 in tuition alone, according to its Web site.

Sound Science Comparisons

So what does unbiased, high-quality scientific research say about nutrient content of organic foods? Essentially, organic foods are no different than non-organic foods, save for slightly lower levels of nitrate (which organic believers claim is toxic, though it isn't — See "Nitrate Nonsense" which appears later in this chapter) and slightly lower levels of protein in some organic grains. Neither difference is nutritionally significant in the context of a normal, balanced diet.

According to research conducted by the University of Guelph and commissioned by Canadian TV (CTV) and one of Canada's leading newspapers, *The Globe and Mail,* there is no difference in nutritional content between organic and conventional foods. Of the 135 comparisons made, conventional produce came out slightly ahead in one or more nutrient 66 times and organic produce 49 times.

According to the subsequent article in *The Globe and Mail,* "The results are no surprise to Phil Warman, an agronomist and professor of agricultural sciences at Nova Scotia Agricultural College. 'In terms of nutritional content, there is virtually no difference. I know this is disappointing for organic growers to hear this and probably for the consumer who has been led to believe the food is nutritionally superior.'"

Leonard Piche, an associate professor in the nutrition program at Brescia College, said that belief in the nutritional superiority of organic foods was wishful thinking and that the evidence against any nutritional differences was good news. "Canadians should feel confident that regardless of whether they purchase organically grown or conventionally grown produce, they can expect to obtain similar nutrient value."

This neatly sums up the view of the vast majority of professional nutritionists, as compared to the "nutritional consultants" like Virginia Worthington and Shane Heaton peddling organic dogma.

The most complete review of published organic food nutrition research was published in 1997 in the *Journal of the Science of Food and Agriculture*.[8] This review examined over 150 research studies published over the last 75 years, including the good, the bad, and the untrustworthy. The conclusion: No clear or consistent differences could be found in the nutritional value of organic versus non-organic foods. This review included plenty of very pro-organic research papers, so it can't be dismissed as a selective look at the research. Some of the research reviewed is downright fringe "crystallization" analysis (See Organic Nutrition Voodoo).

Let's look at what this solid review found, food by food:

Cereals, 30 studies reviewed: No clear differences.

Potatoes, 22 studies: No clear differences.

Vegetables, 70 studies: No clear differences.

Fruits, nuts, and oil seeds, 12 studies: No major differences. *(One study found higher levels of fungal toxins in organic nut products.)*

Wine and beer, 7 studies: Organic beer had slightly lower protein content. (Note: This should not be nutritionally significant, unless beer is the primary source of dietary protein, in which case protein deficiency is likely the least of one's health concerns.)

Bread, 6 studies: No clear differences.

Milk and dairy products, 9 studies: No clear differences.

Meat and meat products, 5 studies: Not enough data to make a meaningful assessment.

Eggs, 1 study: Free-range hen eggs had slightly lower protein content, but slightly higher carotenoid content. Carotenoids are pigments that act as antioxidants, so they may help prevent cancer. Then again, they may not. Research using antioxidant supplements has indicated no cancer protective effect, but this may not be true for antioxidants consumed as part of the food itself. More research must be done before any conclusions can be drawn.

Additional Food Content Research

Research published in 2002 in *Science*, ostensibly the most respected and prestigious scientific journal in the world, reported that 21 years of research

---

[8] Woese K, et al. A Comparison of Organically and Conventionally Grown Foods — Results of a Review of the Relevant Literature. *Journal of the Science of Food and Agriculture* 74:281-293, 1997.

on seven different crops found only "minor differences between the farming systems in food quality."[9] Another research paper on apples published in *Nature*, the second-most respected scientific journal in the world, noted that "Fruit tissue analysis indicated some inconsistent differences."[10]

Two researchers at the University of Otago in New Zealand conducted a review of published studies and published their article in a highly respected, peer-reviewed scientific journal. According to these nutritionists:

> With the possible exception of nitrate content there is no strong evidence that organic and conventional foods differ in concentrations of various nutrients.[11]

A three-year study of carrots, potatoes, cabbages, and sweet corn published in 1996 by researchers at the Nova Scotia Agricultural College found no significant or consistent differences in the levels of 12 macro- and micronutrients or in levels of vitamins C, E, and betacarotene (the carotenoid that makes carrots orange). Year to year variation in vitamin content dwarfed any observed differences between organic and conventional.[12]

A two-year, multi-farm French study comparing carrots and celery grown organically and conventionally found slightly higher betacarotene levels (+12%) in organic carrots and slightly higher vitamin C levels (+11%) in organic celery.[13]

A comparison of carrots and cabbages from 10 Polish organic farms and 10 Polish conventional farms showed only slight differences in nutrient content. The only significant result was a 30% higher vitamin C content in organic cabbages. However, organic carrots had 300% more of the heavy metal cadmium. Moreover, the farms were not matched by vegetable variety grown, so the results may simply be due to different crop varieties.[14]

---

[9] Mader P, et al. Soil Fertility and Biodiversity in Organic Farming. *Science* 296:1694-1697, 2002.

[10] Reganold J. Sustainability of Three Apple Production Systems. *Nature* 410:926-930, 2001.

[11] Bourn D. and Prescott J. A. Comparison of the Nutritional Value, Sensory Qualities, and Food Safety of Organically and Conventionally Produced Foods. *Critical Reviews in Food Science and Nutrition* 42(1):1–34, 2002.

[12] Warman P.R. and Havard K.A. Yield, Vitamin and Mineral Content of Four Vegetables Grown With Either Composted Manure or Conventional Fertilizer. *Journal of Vegetable Crop Production* 2(1):13–25, 1996; Yield, Vitamin and Mineral Contents of Organically and Conventionally Grown Carrots and Cabbage. *Agriculture, Ecosystems and Environment* 61: 155-162, 1997; Yield, Vitamin and Mineral Contents of Organically and Conventionally Grown Potatoes and Sweet Corn. *Agriculture, Ecosystems and Environment* 68:207–216, 1998.

[13] Leclerc J., et al. Vitamin and Mineral Contents of Carrot and Celeriac Grown under Mineral or Organic Fertilization. *Biological Agriculture and Horticulture* 7:339–348, 1991.

This last point is important. When looking for nutritional differences resulting from different growing systems, it is critical to eliminate other variables. This is because different varieties of crops — such as Macintosh apples vs. Granny Smith — may produce nutritionally different products, even if grown using the same methods. What might appear as nutritional differences from growing methods might just be differences between varieties instead. But that being said, the studies to date indicate little difference even without accounting for differing crop varieties.

Other So-called Nutritional Factors

Having failed to demonstrate any meaningful differences in the major nutritional measures — protein content, vitamins, minerals, fiber, etc. — even after 50 years of study, organic believers have turned to the minor components in food to justify their long-held claims of organic food superiority.

The latest "organic nutrient" fad among organic faithful is plant "secondary metabolites." Secondary metabolites (SMs) are basically the huge array of chemical compounds made by plants other than the basics of sugar, cellulose, and proteins. SMs include waxes, oils, fragrances, pigments, fungicides, insecticides, etc. These natural, plant-produced pesticides include nicotine, caffeine, cocaine, morphine, pyrethrum, and hundreds if not thousands more. These pesticidal SMs are often toxic nerve agents made specifically by plants to kill insects, such as nicotine and cocaine. (See Chapter 6 on organic pesticides.)

Research has suggested that crops grown organically may produce more of certain SMs because organic crops aren't as well protected against pests. Some of these natural chemicals are harmful to our health, while some might be beneficial. Little research has been conducted on the vast majority of SMs.

One particular class of SMs called phenolic chemicals has been attracting increased attention recently from organic food supporters. Because some phenolic compounds act as antioxidants, scavenging damaging oxygen free radicals (believed to play a possible contributing role in some cancers), it has been suggested that higher levels of phenolic compounds in organic foods could provide an anti-cancer benefit.

The problem with this theory is that there are literally thousands of different phenolic chemicals produced in plants, and some are actually quite harmful because they are plant-made fungicides and bactericides. Some phenolics

---

[14] Rembialkowska E. The Nutritive and Sensory Quality of Carrots and White Cabbage From Organic and Conventional Farms. IFOAM 2000: The World Grows Organic. *Proceedings of the 13th International IFOAM Scientific Conference*, Basel, Switzerland, 2000.

"discourage herbivory," which means they are meant to be toxic to grazing animals (including human vegetarians!).

In other words, while some phenolic chemicals may have the beneficial effect of scavenging oxygen free radicals and possibly helping prevent cancer, there may well be some definite toxic effects, too. We simply don't know enough about the complexity and levels of various phenolic chemicals in plants to claim which ones are good and which are bad, nor whether having more phenolics overall is a net positive or a net negative to our health.

But organic believers gloss over this complex scientific uncertainty because in their minds, any differences found are proof of organic food's superiority. It's no coincidence that not a single organic organization has even raised the possibility that the slightly higher phenolic content found in this initial research may, in fact, be a health negative.

Another SM that has garnered attention recently is salisylic acid, otherwise known as aspirin. First discovered in the bark of the willow tree, salisylic acid is produced in all plants in varying amounts and is involved in initiating a plant's pest immune/defense systems. Some research has suggested that organically grown foods may have more salisylic acid than non-organically grown foods, and organic supporters suggest this extra salicylic acid may offer health benefits in people. After all, daily low doses of aspirin have been prescribed to reduce the chances of heart attack because they help thin the blood and prevent clots.

PRINCE CHARLES ROYALLY MISINTERPRETS STUDIES ON NUTRITIONAL DEFICIENCIES

The belief that modern, intensive farming techniques result in nutritionally sterile food is clearly popular among the organic intelligentsia. Any scrap of evidence suggesting that organic foods are more nutritious or have higher mineral content is seen as "emerging evidence" of a pattern or trend. Take for instance the following misinterpretation by Prince Charles of Great Britain. (The prince is a long-time organic proponent, farms his Highgrove estate organically, and has his own "Duchy" brand of organic foods.)

The prince gave the keynote Lady Eve Balfour Memorial Lecture at the 50th anniversary of The Soil Association on September 19, 1996. In his speech, the prince stated:

"The evidence is now beginning to emerge. The New Scientist recently reported alarming research results from a study of the long-term effects of the so-called 'Green Revolution' in South Asia. New plant varieties fed

Reality suggests any differences in salicylic acid content between organic and non-organic foods, if they really exist, are far too small to make any health difference.

The Organic Trade Association Web site highlights the research of Dr. John Patterson at the Dumfries and Galloway Royal Infirmary in the U.K. Dr. Patterson examined 11 different varieties of canned, processed organic vegetable soup and compared them to 24 different varieties of canned, processed non-organic vegetable soup in research published in 2002.[15] Overall, the organic soups contained about six times more salicylic acid than non-organic canned soups. This result sounded dramatic and the research was reported widely across the U.K. Patrick Holden, the director of the Soil Association, told the British Broadcasting Company (BBC) that the research "adds to the body of evidence showing the health benefits of organic food."

Not quite. Here's the reality: Patterson's group found less than 1/13,000th of one aspirin tablet's worth of difference per can of soup.[16] At that miniscule amount, you would have to eat a bowl of organic soup every day for 37 years before you'd consume the equivalent of one aspirin.

Dr. Patterson told the BBC that while he is "not an evangelist for the organ-

with high levels of artificial fertilizer have dramatically increased food production, to no one's surprise. But it now becomes clear that those intensively grown crops are nutritionally deficient. They lack vital trace elements and minerals, particularly zinc and iron. This deficiency has been passed on through the food to such an extent that an IQ loss of 10 points has been observed in a whole generation of children who have consumed a diet largely based on crops grown in this way ... could we expect to see the same thing in the developed West? The answer, of course, is that we simply don't know."

Scary sounding stuff, no doubt. However, if one actually reads the studies referred to in The New Scientist article (there are actually two, one conducted by the United Nations' Food and Agriculture Organization and one by the International Food Policy Research Institute), one finds that the nutritional deficiencies in Asia and other Green Revolution areas are the result of a change in the food composition of the overall diet, not changes in the nutrient content of specific foods themselves. In other words, economic and cultural changes in

[15] Baxter G., et al. Salicylic Acid in Soups Prepared From Organically and Non-Organically Grown Vegetables. *European Journal of Nutrition* 40(6):289-92, 2001.
[16] One aspirin contains 325 million nanograms of salisylic acid. A nanogram is 1 billionth of a gram.

ic food movement," his research revealed "a fairly substantial difference." Sure, a 600% difference sounds substantial — unless one knows that the difference is less than 1/13,000th of an aspirin tablet.

Nitrate Nonsense

Food nitrate content is often analyzed in comparing organic to non-organic foods, under the false notion that nitrate (NO_3) is toxic. One of the supposed nutritional advantages of organic foods touted by activists is its lower nitrate content.

However, nitrate is not toxic and is not at all nutritionally harmful. Our bodies produce nitrate constantly, accounting for half of a typical person's total nitrate exposure. Nitrate may, in fact, be an important dietary component, as recent research shows that the human body will manufacture nitrate and concentrate it in our saliva if not enough is consumed in the diet. The head of the pharmacology department at the Royal College of Medicine has been conducting research that indicates nitrates may be important in fighting foodborne microbes.

Nitrates are naturally present in nearly all fruits and vegetables, with leafy green vegetables sometimes having high levels (>2,000 parts per million). Research does suggest that organic fruits and vegetables often have lower nitrate levels, typically 10% to 40% lower. This is because of the lower soil nitrogen levels from the slow-release organic fertilizers. Because nitrogen is so often the limiting factor on organic crop growth, any nitrates absorbed by

these regions over the past 30 years have resulted in a general dietary shift away from fruits, vegetables, and pulses, and toward cheaper cereal grains. As *The New Scientist* article puts it, "because [high-yield rice, wheat, and maize varieties] displaced the local fruits, vegetables, and legumes that traditionally supplied these essentials, the diet of many people in the developing world is now dangerously low in iron, zinc, vitamin A, and other micronutrients." Rice, wheat, and maize are poor sources for these minerals and vitamins, regardless of how they were grown.

So, it's not that the intensively grown high-yielding rice, wheat, and corn varieties are significantly lower in key vitamins and minerals compared to organically grown rice, wheat, and corn. The lesson is that if all you eat is rice, wheat, and corn — regardless of how it was grown — you'll be setting yourself up for nutritional deficiencies.

The prince missed the important distinction between changes in the nutrient content of specific crops/foods versus changes in the composition of the diet itself, illustrating the complexity of the issues involved.

organic crops are rapidly converted into other nitrogen-containing molecules, such as DNA and proteins. Thus, organic produce tends to have lower nitrate levels. But this is nutritionally irrelevant.

There is a serious kernel of truth to the worry over nitrates. Nitrite (NO_2), chemically related to nitrate (NO_3), is toxic at higher exposures. At higher doses, nitrite binds to the oxygen-carrying hemoglobin in our red blood cells, which prevents the blood from transporting oxygen, thus causing a form of chemical suffocation called methemoglobinemia (pronounced *meth-hemo-glo-bin-ee-mia*), or blue baby syndrome. Bacteria can convert nitrate into nitrite through a process called anaerobic respiration.

Young infants are particularly susceptible to methemoglobinemia because of their immature blood system, hence the term blue baby syndrome. There have been a few documented nitrite poisonings (non-fatal) in young infants that were caused by spoiled, bacterially contaminated carrots and spinach.

Carrots typically (and naturally) contain between 100 and 300 ppm nitrate, whether they were grown conventionally or organically. Spinach contains 100 to 1,000 ppm nitrate, organic and non-organic. These are obviously consumed by billions of people safely every day.

The danger for infants is greater than for adults not only because of infants' immature blood systems, but also because of how we prepare infant food. If these vegetables are prepared in purees, juices, or broths for feeding to infants and proper food safety, hygiene, and refrigeration techniques are not followed, bacteria will proliferate in the juice or broth and convert the naturally present nitrates into toxic nitrite. The concentration of nitrite in the juice/broth will increase over time, depending on the bacterial levels.

This bacterial conversion of non-toxic nitrate to toxic nitrite can even happen in the leaves and fruits themselves if the vegetables are improperly stored in hot, humid conditions. Instances of spinach leaves exceeding 2,000 ppm of toxic nitrite have been documented.

It must be remembered, however, that it is nitrite, not nitrate, that is toxic. Moreover, this toxic occurrence can happen just as readily in improperly stored organic foods. Unspoiled, properly prepared purees and juices are fine for infants, even when nitrate levels are seemingly high. Beets and spinach typically have nitrate levels as high as 1,000 to 2,000 ppm but are perfectly safe to feed to infants when prepared and stored properly.

The Committee on Nutrition of the American Academy of Pediatrics, being concerned about nitrite poisoning, stated in 1970, "More than 350 million jars of canned spinach and beets have been used in the United States and Canada over the last 20 years without causing any proven instances of [nitrite poisoning]." To the date of this publication, none have been reported.

Organic Nutrition Voodoo

Organic believers, unhappy that science has not shown a nutrition advantage in organic foods, have resorted to using pseudoscientific methods. So-called "picture forming" methods are popular among organic food believers, and are discussed on many Web sites. The New Zealand Biodynamic Farmers Web site states, "The starting point for this method is that formative forces of a living organism or system are recognizable in each part of the whole. Pictorial imaging methods make these formative forces visible in a picture."

There are multiple picture-forming methods that organic believers have tried to use to "prove" the nutritional benefits of organic, including "sensitive crystallization," chromatograms, "drop picture," etc. Believers claim that these methods show that organic foods have more "vitality." The appeal of these methods is that they use the tools of modern science (chemicals, chromatography papers, and gels) and are discussed using scientific terms. But they are not science, as they measure nothing and tell us nothing of qualitative nutritional value of a food.

The Biodynamic Farming and Gardening Association of New Zealand says, "Pictorial imaging techniques require training and experience before a picture can be read with accuracy. Dr. Ursula Balzer-Graf from the Swiss institute Forschungsinstitut for Vitalqualität has given this method a scientific base."

Figure 2 shows two copper chloride crystal patterns from Dr. Balzer-Graf's work at the Institute of Vital Quality (Forschungsinstitut für Vitalqualität). To make these, she dissolved a drop of carrot juice in a solution of copper chloride in a flat glass dish and allowed the water to evaporate. The crystals that form as the water evaporates create intricate patterns, like huge snowflakes.

The one on the top is from organic carrots, the one on the bottom from conventional carrots. Here is how a colleague of Dr. Balzer-Graf described the "results" at an organic farming conference:

> You can see on the pictures of organic carrots on the top, very fine lines. The centre is packed and the outer perimeter has very fine, very well-defined lines, whereas the conventional carrot grown from the same variety, the same soils, produces a perfectly nice picture but it is much coarser. The lines are much thicker. There are more gaps and

you will see the centre beginning to break up.

I don't really see it, but let's take the presenter at his word, the crystal lines are coarser, thicker, and have more gaps. OK, so what does that mean? What if thicker, coarser lines are signs of greater "vitality"? What if "gaps" and a center "beginning to break up" are evidence of super-healthfulness? How do we know what any of the crystal patterns mean? They're crystals of salt, they don't spell out the words "high cholesterol."

There are other "image forming" techniques. Figure 3 (See page 56) shows the results of three different techniques used in Dr. Balzer-Graf's lab comparing whole wheat to the same wheat milled and cooked as a wheat flake cereal. On the top is the copper crystallization method, in the middle is capillary liquid chromatography, and on the bottom is circular liquid chromatography.[17]

This is how the presenter at the British organic conference described these pictures:

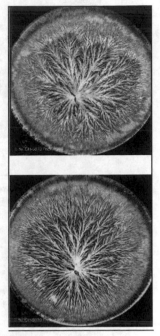

Fig. 2

> This is the penultimate group and this shows the effect of processing. You will see here two lines of pictures, the first picture is of an extract of whole grain. We then take the same grain and mill it into flour ... and we make it into extrusion and make it into breakfast cereal, corn flakes, that is what happens, and that is organic grain. Clever this technology, is it not? So you start off with the grain and you end up with that. You start off with this vitality and you make cereals and you end up with this. It is totally sclerotic. It has completely fallen apart in form. Whether that says anything about anything else is another question. You can draw some conclusions.

So there you have it, whole grain has a whole lot of "vitality" and organic breakfast cereal is "totally sclerotic" and "has completely fallen apart in form."

---

[17] Chromatography is a basic chemical technique for separating solids out of a solution. In capillary chromatography, filter paper is placed upright in a solution and the solid materials separate out as the solution wicks upward. In circular, the solution wicks from the center outward.

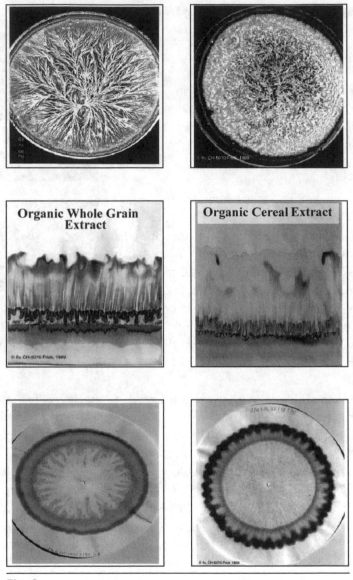

Fig. 3

Then he admits that this means totally nothing in terms of the real world, but suggests we can all draw some conclusions on our own.

Do you think he might want us to conclude that the processed grain will cause our veins to become "sclerotic" and cause our "form" to fall apart, or that whole grains have a whole lot more "vitality"? Just a guess.

The so-called training and experience needed to "read" these "tests" is the same needed to read a crystal ball or conduct a séance. Seriously. If I handed a copper chloride crystal plate or capillary chromatograph to Dr. Balzer-Graf she couldn't tell me whether the drop of juice I tested came from a carrot, corn, a steak, or my car's radiator. She couldn't tell me one thing from any of these that is remotely relevant to the nutritional or health value of the food.

The best that they can do is tell if one set of copper crystal plates came from one food and another set from a different food. The supposed "scientific base"to this method (and training and experience) is grouping plates from the same type of food better than random. That is, if I showed you 10 plates, five from an organic carrot and five from conventional (or even five carrot and five water), you will have "successfully read" the plates if you correctly grouped more than three plates together as "like" — we all did this as kids when we watched Sesame Street. So-called "trained" crystal analysts have been barely able to tell a carrot from a bell pepper, let alone an organically grown carrot versus conventional grown carrot, and did little better than random chance for decades.

Now a group at the University of Kassel, Germany, led by Professor Johannes Kahl, has successfully used computer image analysis to differentiate copper crystals made using juice extracts of organic versus conventional crops. They scan a picture of the copper crystals (such as those in Fig. 2), convert the image to grayscale, and then analyze the grayscale image data numerically using complex linear algebra. It works.

While seemingly "scientific" — complete with analysis of chemical crystal images using powerful statistical software that generates complex-looking graphs — it's meaningless. It is the epitome of voodoo science.

The funny thing is that Dr. Kahl's group says that this method has been "validated according to the requirements of ISO 17025 for the statistically proofed discrimination of products from different farming systems." In other words, his group is seeking to use this technique as a marketing and "certification" tool, to verify that organic food is "different" than conventional, and plans to market a "seal of approval" to food manufacturers and growers.

Reputable nutritionists and food scientists agree that these methods tell you nothing whatsoever about the health or nutrition value of a food. Obviously, processing flour from a whole grain and cooking it into cereal flakes is going to alter how the proteins and carbohydrates interact with crystallizing salts and the chromatography paper, but it doesn't mean that there is less nutritional value in the product. To know that, we would need to analyze the pro-

tein content, amino acid profile, amount and types of fats and oils, carbohy-
drate levels, and vitamin and mineral content. We would need to examine all
of the things that these "holistic" picture analysis methods ignore. It's literally
crystal gazing rather than science.

But as the famous newspaperman H.L. Mencken once said, "No one ever
went broke underestimating the intelligence of the American public." It's a
quote that applies equally well to all cultures. People are gullible, and if you
cloak your baloney in technical jargon and complex-looking graphs, a surprising number of people will believe whatever mumbo jumbo you tell them.

Human society has always had snake oil salesmen, only their snake oils
and technology have changed. Today we're blessed with the miracles of
"biocrystallization" and the "vital qualities" of food measured with plain old filter paper. Welcome to 21st century organic voodoo.

Chapter 3:

Is Organic Healthier?
What the Experts Say

Organic Faithful Say:

"Organic foods are not only better for you, they are better for the environment, and they're actually not more expensive. The shelf price of organic products may be a bit higher because farmers must deal with the same costs of conventional food production — such as harvesting, transportation and storage — but they also have to adhere to stricter handling and production standards. In the end, if you add up the indirect costs of conventional agribusiness, like cleaning up sludge, replenishing depleted soils, and the expense of health care for workers exposed to toxic pesticides, organic foods are considerably cheaper."

Katherine DiMatteo, executive director of the Organic Trade Association ($)[1]

http://recipestoday.com/resources/articles/organic.htm

"Our mission statement is clear: The Rodale Institute works worldwide to achieve a regenerative food system that improves environmental and human health. We believe that Healthy Soil = Healthy Food = Healthy People®, it's a matter of human survival."

Rodale Institute Web site page, "What We Do" ($)

http://www.rodaleinstitute.org/about/what_set.html

---

[1]($) Indicates that the person quoted has a profit motive or other financial interest in promoting organic food.

"Is organic food better for you? 'There's no question! Organic food is grown and stored without the use of artificial pesticides and fertilizers. The fact that residues remain on conventional foods and are consumed by us over decades, accumulating in our fatty tissues, is well documented. Ignoring this danger to health completely, as there has been no comparative long-term research about the difference between the long-term effects of consuming conventional versus organic foods, it is still obvious that organic food is better for you."

> Renée J Elliot, founder of Planet Organic, an organic and natural food supermarket ($)
> From interview in Organicfood.com.uk
> http://www.organicfood.co.uk/sense/betterforyou.html

"Is organic food better for you? 'There is so much research that confirms that organic food is better for you that it is amazing that the Food Standards Agency are either ignorant of it or don't understand what organic food is about.'"

> Craig Sams, president of Whole Earth Foods and Green & Blacks, organic food companies ($)
> From interview in Organicfood.com.uk
> http://www.organicfood.co.uk/sense/betterforyou.html

"Organic food is not only better for your health, but is also better for the environment. No one in their right mind trusts government or industry assurances that agrochemical residues in food are safe — we've heard it all before. Salmonella, listeria, BSE, and now foot and mouth disease all point to the failings of factory farming … The assumptions on safety do not hold water, especially when the precautionary principle of proving safety rather than demonstrating minimal risk, is not applied."

> Michael van Straten, "naturopath," "acupuncturist," and "nutritional consultant" ($)
> From interview in Organicfood.com.uk
> http://www.organicfood.co.uk/sense/betterforyou.html

Reality Says:

"There are numerous studies demonstrating no nutritional difference between organic and conventional fresh produce."

> Shane Heaton, owner of an Australian organic food company,
> organic "nutritional consultant," and paid consultant to the Soil Association ($)
> From interview in Organicfood.com.uk
> http://www.organicfood.co.uk/sense/betterforyou.html

"Organic food is an important addition to consumer choice, but no independent scientific evaluation has ever shown that it is any healthier. [Organic consumers are] not getting value for money, in my opinion and in the opinion of the Food Standards Agency, if they think they're buying food with extra nutritional quality or extra safety. We don't have the evidence to support those claims."

Sir John Krebs, chairman of the UK's Food Standards Agency
Letter to editor of The Guardian newspaper, published May 27, 2003

"The organic industry and the whole organic myth-promoting machine basically make up the rules as they go along to suit themselves. ... Moreover, the organic industry is not allowed [by the Advertising Standards Authority] to make any claims about the product being healthier, tastier, or more nutritious than conventionally grown crops, as there is no sound scientific evidence to support any of these claims. Science, facts, and reason clearly have no place in the massive con-trick that surrounds the Emperor's New (Organic) Clothes."

Dr. Michael A. Wilson, fellow of the Royal Society of Edinburgh
chief executive, Horticulture Research International, UK

Organic foods are widely marketed by companies and proponents as "healthier" and "better for you" than non-organic foods. If you doubt this, then you haven't paid much attention to the writings, promotions, and marketing of organic foods. But it's an easy enough fact to verify. A simple Internet search using the terms "organic" and "health" returns over 7 million pages from countless Web sites hawking organic food as better for you.

Yet there is simply no evidence whatsoever that a diet high in or exclusively of organic foods is any healthier for you than a diet of regular food. There is plenty of evidence that a diverse diet, high in fruits, vegetables, diverse whole grains, and fish is healthy. But the studies that support this dietary advice were conducted using conventional foods, not organic. In fact, there have been no short or long-term human studies conducted to support the organic marketing claims — claims that organic activists have made for more than 50 years.

In early March of 2005, the Advertising Standards Authority in the United Kingdom — a quasi-government "truth in advertising" watchdog — upheld a complaint against the organic industry group The Soil Association for fund- raising leaflets implying that organic foods were healthier.[2] The ASA's ruling noted that "[The Soil Association] did not show organically-produced food conveyed noticeable health benefits over and above the same food when conventionally produced or that a diet of organic food could guarantee no harmful effects."

---

[2] http://www.asa.org.uk/asa/adjudications/Adjudication+Details.htm?Adjudication_id=39414

Despite the near total lack of evidence, the number of so-called experts extolling the health benefits of organic foods is large and, arguably, growing. Organicfood.co.uk, which bills itself as "your organic lifestyle magazine," asked a number of people on both sides of this issue a simple question: Is organic food better for you?

While the issues addressed by the respondents varied, most interesting was the contrast between the qualifications and motivations of the organic food supporters and those of the two individuals quoted in the article who didn't see additional health merits in organic foods.

On the pro-organic side were:

- Ms. Renee Elliot, founder of the Planet Organic supermarket and a council member of the U.K. organic lobby group, the Soil Association;

- Mr. Craig Sams, president of Whole Earth Foods and Green & Blacks, an organic candy company;

- Mr. Patrick Holford, founder of the New Age, pro-organic Institute for Optimum Nutrition, which "certifies" organic nutritional consultants;

- Ms. Charlotte Reynolds, owner of Swaddles Green Farm, which sells organic food via the Web and through direct delivery;

- Mr. Michael van Straten, a "naturopath," "acupuncturist," and "nutritional consultant" who promotes organic food via his own radio program;

- Mr. Shane Heaton, an organic food retailer and "nutritional consultant" — "certified" by the Institute for Optimum Nutrition;

- Ms. Carol Charlton, who runs the "Organic Café," the UK's first organic-certified restaurant;

- Ms. Lizzie Vann and Ms. Diane Mulligan, founder and marketing manager of Organix, an organic children's food company.

Every one of these people makes their living by selling organic food or organic nutrition advice. Not one of them is an independent professional nutritionist or food scientist looking at this issue from an objective position. Not one has a scientific degree or any rigorous formal training in food nutrition or health. (As noted in Chapter 2, the Institute of Optimum Nutrition is not a widely respected academic institution.)

Contrast this with the qualifications of the two individuals included in the article who didn't believe that organic foods were healthier:

- Dr. Richard Harding, director of the U.K. Food Standards Agency's Food

Chain Division, whose job is to lead focal investigations into food safety and standards in specific areas from the farm onwards;

- Dr. Philip Stott, professor of Biogeography in the University of London and editor of the *Journal of Biogeography*.

I should note that the article also includes the opinion of an executive with the agribusiness corporation Monsanto, an odd choice likely made by the editors to highlight "corporate interest" in denying the benefits of organic foods.

There are, in fact, many highly qualified professionals who have weighed in on this question over the years that Organicfood.co.uk could have asked and/or quoted.

The following is a collection of the statements and comments of credentialed, independent scientists, scientific organizations, and other experts that have expressed an opinion on the merits (or lack thereof) of organic foods. It is by no means a complete list, but illustrates the depth and breadth of learned scholars — food and farming experts all — who have studied organic foods and farming methods and come to the opposite conclusions of organic believers. These should be measured against the extremely small number of credentialed scientists who support organic and whose own organic research has mostly failed to support the claims of superiority. The organic lobby would have you believe that all of these experts are ignoring reality because they are in the pocket of the "chemical farming industry." Decide for yourself after reviewing their statements, qualifications, and motivations.

Norman Borlaug, Ph.D., Nobel Peace Prize Laureate, "Father of the Green Revolution" that saved an estimated 1 billion humans from starvation. Interview from *Reason Magazine*
Question: What do you think of organic farming? A lot of people claim it's better for human health and the environment.

Borlaug: "That's ridiculous. This shouldn't even be a debate. … If people want to believe that the organic food has better nutritive value, it's up to them to make that foolish decision. But there's absolutely no research that shows that organic foods provide better nutrition. As far as plants are concerned, they can't tell whether that nitrate ion comes from artificial chemicals or from decomposed organic matter. If some consumers believe that it's better from the point of view of their health to have organic food, God bless them. Let them buy it. Let them pay a bit more. It's a free society."

American Society for Microbiology (non-profit representing more than 40,000 microbiologists)
Comment to USDA on Proposed National Organic Program
"In response to the notice published [in March of 2000] the American Society for Microbiology would like to comment on the proposed rule to establish the National Organic Program. … The ASM is concerned that the USDA organic foods' seal will be perceived by consumers as an assurance of both safety and quality. Before this conclusion can be drawn a comprehensive survey of organic foods for foodborne pathogens is needed to evaluate the safety of such foods. … The proven association of foodborne pathogens with both fresh produce and manure raises concerns regarding the microbiological safety of fruits and vegetables grown in soil fertilized by manure. Research is needed to identify conditions for the safe use of manure in fruit and vegetable production. In addition, copper, a heavy metal, is allowed in production and its use need not be identified in the final product. Studies on the microbiological safety of organic foods are limited. Available data on pathogen and copper prevalence indicate that organic foods are no safer than, and may not be as safe as, conventionally grown foods. … Thus, [the American Society for Microbiology] proposes the USDA explicitly include in its seal of approval, a disclaimer that the food in question does not meet safety standards. It is disingenuous to not provide such information."

Federation of Animal Science Societies (non-profit representing collectively tens of thousands of scientists with government, academia, and industry)
Statement released March 26, 2003
"An important point is that the National Organic Program is a marketing program, not a food safety, nor food healthfulness program. The NOP regulations do not address nutritional content of foods, food safety, nor animal well-being. … it is erroneous to imply that organic foods are safer and more healthful than conventional foods, or vice versa. … However, studies that have been conducted on the microbiological safety of organic foods show evidence for concern. … In conclusion, while organic foods offer the consumer a choice, there is no evidence of nutritional difference between organic and conventionally produced meat, milk, and eggs. Furthermore, there is no evidence that organic foods are any safer than conventional foods. In fact, there may be more risk associated with the use of organic foods due to their potential for introducing Campylobacter or other harmful microorganisms into the food chain."

Institute of Food Technologists (non-profit representing thousands of sci-entists with government, academia, and industry)
Press Release, November 5, 2002
"Organic foods are not superior in nutritional quality or safety when com-pared against conventional foods, yet organics do have the potential for greater pathogen contamination. Thus, purchasing organically grown pro-duce is not necessary for safety or nutritional reasons, according to the Institute of Food Technologists, an international, not-for-profit scientific society. 'Consumers need to understand that organic production does not mean pesticide-free and pathogen-free production,' says IFT food science expert Carl Winter, the director of the FoodSafe Program at University of California at Davis."

American Phytopathological Society (non-profit representing thousands of plant health scientists with government, academia, and industry)
Comment on USDA Organic Program
"In response to the notice published March 13, 2000, in the Federal Register, the APS would like to comment on the proposed rule on the establishment of the National Organic Program. ... The proven association of foodborne pathogens with both fresh produce and manure raises concerns regarding the microbiological safety of fruits and vegetables grown in soil fertilized by manure. Research is needed to identify conditions for the safe use of manure in fruit and vegetable production, which is not dealt with in the cited com-posting standards. ... Studies on the microbiological safety of organic foods are limited. Available data on pathogen and copper prevalence, as well as tox-ins produced by fungi (mycotoxins), indicate that organic foods are no safer than, and may not be as safe as, conventionally grown foods. ... The USDA should require a disclaimer on all labels that the organic seal is unrelated to safety standards."

Sir John Krebs, chairman of the UK Food Standards Agency
"Organic food is an important addition to consumer choice, but no independ-ent scientific evaluation has ever shown that it is any healthier. ... [Organic food consumers are] not getting value for money, in my opinion and in the opinion of the Food Standards Agency, if they think they're buying food with extra nutritional quality or extra safety. We don't have the evidence to support those claims."

Dr. Ian Brown, B.Sc. of Agriculture and fellow of the Royal College of Physicians
Chairman, Pesticide Residues Committee, UK:
"The [pesticide residues] are not only low, but are usually hardly measurable at all, they are parts per million or per billion. I monitor the system to make sure public health is not being compromised and so far I am satisfied that it has not been. There is nothing to worry about, our food is safe."

Dr. Hugh Pennington, Ph.D.
Scotland's top food expert
"I don't think organic food is healthier. It may use less pesticides but the amount of pesticides used in non-organic food is unlikely to do anybody any harm. It is about zero. Supermarket food is much safer than 30 years ago. Organic food is just as likely to give you food poisoning. People seem to think that just because it's organic, it's healthier — it is not. Just because an animal is free-range doesn't make it safer to eat. [Biotech food] is perfectly safe, possibly far safer than organic."

Dr. Michael A. Wilson, fellow of the Royal Society of Edinburgh
Chief executive, Horticulture Research International, UK
"The organic industry and the whole organic myth-promoting machine basically make up the rules as they go along to suit themselves. ... Moreover, the organic industry is not allowed [by the Advertising Standards Authority] to make any claims about the product being healthier, tastier, or more nutritious than conventionally grown crops, as there is no sound scientific evidence to support any of these claims. Science, facts and reason clearly have no place in the massive con-trick that surrounds the Emperor's New (Organic) Clothes."

Also: "The view of molecular scientists and biochemists is that the pro-organic lobby support their message with scare stories designed to scare the public and promote their products. To senior academic colleagues, that is crossing the line into unethical behavior. If you stick to the science, organic farms produce lower yields and more pests and there is no evidence to substantiate their claims."

Richard Gallagher, editor, *The Scientist*
Excerpt from "The Organic Food Placebo," October 11, 2004, editorial
"I find myself at the same pole as Dick Taverne. ... He characterizes the organic food movement as a massive con trick: '... the craze for organic food is built

on myth. It starts with a scientific howler, has rules with neither rhyme nor reason. None of the claims made for it have ever been substantiated, and if it grows it will damage the nation's health.' The 'scientific howler' in question is that 'natural' chemicals are good and synthetic chemicals bad. Are organic foods safer? No. ... Well how about taste? No again. ... Given all this, how has the organic movement become so successful? Why have so many been taken in? We now have our answer: the placebo effect writ large ... a recent super-market-commissioned poll, which revealed that, yes, simply making the choice to buy organic food can induce a sense of well-being. According to the BBC, 'One nutritionist says people feel [that] organic food can even boost emotional and mental health, increasing their sense of well-being and optimism when they choose the food they think is healthier.'"

Dr. Tony Trewavas, Ph.D.
Institute of Cell and Molecular Biology
University of Edinburgh, Scotland
"Organic food is more expensive because it uses land more wastefully."

"It would be difficult to make a case for organic farming on any reasonable basis for environmental benefit."

"There is no basis for the [superiority assertions] of organic farming once [farm management] is taken into account. Proper experimentation indicates that organic agriculture is just another form of agriculture with its own problems and difficulties and no better than other alternatives."

Experts vs. Experts

You might ask yourself why one should believe the opinions of these scientists over the opinions of other health activists and individuals. After all, nobody has absolute knowledge, and scientific opinions seemingly change constantly as new knowledge is gathered and examined. This is all certainly true. Science is never absolute and is always subject to change. However, there are other reasons to doubt the self-serving claims of organic food proponents — especially ones who earn their living peddling organic foods.

Most important is the track record of so-called "healthy lifestyle" experts of the past, who made their living telling people that the medical establishment and food scientists were wrong. Here are a few of these past "lifestyle" experts and the stories of their average or early demise.

U.S. organic pioneer, Jerome Rodale: Widely considered the founder of the U.S. organic farming movement and founder of the Rodale Institute and organic publishing empire, Rodale Press, Rodale was inspired by the early teachings of organic activists in Europe, including Rudolf Steiner.

Rodale began farming organically in the U.S. in 1940 and immediately began promoting himself and his organic beliefs. He launched *Organic Gardening* magazine in 1942 and *Prevention* in 1950, so named because Rodale believed that eating organic foods would prevent the onset of disease, cancer, and poor health. Today, Rodale Press publishes an array of popular magazines, including *Prevention, Organic Gardening, Men's Health, Runner's World, Backpacker, Bicycling,* and more. Most people are completely unaware of the organic philosophy behind these publications because most of the publications soft-peddle it so as not to come off as extreme.

On June 7, 1971, Mr. Rodale told the *New York Times Magazine*, "I'm going to live to be 100, unless I'm run down by a sugar-crazed taxi driver." The next day, Rodale died of a heart attack at age 73 during a taping of the Dick Cavett television talk show.

Cavett recalled the incident in a 2006 interview. "Rodale had finished a very funny half-hour — he had talked about his own health and how good he felt. He had said, 'I plan to live to be 100.' It happened not long after he offered me asparagus boiled in urine, which I promised to take home and sample there — somehow the uric acid made some healthful combination."

Later during the taping of the show, Cavett says he and journalist Peter Hamill were discussing politics when they suddenly heard what sounded like a loud snore and noticed Rodale's chin had dropped to his chest. The episode never aired, but accounts reported that Cavett, thinking his guest had dozed, quipped, "Are we boring you Mr. Rodale?"

Cavett says he's not sure if he said that. "I can't imagine that I would. My memory is, my first thought was this guy is dead. He has joined the silent majority." Audience members at first laughed, thinking it was all a joke, then cried as firefighters tried to revive him.

Linda McCartney, wife of Beatle Paul McCartney: Linda was a long-time organic and meat-free food advocate. She created her own line of meatless frozen foods, "Linda McCartney Kitchen Garden," that includes a range of organic products. The brand is now owned by H.J. Heinz Company foods. She died of breast cancer at age 56, in 1998.

Roy Walford: Dr. Walford was a longevity scientist and UCLA medical school professor. He studied why mice fed a calorie-restricted diet seemed to live 30% to 40% longer than mice fed a normal diet. Dr. Walford wrote many books on the topic, including *Maximum Life Span, The 120 Year Diet, The Anti-Aging Plan: Strategies and Recipes for Extending Your Healthy Years,* and *Beyond the 120 Year Diet: How to Double Your Vital Years.* Dr. Walford also participated in the infamous Biosphere 2 experiment that attempted to re-create all of earth's ecosystems in a self-sustaining mega-greenhouse in an Arizona desert. During the experiment, food ran critically short because of crop failures inside the greenhouse — they had refused to use chemical pesticides and instead had tried to control pests with "biocontrol" organisms and integrated pest management. Despite the lack of adequate food, Dr. Walford convinced the other seven participants to stay and try to eke out their remaining time on a highly restricted diet with meat eaten only once per week. They had to resort to eating the crop seeds reserved for planting future crops, yet even that wasn't enough.

Dr. Walford practiced what he preached outside the failed Biosphere 2 experiment. For over three decades he restricted his diet to just 1,600 calories per day and kept himself to a tiny 130 pounds. He also ran religiously and followed much of the popular wisdom on a healthy lifestyle. His work and activism lead to the creation of the Calorie Restriction Society and an army of followers who are to this day leading austere, calorie-limited lives in the hopes of living to 120 or more.

Yet despite all of his efforts, in 2004 Dr. Walford succumbed to Lou Gehrig's disease at the age of 79, just over three years older than the average U.S. life expectancy for white males.

Paavo Airola: Dr. Airola was a self-proclaimed "health expert" in the United States who wrote more than a dozen books on how to use diet and nutrition to improve your health. His books included *Are You Confused, There Is a Cure for Arthritis, How to Get Well* (over 800,000 sold), and *How to Keep Slim, Healthy and Young With Juice Fasting,* among others. Many of his books are still sold today through health food stores. The book jacket to one states that Dr. Airola was "an internationally recognized nutritionist, naturopathic physician, award-winning author, and renowned lecturer. He studied nutrition, biochemistry, and biological medicine in Europe, then spent many years studying ancient, herbal, and alternative healing methods during his worldwide travels. He acquired his clinical experience while directing various biological medical clinics in Europe and Mexico. Because of his pioneering work and extensive knowledge, Dr. Airola is looked upon as a world-leading authority on nutrition and holistic medicine."

Dr. Airola died of a stroke at age 64, more than a full decade short of the average for white males in the U.S.

Nathan Pritikin: He dropped out of college after just two years. After working as an engineer, Pritikin founded a chain of Longevity and Wellness Centers. He authored or coauthored several books, including *The Pritikin Program for Diet and Exercise, The Pritikin Promise: 28 Days to a Longer and Healthier Life,* and his last book, *Diet for Runners.* The "Pritikin Diet," as it has become known, consists mainly of fresh and cooked fruits and vegetables, whole grains, breads and pasta, and small amounts of lean meat, fish, and poultry, all coupled with a daily regimen of aerobic exercise — all pretty sound and commonsensical health and diet advice.

Yet despite his following and his many "longevity and wellness" spas, Nathan Pritikin died at the fairly typical age of 69 in 1985. His followers claim that he died as a result of complications from an experimental drug therapy used to treat the leukemia that he suffered from. In reality, he committed suicide because of his rapidly declining health.

As John MacGregor writes, "Australian health writer Ross Horne, a friend of Pritikin's, says he would have lived years longer had he only embraced 'man's natural diet,' fruitarianism." Speaking of which …

T.C. Fry: Fry was a promoter of fruitarianism and a leader in the "Natural Hygiene" and Raw-Food movements in the U.S. Most "Natural Hygiene" and raw-foods fanatics are also heavily into organic foods. Fry wrote numerous booklets on his diet philosophy, including *The Great AIDS Hoax, How to Determine Your Natural Dietetic Character, The Great Fruitarian Debate,* and *The Incredible Diet.*

Yet for all his teachings on how to live a long and healthy life, Fry died at age 70 from a coronary embolism, consequent to severely clogged arteries. As one devotee wrote after his death, "Many people want to know why Fry died at the early age of 70 years of age of a coronary embolism, why he had multiple atherosclerotic thrombi of his lower legs, why he had edema of both his ankles, why he had a lesion of the upper lobe of his left lung, why he was anemic, why he had a high acid blood pH, why he had difficulty breathing, why he was lacking energy, why he lost so much weight, … why he was osteoporotic, why his teeth and mouth were in such poor shape." All are good questions about a guy who pontificated for most of his adult life on his "superior" physical health and fitness due to his supposedly strict fruitarian diet. Some of his followers and employees contend that they used to hear "suspicious plastic wrapper" noises when Fry would shut himself in closets or empty rooms at a Missouri "wellness" clinic he founded.

Jim Fixx: Fixx is considered to have founded the U.S. runners movement (for good health) in the 1970s via his best-selling book, *The Complete Book of Running*. At the time it was published in 1977, it was the best-selling non-fiction book in history. One chapter was a fierce rebuttal of a *Playboy* magazine article titled, "Jogging Can Kill You." Fixx ardently believed that running was a key to good health and longevity. In an ironic tragedy, Fixx died of a heart attack while jogging at age 52. An autopsy revealed that his coronary arteries were nearly completely blocked with fatty deposits and he had apparently suffered three previous heart attacks in the weeks before his death.

George Ohsawa: He was the inventor of the macrobiotics diet (macrobiotics literally means "long life"), author of *Zen Macrobiotics*, and founder of the Macrobiotics Foundation. Macrobiotics is a diet heavy in grains. Ohsawa died of lung cancer at 73.

Adelle Davis: Davis was the author of *Let's Eat Right*, which sold more than 10 million copies, and many other best-selling health-through-diet books throughout the 1960s and 1970s. Davis used to say that she never saw anyone die of cancer who drank a quart of milk per day. She died of cancer at age 70, several years below the average for white women in the U.S.

Dr. Stuart Berger: He advocated vitamins, minerals, and exercise for good health and a long life. Berger authored numerous diet and health books, including *How to Be Your Own Nutritionist*, *Stuart Berger's Immune Power Cookbook*, and *The Southampton Diet*. Dr. Berger died at age 40 of obesity-related health problems, weighing 365 lbs. at the time of his death.

Most of these so-called "health experts" died at or before the averages for their gender, averages that are created by the vast majority of consumers out there who don't follow austere, stringent, or particularly regimented diets; averages that are created by the vast majority of consumers who do NOT eat organic foods. In fact, these averages include those who die of accidents and other non-diet-related causes. They also include smokers, drug users, the sexually promiscuous, heavy drinkers, and the overweight — all of which are generally bad for one's health.

While this isn't a recommendation to forget common-sense health advice, such as to not smoke cigarettes, to eat a balanced diet, and to engage in regular exercise, it demonstrates that those who claim to have "the answers" to a healthy or long life usually don't.

I'll say it one last time: There simply isn't any evidence whatsoever that eating an organic diet and living an "organic lifestyle" prolong one's life or are in any way healthier than eating a balanced diet of plain, old, regular, non-organic foods.

I challenge anyone to provide me with the evidence otherwise. It simply doesn't exist.

Chapter 4:

Is Organic Food Safer?
Think Again

Organic Faithful Say:

"Organic products are no more or no less susceptible to *E. coli* contamination than are foods produced by non-organic methods."

Whole Foods Market: Issues & Actions: Food Safety : *E. coli* ($)[1]
www.wholefoods.com/issues/ecoli.html Nov. 12, 1996

"Are organic products more likely to be contaminated by *E. coli*? No, there is no reputable scientific evidence to indicate this. All food — whether conventional or organic — is susceptible to *E. coli*."

Organic Trade Association Web site ($)
http://www.ota.com/organic/foodsafety/ecoli.html

"Our research found that organic farming practices can reduce the risk of bacteria such as *E. coli* in food. Those critics who slam organic food for being high risk and more likely to cause food poisoning are wrong."

Adrian Long, head of Communications for the British-based Soil Association ($)
"Organic Myths Busted in New Report," press release, August 13, 2001

---

[1]($) Indicates that the person quoted has a profit motive or other financial interest in promoting organic food.

"There is no real reason or evidence that organic farming has higher levels of mycotoxin."

Anonymous spokeswoman, U.K. Soil Association ($)
Times Higher Education Supplement, October 21, 2003

"Accusations of organic food being a greater toxicological risk (from *E. coli* 0157 or aflatoxins) are unsubstantiated, with no real evidence or logic to justify them."

Craig Sams, president of Whole Earth Foods organic retailer and paid consultant of the Soil Association ($)
From interview in Organicfood.com.uk
http://www.organicfood.co.uk/sense/betterforyou.html

Reality Says:

"The percentages of *E. coli*-positive samples in conventional and organic produce were 1.6% and 9.7%, respectively. ... Organic lettuce had the largest prevalence of *E. coli* (22.4%) compared with other produce types."

University of Minnesota study published in the *Journal of Food Protection*, May 2004
(J of Food Prot 67, vol. 5, pages 894-900)

"The real bad news for you organics buyers is that the average concentration of *E. coli* in the contaminated [organic] spring mix was much higher ... the organics were twice as likely to have E. coli and had larger amounts."

ABC NEWS 20/20 How Good Is Organic Food?
February 20, 2000

"Experts say that increased consumption of organically grown, unprocessed foods produced without synthetic fertilizers, pesticides, or preservatives may also be contributing to the [problem of increased foodborne illness from produce]. "Organic 'means a food is grown in animal manure,' noted Robert V. Tauxe, M.D., MPH, chief of the CDC's foodborne and diarrheal diseases branch"

Journal of the American Medical Association, Medical News and Perspectives — January 8, 1997
(JAMA 277:97-98)

"By not applying normal plant protection measures, such as fungicides, organic food would appear to be more at risk from mycotoxins contamination."

Dr. Jim Duncan, Ph.D., senior scientist, Scottish Crop Research Institute
Times Higher Education Supplement, October 21, 2003

The U.K.'s Food Standards Agency (FSA) found that all six organic corn meal products the agency purchased from supermarket shelves and tested failed the proposed European Commission safety limit for fumonisin of 500 parts per billion. The average level found on the organic corn meals was 1,800% above this limit, with the lowest fumonisin level in organic corn still six times the safety limit. In comparison, the fumonisin level of 20 non-organic corn meals was only 121 ppb. Fumonisin is a fungal toxin that is a likely human carcinogen and suspected of causing devastating birth defects such as spina bifida.

> Results of Food Standards Agency product testing survey and recall, September 2003
> http://www.food.gov.uk/news/newsarchive/2003/sep/moremaize

Perhaps the biggest myth about organic foods is that they are demonstrably safer than conventional foods. In fact, the available evidence indicates that organic foods pose more, not fewer, food safety risks than conventional foods.

But there are no doubts that consumers believe organic foods are safer. Just listen to the response of a consumer asked by ABC News 20/20 at a supermarket why she is buying organic foods: "Safer, yes, safer and better, because I just really believe it's better for the whole family."

A 2004 survey of organic food consumers by the Chicago market research firm Mintel found that roughly half of organic food consumers said they were "highly concerned" about food safety while another third had a "medium" level of concern. That's over 80% of respondents. Why do so many consumers believe that organic foods are safer?

Organic proponents underscore that organic foods generally have lower levels of synthetic pesticide residues than conventional products. These supposed pesticide risks are tiny and purely theoretical. These proponents refuse to acknowledge the clearly higher risk of food-borne illnesses and fungal toxins posed by organic foods, which are both real and potentially fatal.

Instead, the organic faithful continue to claim or strongly imply that organic foods are safer in all ways than conventional foods. They dismiss documented cases of people sickened by organic foods as exceptions caused by mishandling or "bacterial pollution" from non-organic farms. They completely ignore the higher fungal contamination levels in their grains. They embark on incredible disinformation campaigns, attempting to get fired any reporter who dares to look critically at organic foods. (This really happened to John Stossel of ABC News' "20/20" program. You can read all about it in his book *Give Me a Break*, 2004).

They seem to be unable to acknowledge the real and potential food safety shortcomings of organic farming methods, while exaggerating beyond all reason any real or imagined shortcomings of "conventional" farming.

The food safety risks from organic foods are comparatively low in global and historical terms, but they are not insignificant. Consumers should be well aware of organic food's susceptibility to foodborne pathogens and fungal toxins, as these threats are the most serious food safety risks in our food supply today.

More than 70 million people in the U.S. are afflicted with a foodborne illness each year, many of them exposed to pathogenic bacteria via fresh, uncooked vegetables and fruits. Hundreds of thousands of these victims are hospitalized every year, with an estimated 5,000 losing their lives. Many of the survivors will have permanent organ damage.

The available evidence indicates that organic produce is considerably more likely to carry these foodborne bacteria, due to organic farmers' heavy reliance on animal manure for fertilizer. Animal manures are a primary source of these infectious microbes. While conventional farmers use animal manure as well, they don't often use it on food crops such as fruits and vegetables. Instead, they mostly apply it to fields growing crops such as corn for livestock feed.

Organic foods are also more likely to be contaminated by fungal toxins, where the risks range from birth defects and esophageal cancer to liver and kidney diseases. Recent testing by the British Food Standards Agency showed that organic corn meals had radically higher contamination rates for the dangerous fungal toxin fumonisin. All organic brands of corn meal tested by the agency were beyond safety limits and had to be recalled. Contamination of homemade corn tortillas by this toxin is suspected of causing an epidemic of birth defects in Brownsville, Texas, in the early 1990s.

The Facts

There are several published scientific studies that indicate the higher risk of foodborne pathogens and fungal toxins in organic foods.

The most recent study finding an increased risk in organic foods was conducted at the University of Minnesota by Dr. Francisco Diez-Gonzalez and his students.[2] They examined fresh fruits and vegetables from 32 organic farms and compared them to produce from eight non-organic farms in Minnesota, looking for *Escherichia coli*, Salmonella, and the pathogenic strain of *E. coli* O157:H7.

---

[2] Mukherjee A, et al. Preharvest Evaluation of Coliforms, *Escherichia coli*, *Salmonella*, and *Escherichia coli* O157:H7 in Organic and Conventional Produce Grown by Minnesota Farmers. *Journal of Food Protection* 67:894-900, 2004.

Salmonella is estimated by the U.S. Centers for Disease Control (CDC) to cause over 1.3 million illnesses per year. *E. coli* O157:H7 is estimated to cause over 60,000 illnesses per year. Salmonella and *E. coli* O157:H7 are the leading causes of produce-related illness outbreaks, accounting for 30% and 20% respectively. Generic *E. coli* is an indicator of fecal contamination and is used by health authorities as a red flag for food bacteria risks.

The Minnesota research found that organic produce was six times more likely to be contaminated by generic *E. coli* than conventional produce. Generic *E. coli* was present in only two out of 129 samples (1.6%) of conventional fruits and vegetables compared to 46 out of 476 samples (9.7%) of organic produce.

Some organic foods were contaminated more than others. For example, fully one-third of the study's organic onions were contaminated by *E. coli* compared to zero for conventional onions. Organic cabbage, broccoli, zucchini, and bok choi were contaminated by *E. coli* at least 10% of the time, compared to zero contamination of their conventional counterparts. Nearly one in four heads of organic lettuce was contaminated by *E. coli* (22.4%) compared to only one out of six conventional (16.7%).

Additionally, the Minnesota researchers found Salmonella in organic green peppers and lettuce, but not in any conventional foods they tested.

The researchers did not find any *E. coli* O157:H7 in any produce. However, this is not surprising given how difficult it is to isolate O157:H7 from produce. Health authorities have found very strong evidence linking fresh vegetables as the source of *E. coli* O157:H7 in 19 separate *E. coli* outbreaks in the U.S. but were unable to isolate any O157:H7 in the contaminated products. An examination of some 4,000 fruit and vegetable samples also failed to isolate any O157:H7.

Curiously, the Minnesota researchers did not compare the amounts of *E. coli* on organic to the amounts of *E. coli* on conventional produce. Instead, they report only the average *E. coli* level of all positive food samples, both organic and conventional (~1,200 Colony Forming Units per gram). When contacted, Dr. Diez-Gonzalez stated that he didn't believe there were any differences in *E. coli* levels between the contaminated organic and contaminated conventional foods, yet would not share data to support this claim. He clearly has these data; otherwise he could not have calculated the average bacteria level for all positive samples.

Previous research by the University of Georgia has shown that organic foods may have more than 100 times more *E. coli* when contaminated than conventional. It stands to reason that if a higher proportion of organic samples are contaminated, contamination levels would be higher too.

The comparatively high "fecal contamination" rate for organic produce makes sense. All 32 organic farms included in the Minnesota study reported using "aged or composted animal manure regularly as a main source of fertilizer." One spread untreated manure as a fertilizer right through harvest time! In comparison, only four of the eight non-organic farms reported using any manure at all, and it is unlikely they used it as extensively as the organic farms.

Of the 15 farms where *E. coli*-contaminated foods were found, two were conventional and 13 were organic. But only 5.5% of the samples from the conventional manure-using farms were contaminated, versus 20% of the samples from the organic manure-using farms.

Dr. Michael Doyle at the University of Georgia has also found more bacterial contamination of organic foods. Dr. Doyle's research found Salmonella in 7.7% (three of 39 samples) of organic sprouts but none in 39 samples of conventional sprouts. He also found *E. coli* in 16.7% (eight of 48 samples) in organic "spring mix" lettuce versus only 8.3% in conventional spring mix.

Importantly, there was 100 times more *E. coli* in the contaminated organic spring mix compared to the conventional spring mix (1 million CFU per gram in organic versus 10,000 CFU in conventional).

When Dr. Doyle was hired by ABC-TV's "20/20" program to look for *E. coli* in produce and mixed spring greens for a story on the safety of organic foods, he again found about twice as much *E. coli* on organic "spring greens" compared to conventional — finding it both on a higher proportion of samples and at significantly higher levels.

Finally, there have been outbreaks of *E. coli* O157:H7 associated with organic lettuce and salmonellosis from organic sprouts. Organic lettuce caused outbreaks of *E. coli* O157:H7 in Connecticut and Illinois in May and June of 1996. The lettuce was traced back to a California organic farm.

Organic believers, seemingly incapable of accepting that organic farming isn't perfect, have claimed that the lettuce was contaminated in the shed where the lettuce was packed for shipping, which was located near or adjacent to a cattle holding facility, rather than in the field. This may or may not be the case.

Generic *E. coli* was found both in the lettuce rinse water and in the finished lettuce at this organic farm. However, it is impossible to know for sure the source of the *E. coli* in the rinse water and finished lettuce. Did it come from the manure-fertilized organic field or from manure in the cattle holding pen adjacent to the packing shed? It is far more plausible that *E. coli* O157:H7 contaminated some of the lettuce in the field and was brought into the packing shed via the harvested organic lettuce — thus contaminating the lettuce rinse water and subsequent heads of lettuce — than any scenario whereby manure from a nearby cattle holding pen contaminates the rinse water. How would manure from the cattle pen get into the lettuce rinse water?

The worry over vegetable and fruit contamination of organic foods runs deeper than simply adequate pre-washing of foods before eating them. Research published in the *Journal of Applied Environmental Microbiology* indicates that E. *coli* O157:H7 can enter crops via the roots and migrate to edible portions of the plant. This makes washing pathogens from the foods essentially impossible.[3] As the researchers wrote, "E. *coli* O157:H7 migrated to internal locations in plant tissue and was thus protected from the action of sanitizing agents by virtue of its inaccessibility."

Chicken Soup

Organic food consumers should also be aware of the risk of Salmonella and other illness bacteria, such as Campylobacter, from organic and free-range chickens. Campylobacter is the leading cause of foodborne bacterial illnesses. The CDC estimates it causes nearly 2 million cases per year. These bacteria have been found more often and at higher levels in organic and free-range birds.

A study in Denmark in 2001 found that organic chicken are three times more likely to be contaminated by Campylobacter than conventional chickens. Whereas all 22 organic chicken flocks were infected with the bacteria (100%), only 29 of 79 conventional chicken flocks were infected (36.7%).[4]

Britain's Food Standards Agency found similar patterns of higher organic contamination with Campylobacter when it studied the issue in 2002. The agency found that more than 99% of organic chicken flocks were infected with Campylobacter, compared to only 56% of conventional flocks.

Experts theorize that the higher Salmonella and Campylobacter contamination rate of organic chickens is due to more time spent outdoors where they are exposed to wild bird feces and other sources of the bacteria. Organic birds

---

[3] Solomon E.B., et al. Transmission of *Escherichia coli* O157:H7 from Contaminated Manure and Irrigation Water to Lettuce Plant Tissue and Its Subsequent Internalization. *Applied and Environmental Microbiology* 68:397-400, 2002.

[4] Heuer O.E., et al. Prevalence and Antimicrobial Susceptibility of Thermophilic Campylobacter in Organic and Conventional Broiler Flocks. Letters in *Applied Microbiology* 33:269-274, 2001.

also take nearly twice as long to reach a marketable weight, thus providing greater opportunity for the bacteria to infect the birds.

While proper cooking of the chicken will kill these illness-causing bacteria (i.e., thoroughly cooking the meat up to 160° F), they can also contaminate any cutting boards and kitchen utensils used to prepare the raw meat. Therefore, unless stringent food hygiene procedures are followed, such as washing everything that has contacted the raw poultry meat, the risks of contracting a foodborne illness from organic birds are higher.

E. coli Hullabaloo

My group at the Hudson Institute first noted the likely higher *E. coli* contamination rate of organic foods in 1998, after we ran across the comments of Dr. Tauxe, head of the CDC's foodborne illness division, published in early 1997 in the *Journal of the American Medical Association (JAMA)* (quoted at the beginning of this chapter).

Dr. Tauxe suggested during a talk at a scientific meeting that the apparent increase in the number of *E. coli* O157:H7 cases originating from fruits and vegetables in the mid-1990s was linked to increased consumption of organic foods. Here is an excerpt of the Medical News & Perspectives article published in JAMA in January 1997:

> Experts say that increased consumption of organically grown, unprocessed foods produced without synthetic fertilizers, pesticides, or preservatives may also be contributing to the problem.
>
> "'Organic' means a food is grown in animal manure," noted Robert V. Tauxe, M.D., MPH, chief of the CDC's foodborne and diarrheal diseases branch, at the 36th Interscience Conference on Antimicrobial Agents and Chemotherapy, also held in New Orleans.
>
> Studies have found that E. coli *can survive in cow manure for 70 days and can multiply in foods grown with manure, unless heat or additives such as salt or preservatives are used to kill the microbes.*
>
> But there are essentially no regulations related to the use of animal manure in agriculture, said Tauxe, who predicted that oversight of the problem will ultimately be instituted by some government agency.
>
> "We got rid of human waste in our food and water, and I think we're going to have better control in the future of manure in our food and water," he said.

Dr. Tauxe's comments were based on the CDC's 1996 data on outbreaks of *E. coli* O157:H7, (See Table 1, page 82). According to these data, 24% of all O157:H7 cases that were traced back to a source by the CDC in 1996 were attributed to organic and natural foods. In fact, more than one-third of all traced cases caused by contaminated food (i.e., excluding cases resulting from person-to-person contact or from swimming pools) were from organic and natural foods.

My group (The Center for Global Food Issues) first wrote about organic food's potentially higher food safety risk in the fall of 1998 in a magazine published by the Hudson Institute, of which the Center for Global Food Issues is a part. The backlash against us from the organic faithful and industry was incredible. The CDC was inundated with angry phone calls demanding to see "the study" on which our article was written. But we had not claimed that the CDC had conducted a detailed study comparing the risk levels of organic and conventional foods. The first sentence of our article stated clearly, "According to recent data compiled by the U.S. Centers for Disease Control."

In response to the avalanche of angry phone calls from irate organic activists, the CDC released a public statement (not a press release) hoping to quell the furor:

> "Since 1982, most of the outbreaks of *Escherichia coli* O157:H7 have been associated with foods of bovine origin (e.g. ground beef). In recent years, a wider spectrum of foods, including produce, have been recognized as causes of outbreaks. The Centers for Disease Control and Prevention (CDC) has not conducted any study that compares or quantitates the specific risk for infection with *Escherichia coli* O157:H7 and eating either conventionally grown or organic/natural foods. CDC recommends that growers practice safe and hygienic methods for producing food products and that consumers, likewise, practice food safety within their homes (e.g., thoroughly washing fruits and vegetables). These recommendations apply to both conventionally grown and organic foods.
> — Dr. Mitch Cohen, CDC

Organic activists immediately seized on the CDC statement to claim that we had fabricated the CDC data. The Organic Trade Association posted a statement on its Web site saying, "According to Robert Tauxe, M.D., chief of the foodborne and diarrheal diseases branch of the CDC, there is no such data on organic food production in existence at their centers."

The debate quickly became absurd. The Henry A. Wallace Institute for

Table 1:

CLUSTERS/OUTBREAKS OF *E. COLI* O157:H7 INFECTIONS REPORTED TO CDC IN 1996.

#	Month	State	Setting	Number ill	Likely vehicle or mode of spread
1	4	TX	Home	3	Ground beef
2	5	CT & IL	Home	47	Lettuce (organic)
3	6	WA	Pool	4	Swimming
4	6	MN	Lake	8	Swimming
5	6	NY	Restaurant	61	Unknown
6	6	MI & OH	Restaurant	10	Unknown
7	6	NH & MA	Community	29	Unknown
8	6	MN	Day-care	7	Person-to-person
9	6	OR	Picnic	38	Unknown
10	6	NY	Nursing home	5	Person-to-person
11	6	PA	Day-care	3	Person-to-person
12	6	NC	Day-care	2	Person-to-person
13	7	NV	Party	2	Ground beef
14	7	GA	Pool	18	Swimming
15	7	MO	Community	3	Unknown
16	8	PA	Party	9	Ground beef
17	8	MN	Day-care	8	Person-to-person
18	8	MS	School	36	Person-to-person
19	8	MN	Day-care	63	Person-to-person
20	9	VT	Fair/Festival	11	Unknown
21	9	RI	Community	5	Unknown
22	9	NY	Day-care	9	Person-to-person
23	9	OR	Restaurant	7	Ground beef
24	10	CA,WA,CO	Community	71	Apple juice (unpasturized natural)
25	10	CT	Home	14	Apple cider
26	10	MN	Day-care	3	Person-to-person
27	10	WA	Fair/Festival	8	Apple cider
28	11	IL	Home	2	Venison
29	12	OR	Home	4	Venison
			Total	488	

Alternative Agriculture (an organic activist group) issued a press release with the headline, "Contrary to Avery article, CDC has never conducted study of the risk of organic food." At one point, a publication called *PR Watch*, published by the Center for Media & Democracy, even claimed we had fabricated the quotes from the CDC's Dr. Tauxe published in the *Journal of the American Medical Association*.

However, the more recent research by Dr. Doyle and Dr. Diez-Gonzalez has completely supported Dr. Tauxe's initial concerns and the CDC's 1996 data. All of the available research indicates that organic produce carries a markedly higher foodborne illness risk due to organic farmers' heavy reliance on manure fertilizers.

In fact, the Minnesota research indicates that manure-handling regulations should be tightened for all growers of fruits and vegetables, organic and conventional. Produce from farms that used manure aged or composted for less than one year had a 19-fold (1,900%) higher *E. coli* contamination rate than produce from farms that used manure more than one year old.

Current USDA National Organic Program rules allow raw, uncomposted manure to be applied as close as 90 to 120 days before harvest, even for crops intended for human consumption. In fact, composted manure can be applied after as little as three to 15 days of composting!

The Minnesota research indicates that these "pre-harvest intervals" need to be vastly increased. Yet organic farmers are already finding it difficult to comply with the current rules. I have been told by several organic farmers that the composting regulations are too strict and cost them too much time and money (manure loses nitrogen the longer it sits, so its value as fertilizer decreases the longer the required pre-harvest interval). They have a financial stake in keeping the manure-handling regulations as lax as possible. But food safety must come before financial gain.

Fungal Toxins

The second serious food safety risk in organic foods is fungal toxins, also called mycotoxins, produced by fungi growing on grains, fruits, and vegetables. While some mycotoxins, such as aflatoxin, have been known for decades and are strictly regulated in the food supply, many others have only recently been discovered and have yet to be regulated. The list of known health impacts from fungal toxins is growing each year.

Fungal toxins are probably the fungi's way of preventing other microorganisms and animals from competing for their food sources. Fungal toxins are a way of making grains and foods usable only to the fungus.

There are a large variety of fungal toxins produced by many different fungi. Some mycotoxins damage the liver and kidneys, while others cause general cell death or interfere with DNA replication. Fungal toxins pose both short-term (acute) and long-term (chronic) food safety risks. Bottom line: mycotoxins are a real and serious food safety risk and their presence in the food supply should be avoided and minimized as much as possible.

Fungal toxins are particularly a problem in organic foods because organic farmers are prohibited from using the most effective fungicides, which are all synthetic. The fungicides that they are allowed to use, copper and sulfur chemicals, are expensive and not very effective. Thus, most organic farmers avoid using them and even when they are used, they don't suppress fungi very well.

For example, the main reason why organic potato yields are only about 50% to 60% of conventional potato yields is fungal diseases like late blight (Phytophthora infestans). Yet these low yields are harvested despite the routine preventative use of copper and sulfur as fungicides in organic potato production (copper and sulfur must be applied *before* the disease hits). Without these organic fungicides, potato yields would be even lower still.

While the research data are limited, the fact of organic foods' higher mycotoxin risk is clear. The most recent evidence is from the UK, where the food safety authorities are beginning to implement new limits on the amounts of a toxin called fumonisin in grains, especially corn.

Fumonisin was first isolated and identified by South African researchers looking for the cause of persistent livestock miscarriages and still-births. After 18 years of research, they eventually identified the cause as fumonisin in feed grains.

Since the discovery and characterization of fumonisin, South African medical authorities have established a link between high fumonisin levels in corn and high esophageal cancer rates in the people from the Transkei region of South Africa. More recently, fumonisin contamination of homemade corn tortillas has been linked to an outbreak of birth defects (including spina bifida) near Brownsville, Texas.

As a result of these real and serious risks, food safety authorities in numerous countries have begun establishing limits on fumonisin levels allowed in human food. The EU has proposed and will soon begin enforcing a limit of 500 parts per billion (ppb) of fumonisin in food. Ahead of this new regulation, the British Food Standards Agency (FSA) began testing corn meal products in British supermarkets for fumonisin in 2003. After the FSA tested 33 corn meal brands purchased from food stores, 10 brands were found to contain above the 500 ppb limit.

All six organic corn meals tested failed this new standard, with an average fumonisin level of over 9,000 ppb. That's an abysmal 100% failure rate for organic corn. Two organic corn meals were above 16,000 ppb.

In contrast, only four of the 27 non-organic corn meal products were above the safety limit. These were mostly from Turkey and other developing countries. Of the 23 conventional corn meals that didn't fail, the average fumonisin level was only 120 ppb.

Dr. Tony Trewavas, a professor of food biochemistry at Edinburgh University who wrote to the FSA calling for an investigation into the problem, noted, "No one knows what fumonisin levels are dangerous."

We do know that fumonisin begins causing "excess tumors" (cancer) in rats somewhere between 25,000 and 50,000 ppb. This means that the more contaminated organic corn meals had fumonisin levels over one-third the level proven to cause cancer in rodents!

Dr. Michael Wilson, chief executive of the government-funded Horticulture Research International, says, "We don't have a proper grasp on the problem because no systematic analysis has been undertaken. If any Genetically Modified [food] product had the levels of toxin found in the organic corn, it would be the end for GM."

Many more food safety experts expressed alarm over the FSA's organic contamination findings and warned that these problems are inherent in organic food production due to organic growers' refusal to use effective fungicides.

Dr. Jim Duncan of the Scottish Crop Research Institute says, "By not applying normal plant protection measures, such as fungicides, organic food would appear to be more at risk from mycotoxins contamination."

Dr. Richard Mithen, head of plant foods for health protection at the Institute of Food Research, noted, "I have been concerned that more widespread adoption of organic systems will lead to a resurgence of [crop] diseases such as bunt in [cereal crops] and, with important implications for human health, a resurgence of fungal diseases that produce toxins for consumers."

Dr. Ian Crute, director of the Rothamsted Research Institute, warns, "The lack of control of plant pathogenic fungi — such as ergot — that have the potential to produce toxic metabolites is definitely an 'Achilles heel' for organics and is a food scare waiting to happen."

Dr. Peter Goodenough, principal research fellow at Reading University and editor of the *International Journal of Food Science and Technology,* said, "If growers in some climatic regions regularly grow their crops without fungicides, sooner or later ergot poisoning will occur again."

Ergot is a fungal disease of cereal crops that produces ergotomine, a dangerous fungal toxin. Famously known as St. Anthony's Fire, ergot poisoning causes hallucinations (ergot is a natural source for the recreational drug LSD), convulsions, retching, and an excruciatingly painful burning sensation in the hands and feet. Eventually, the fingers, toes, hands, and feet will fall off due to dry gangrene — caused by lack of blood flow due to constricted blood vessels. Medieval wood cuts show St. Anthony, patron saint of those who suffer in pain, surrounded by the lost hands and feet of ergot victims. Ergot poisoning killed hundreds of thousands in Europe in the 10th through 16th century.

When asked about the high levels of fumonisin found in the organic corn meals, the spokeswoman for the UK organic lobby group, the Soil Association, responded that "there is no real reason or evidence that organic farming has higher levels of mycotoxin."

The Soil Association spokeswoman even went so far as to cynically attempt to deflect attention to the theoretical and tiny risks of pesticide residues on non-organic foods. "Comparison of the levels of these compounds and the possible risks associated with them is of great importance, particularly when compared with the possible effects of the cocktails of fumigants and fungicides that may be detectable on non-organic products," she said.

According to Britain's *Times Higher Education Supplement*, the Soil Association spokeswoman "said anecdotal evidence suggested organic crops were less susceptible to fungi than conventional crops, as they possessed thicker plant-cell walls. She said fungal infections were best controlled through crop rotation, lower applications of nitrogen, and the selection of resistant crops."

But the FSA fumonisin data and years of impartial research indicate that these methods are totally inadequate at controlling fungi and the statements of the Soil Association are simply self-serving organic propaganda. Reputable, independent crop scientists have repeatedly said that by not using effective synthetic fungicides, organic farmers expose consumers to significantly higher fungal toxin risks.

Other Fungal Toxins

There are many other fungal toxins to worry about, and many that are still unknown or only poorly understood. Remember, it took 18 years of research to identify fumonisin. There are more than 300 mycotoxins known, produced by more than 350 different food-associated molds and fungi. Aside from fumonisin and ergotomine, there are aflatoxin, patulin, ochratoxin, and even vomitoxin (yes, it causes severe vomiting!).

Aflatoxin has been extensively studied and there are strict aflatoxin limits on susceptible foods, such as grains and peanuts. Because of these strict regulations and testing, organic foods for humans are no more likely to have higher levels of aflatoxin than non-organic foods. However, they do have a higher contamination rate and this means a higher percentage of organic grains and nuts are diverted to animal feeds or are destroyed as unfit for consumption.

Patulin is a fungal toxin of particular concern in apple juice. Patulin causes premature death in rats, and as a result the FDA has set an "action limit" for patulin in juices and ciders of 50 ppb. Organic apple juice has been shown to have up to 10 times higher amounts of patulin than non-organic apple juice.

Proper control of insects and fungus during apple fruit development is important, along with not using dropped apples to make ciders/juices, and culling all bruised and rotten apples before making ciders. Organic apples are more likely to suffer from the insect and fungal damage that leads to high patulin levels because of the lower effectiveness of their pesticides and fungicides.

The FDA does not test apple juices for patulin. The agency conducts only periodic surveillance and relies almost entirely on apple juice makers to comply through their processing procedures. Also, small cider makers that sell directly to consumers are exempt from the pathogen reduction requirements.

While the larger apple juice makers have established detailed handling, culling, and quality-control procedures to comply with the FDA limit and to avoid lawsuits, smaller juice makers may not. Be very careful to buy only pasteurized juice from a high-quality maker where you're reasonably sure these safety measures have been taken. Understand that pasteurization does not destroy the patulin toxin, so ensuring the cider is made from only high-quality, undamaged apples is key.

Conclusion: Moundhills?

In the final analysis, the food safety risks from organic foods aren't very high in historical terms. Our entire modern food system is vastly safer than it was even 50 years ago. We've made incredible strides in reducing the risks from bacteria and natural contaminants in our food supply and in curing illnesses after we contract them.

Despite this relatively low risk in historical terms, all the available objective evidence indicates that the food safety risks from organic foods are significantly higher that those from conventional foods. Foodborne bacterial risks are significantly higher in organic produce, as are fungal toxin risks. These higher risks have been demonstrated by multiple independent studies by researchers that are both skeptical and friendly to the organic philosophy.

This relative risk disparity shouldn't be a huge surprise, as the incredible strides in food safety over the past 50 years are the direct result of the very science and technology systematically rejected by organic farmers and consumers.

If you buy organic foods because you think you are getting a safer product, you're simply fooling yourself. In fact, you might be fooling yourself sick.

Chapter 5:

Pesticide Residue Realities

Organic Faithful Say:

"There are no pesticides ... in organic farming."
Katherine DiMatteo, executive director of the Organic Trade Association ($)[1]
From "U.S. Sets 'Organic' Standard,"
Washington Post, December 21, 2000

"Organic food excludes pesticides."
Craig Sams, president, Whole Earth Foods, London ($)
Landmark September/October 2000

Reality Says:

"Organic can never be defined as pesticide-free."
Institute for Food Science and Technology, U.K., March 16, 2001

"While synthetic pesticides are prohibited in organic farming, some 'natural' pesticides may still be used, and they are not necessarily less worrisome just because they're 'natural.'"
Ned Groth, Senior Scientist, Consumers Union (publisher of *Consumer Reports*)
quoted at: http://www.babycenter.com/expert/baby/babyfeeding/11803.html

"A cup of coffee contains natural carcinogens equal to at least a year's worth of carcinogenic synthetic residues in the diet."
Sir (Dr.) John Krebs, chairman of the United Kingdom's Food Standards Agency
quoted in: http://www.guardian.co.uk/life/lastword/story/0,13228,1438870,00.html

---

[1] ($) Indicates that the person quoted has a profit motive or other financial interest in promoting organic food.

One-quarter of organic fruits and vegetables carry measurable residues of synthetic pesticides. In fact, nearly 10% of organic fruits and vegetables have more pesticide residues than the average found on non-organic produce.[2] How did they get there? From drift and contact with processing machinery or by fraud of some unethical organic growers?

We'll return to this in a moment. But first I want to point out that the levels of synthetic pesticide residues are only half of the picture because essentially nobody is looking for residues of organic pesticides. There are no inexpensive and rapid testing methods to look for residues of organic pesticides as there are for virtually all synthetic pesticides, so the government simply doesn't look for them. Instead the government assumes that these products break down rapidly enough that there aren't enough residues to be concerned about. Governmental regulators may be right about not needing to worry, as is the case with synthetic pesticides. However, the lack of testing leaves consumers with the false impression that there aren't any organic pesticide residues. But there are.

Take rotenone, an organic pesticide extracted from the roots of several tropical plants. Often sold as "cube root" or "derris extract," rotenone is considered highly toxic to man and is extremely toxic to fish (it is often used to rid ponds of all fish for restocking with preferred species) and causes symptoms highly similar to Parkinson's disease when given to rats. In the U.S. it has been used mainly in organic tomato and lettuce crops. As of early 2006, there is no required preharvest interval for rotenone in the U.S. In other words, farmers can apply it to right up to harvest time.

Yet scientists using expensive and time-consuming laboratory detection methods have found 200 to 300 parts per billion of rotenone on lettuce up to two weeks after treatment, in addition to several hundred parts per billion of toxic breakdown products.[3] Italian researchers recently found that rotenone persists particularly long on olives and concentrates in the olive oil. They found 500 parts per billion of rotenone in the oil even 12 days after it was sprayed. This is more than 10 times the legal-

---

[2] Baker B.P., et al. Pesticide Residues in Conventional, Integrated Pest Management (IPM)-Grown and Organic Foods: Insights From Three U.S. Data Sets. *Food Additives and Contaminants* 19(5):427-446, 2002.

[3] Newsome W.H., et al. Residues of Rotenone and Rotenolone on Lettuce and Tomato Fruit After Treatment in the Field With Rotenone Formulations. *Journal of Agricultural and Food Chemistry* 28:722-724, 1980.

ly allowed residue in Italy.[4]

Organic activists have resisted even acknowledging that organic pesticides exist and that their farmers use them. Examine the USDA regulations and those of other groups, such as the Soil Association in Britain, and you'll see that they go to amazing lengths to avoid using the word pesticide. Instead they call the products "botanical extracts" or "mineral dust." They know that most consumers purchase organic foods because of fear over pesticide residues. To acknowledge the use of organic pesticides — and residues of these pesticides on food — would erode the foundation of fear that supports a sizable portion of their consumer base.

Pesticide Residues in Organic Foods

The notion that organic foods are pesticide-free is a carefully cultivated illusion.

Just ask Consumers Union (CU), the consumer group that publishes *Consumer Reports* magazine. CU's senior scientist, Dr. Ned Groth, along with a researcher from the Organic Materials Review Institute (OMRI), analyzed extensive government testing data of pesticide residues on fresh fruits and vegetables — the foods most likely to contain pesticide residues. (Processed foods are far less likely to contain any pesticide residues because processing usually breaks down remaining pesticide traces.)

The data reviewed by CU and OMRI researchers included data gathered by Consumers Union and comprehensive government data on more than 26,000 samples of "conventional" fruits and vegetables. In contrast to this huge database of non-organic foods, Groth and OMRI were only able to find government or Consumers Union data on 194 samples or organic fruits and vegetables. While this was a comparably small sampling compared to the 26,000 conventional food samples examined, one-quarter of the organic fruits and vegetables were found to contain measurable residues of synthetic pesticides. As these researchers stated in a paper published in the journal *Food Additives and Contaminants*, "none of the choices available to consumers [organic, conventional, or 'no-detectable residues'] is completely free of pesticide residues."

The seemingly high percentage of organic samples that tested positive for synthetic pesticides may indicate that organic farmers are taking advantage of the rather glaring gaps in the regulation of their operations. The USDA

---

[4] Cabras P., et al. Rotenone Residues on Olives and in Olive Oil. *Journal of Agricultural and Food Chemistry* 50:2576-2580, 2002.

requires no mandatory pesticide residue tests for any organic foods. No routine testing of any kind is conducted on the food. Organic farms undergo only a once-per-year audit and inspection of their records and facilities by a USDA-accredited organic certification agent. The less-than 100 independent agents deputized by the USDA decide if and when any pesticide residue testing is needed (presumably based on suspicion or a tip) and must pay for the cost of such testing out of the fees they charge the farmers. Certification agents compete with each other in an open market and decide their own fee, which discourages expensive pesticide residue testing.

The CU/OMRI review of its own and government data showed that up to half of some kinds of organic fruits and vegetables carry synthetic pesticide residues. For example, USDA testing found synthetic pesticide residues on half of the organic peaches, broccoli, and celery it tested. One-third of organic cantaloupe and lettuce had synthetic pesticide residues. CU testing found synthetic pesticide residues on one-third of organic apples and peaches.

Nearly 10% of organic produce that was examined contained higher levels of synthetic pesticides than the average found on non-organic foods. And remember, the USDA and CU only looked for residues of synthetic pesticides, not for traces of organic pesticides — the ones most likely to have been used on organic farms.

Why are pesticide traces present at such a high frequency in organic foods? The answer is modern science. We now have incredible chemical detection technology that can detect even the tiniest traces of synthetic chemicals. We can almost literally find the molecule in the haystack. Analytical methods now detect most pesticide residues at parts per billion (ppb) concentrations, equivalent to one second in 32 years! These are incredibly low levels. As a result, most foods — even organic foods — have detectable pesticide residues.

But all the food is still perfectly safe to eat. None of these low residues poses appreciable food safety risks. The traces of synthetic pesticides found on both the conventional and organic foods were far below government-established safety levels. The government safety levels, called reference doses, are established with built-in 100 to 1,000–fold safety margins. As Paracelsus, the grandfather of toxicology, said over 500 years ago, "All substances are poisons. There is none that is not a poison. The right dose differentiates a poison from a remedy." (See Toxicity and Consumer Risk).

Another reason why organic foods (and non-organic foods) show pesticide residues is that traces of older, banned pesticides remain in our environment. The early synthetic pesticides (such as DDT) were designed to be long-lived to protect crops throughout the growing season. This means there are traces of these chemicals still out there in the environment that show up at extremely low levels in our food. These residues pose no health threat, however.

Blind to Organic Pesticides

But what about the organic pesticide residues, such as the rotenone found on organic lettuce, tomatoes, and olives? These pesticides carry the same theoretical food safety risks as synthetic pesticides. If you are worried about the residues of synthetic pesticides in foods, you should also worry about residues of organic pesticides. Yet as has been discussed, nobody, including the government, has any real residue data for organic-approved pesticides. In fact, a rapid residue test exists for only one organic-approved pesticide: pyrethrum. This

---

TOXICITY AND CONSUMER RISK: THE DOSE MAKES THE POISON

The physician Paracelsus, who lived just as Christopher Columbus was discovering the New World, is credited with penning the first principle of modern toxicology (the study of toxic substances and why they are toxic). Paracelsus wrote: "All substances are poisons. There is none that is not a poison. The right dose differentiates a poison from a remedy."

It was a surprisingly cogent thought, given the primitive state of science at that time. It remains as apt today as when it was first written more than 450 years ago. Odd, then, that in today's society, with its strong emphasis on science, reason, and knowledge, the public must be continually reminded of a fact that has been known for so long.

Every substance is poisonous at a high enough dose. Water, critical to life, can poison as well. Consider the fate of the 4-year-old adopted daughter of a Salt Lake City, Utah, couple. The girl was forced to drink large amounts of water in an unusual form of therapy meant to promote bonding with her new parents. (The girl was encouraged to go to them for solace for the discomfort caused by her over-full bladder.) The girl died due to fatal brain swelling caused by a low salt concentration in her blood resulting from excessive water intake.[5] Sadly, there was a spate of water overdose deaths among marathon runners during 2000-2004, notably several in the Boston Marathon. These runners mistakenly believed the myth that it is impossible to drink too much water.

---

[5] Paul Foy, *Associated Press*, "Parents Charged in Death of Girl Forced to Drink Water; Lawyer Said Was Bonding Therapy," September 17, 2002.

test is really only a byproduct of the test created to find residues of synthetic pyrethroids, but it also detects natural pyrethrum. If you want to search for residues of the other commonly used organic pesticides, you must conduct extremely expensive and time-consuming laboratory chemical analyses.

Why are our food safety authorities so careless of organic pesticides? Many of the organic pesticides were in use well before modern regulatory agencies and didn't appear to cause any health problems. Therefore, these pesticides were exempted from most of the regulations required for synthetic pesticides. In fact, many have yet to be fully tested for carcinogenicity and other health risks.

Pyrethrum, a nerve toxin extracted from African chrysanthemums, has been used as a pesticide on food crops for over a century. It continues to be widely used by organic farmers. Yet the EPA didn't get around to testing natural pyrethrum for cancer-causing effects until the 1990s. The EPA finally officially listed pyrethrum as a "likely human carcinogen" in 1999.[6]

The CU/OMRI researchers said this about the lack of safety and residue data for organic pesticides:

> *"The lack of residue data ... and the lack of complete toxicological data for most [organic] insecticides, have seriously limited ability to carry out risk assessments for these pest management products. ... It seems essential that the widely used [botanical organic pesticides] be more completely tested for the full range of toxic effects that conventional pesticides are currently tested for. Expanded efforts to collect data on possible residues of the natural pesticides in organic and non-organic foods are also needed. Better toxicity data and residue data will improve the basis for risk assessments of these pest-management tools."*

Such testing should certainly be done, at the very least to give consumers a legitimate and balanced frame of reference from which to examine the risks from non-organic foods. But extensive testing of organic pesticides is unlikely to reveal any real-world human health risks. The National Research Council (NRC) — part of the prestigious National Academy of Sciences — concluded in 1999, after an exhaustive examination of the available research, that residues of synthetic pesticides in foods posed a lower theoretical cancer risk than the natural plant-produced pesticides and other natural chemicals found

---

[6] U.S. EPA. Report of Cancer Assessment Review Committee, 1999. Available on this book's companion Web site, www.TheTruthAboutOrganicFoods.org.

commonly in our food. However, the NRC also said that neither the natural nor synthetic carcinogens were present in large enough amounts for consumers to worry. In fact, the scientists reiterated that the best way to reduce the risks of cancers of all types was to increase one's consumption of fruits and vegetables. They did not recommend eating organic fruits and vegetables, but surely they would not be excluded.

Better Safe Than Sorry?

Doesn't eating organic food lower your exposure to pesticide traces? Isn't that important, at least for children? After all, recent research shows that children who eat a mostly organic diet have one-sixth of the levels of organophosphate (OP) insecticide metabolites in their urine than children who eat conventional foods have.[7] The problem with relative risk comparisons (i.e., consumers who eat conventional food are exposed to six times more pesticide residue than are consumers who eat organic foods) is that they can be highly misleading if they aren't placed in their proper context of dose.

Suppose a wealthy aunt of yours dies, leaving behind a $10 million estate. You and your sibling are notified that you will each get a share, but that your share will be six times larger than your siblings because you've always been there for her. You might get excited, presuming that you'll get most of the money, and your sibling might get upset for the same reason. But how excited would you be, and how upset would your sibling be, if when you went to the executor's office you discover that $9,999,999.93 of the estate was left to a very worthy charity, you get six cents and your brother gets a penny?

You and your brother had gotten worked up over the relative size difference of your respective inheritances — 600% — without considering the actual size of the inheritance. Seven cents isn't worth getting excited or upset about. The same is true of pesticide residue exposures and the relative difference in exposure between organic and conventional foods. An organic diet may expose us to only one-sixth as much pesticide residue, but it's a difference without real meaning.

In fact, the research indicates that we're most likely exposed to even less residue than had been previously thought. In the 2003 paper concluding kids who consume organic foods are exposed to one-sixth of the amount of residues

[7] Curl C.L., Fenske R.A., Elgethun K. Organophosphgate Pesticide Exposure of Urban and Suburban Preschool Children With Organic and Conventional Diets. *Environmental Health Perspectives* 111:377-382, 2003.

found on conventional foods, the researchers measured the amounts of harmless byproducts of OP pesticides called dialkylphosphates (DAPs) in the urine of two groups of children. The researchers garnered headlines in newspapers all over the world by highlighting a relative six-fold difference in DAP amounts in the urine, hence they assumed a six-fold difference in pesticide exposure. But what they ignore is the astronomically low level of overall risk.

The average concentration of the OP pesticide metabolites in the urine was three parts per billion, indicating exposure of far less than three ppb, which is well within EPA reference doses. Moreover, subsequent research from 2005 showed that these metabolites are cleared from the body in less than 24 hours, indicating that our bodies are readily able to metabolize and detoxify pesticide chemicals quickly.

In fact, most pesticides are readily detoxified on the surface of plants (and produce) well before they reach consumers. One group of researchers says that its work shows that half or more of the DAPs in the urine of the kids in the 2003 study were consumed in this benign form. As the researchers wrote, "DAP in urine is the sum of metabolites from trace OP residue in the food and pre-formed DAP from produce. The sources of these nontoxic DAPs will vary with individual produce, and they cannot be distinguished by urine testing. Scientific studies intended to detect extremely low, benign levels of DAP must consider all sources that contribute to human exposure."[8]

The latest research from scientists at the U.S. CDC confirms that children are exposed to totally non-worrisome traces, even when they are examined for the most worrisome OP pesticide. According to the scientists' estimate from 2006, children are exposed on average to just one-fifth of the acceptable daily lifetime exposure. Even the most theoretical vegetarian children consumed one-half of the EPA's ultra-cautious daily lifetime acceptable exposure. How cautious is it? We're talking one two-thousandths of a totally non-toxic daily dose. One aspirin is one-seventieth of an immediately toxic dose, so these exposures are incredibly safe.[9]

All of this research merely confirms what we already knew: There are only trace residues of pesticides in our foods, and our bodies rapidly metabolize and excrete these traces. Residues found on food through extensive testing of the U.S. food supply by the USDA and EPA have repeatedly been at levels far below those

---

[8] Krieger R.I., et al. Preformed Biomarkers in Produce Inflate Human Organophosphate Exposure Assessments. *Environmental Health Perspective* 111(10): 688, 2003.
[9] Barr D.B., et al. Concentrations of Selective Metabolites of Organophosphorus Pesticides in the United States Population. *Environmental Research* 99:314-326, 2005.

that would be worrisome. This government testing reveals that a sizable percentage of our fresh produce (and vast majority of processed foods) has no detectable pesticide residues whatsoever, despite our incredible detection technologies.

Real World Exposures

Using the U.S. Department of Agriculture's extensive food pesticide residue database, let's examine a more realistic scenario: How much actual pesticide residue would you consume in a pound of non-organic apples? (One pound is about three average apples.)

According to the USDA's surveillance data, there were traces of 13 different synthetic pesticides found on 2,300 separate non-organic apple samples. (Usually a sample is five pounds of a food, blended up and homogenized.) The USDA found an average of three different pesticides detected per sample. To make a "worst-case" scenario, we'll use the pesticide that USDA found at the highest residue levels in apples: thiabendazole, a fungicide that when detected on apples occurred at an average level of 0.8389 parts per million (ppm), or 839 parts per billion.

Assuming that all of the apples had the average level of thiabendazole found in the thiabendazole-positive samples — even though thiabendazole was detected in less than half of all samples — you would ingest a total of 380 micrograms of thiabendazole by eating the pound of apples.[10] Let's be conservative and round that number up to 400 micrograms, or 0.4 milligrams. Is 0.4 milligrams of thiabendazole enough to be worried about? I'll let you be the judge.

The EPA establishes reference doses for each pesticide based on extensive animal testing. The reference dose is the amount of a pesticide that the "EPA judges an individual could be exposed to on a daily basis for a lifetime with minimal probability of experiencing any adverse effect."[11] The agency looks at both the long-term (chronic) and short-term (acute) toxicity of a chemical. (See Establishing Reference Doses, page 98).

Thiabendazole has shown no chronic health impacts whatsoever in several animal species, even at doses thousands of times higher than realistic consumer exposures. It did not cause mutations, cancers, or birth defects, nor did it "bioaccumulate" in foods or people's bodies. Therefore, the EPA established a daily reference dose for thiabendazole based on acute toxicity testing, which

---

[10] There are 2.2 lbs per kilogram, and 839 ppb is equal to 839 micrograms per kilogram. Thus, dividing 839 by 2.2 equals 381 micrograms per pound.

[11] EPA publication 735-F-98-034, "Protecting the Public From Pesticide Residues in Food," EPA Office of Pesticide Programs. http://www.epa.gov/pesticides/factsheets/protect.htm

showed no observable health effects at 250 milligrams per day. For an adult male weighing 70 kilograms (155 lbs), this works out to about 3.5 milligrams per kilogram of body weight (250 mg/70 kg = 3.57). Dividing this number by a 100-fold "uncertainty factor" for extra safety, the reference dose for thiabendazole was set at 0.035 mg per kilogram of body weight per day. For an average sized adult, this is 2.45 mg total.

Our theoretical pound of residue-laden apples contained less than 0.4 mg, or one-sixth the EPA reference dose. And remember the 100-fold uncertainty factor. The 0.4 mg of thiabendazole is less than one five-hundredths of the amount that caused no observable health effects whatsoever in human testing, even when consumed in concentrated pill form every day.

There are far more significant health risks in our food to worry about than these, such as foodborne bacteria and carcinogenic fungal toxins (all natural, by the way). The EPA has yet to identify a single person who has died, or even gotten a stomachache, from residues of properly applied pesti-

ESTABLISHING REFERENCE DOSES

Let's walk through the process by which thiabendazole's reference dose was established and you'll see how conservative reference doses actually are.

When establishing a reference dose, EPA toxicologists first look for any chronic health effects a pesticide might cause, such as cancer or birth defects. They test the chemicals in several animal species. If any long-term effects are seen, reference doses are established based on the lowest No Observable Effect Level (NOEL) dose — i.e., the NOEL in the most sensitive animal species. The NOEL dose from the animal studies is then divided by 100 or 1,000 to account for uncertainty in the differences in susceptibility between laboratory animals and humans (divide NOEL dose by 10), differences in susceptibility among individual people (divide by another 10), and between adults and children (divide by another 10).

Thiabendazole showed no chronic health impacts in several species. Therefore, to set the reference dose, human volunteers consumed 250 mg/day of thiabendazole for two weeks under the supervision of physicians. No health effects were observed.

For an average 70 kilogram adult male, 250 mg/day is a dose equivalent to 3.5 mg/kg/day. The EPA then cut this NOEL dose by 100, resulting in a daily reference dose of 0.035 mg/kg/day. (If the tests were done on an animal instead of humans, they would have cut this dose by another 10, resulting in a reference dose of 0.0035 mg/kg/day.)An easy comparison is with beer. If a couple of beers is an "effective dose" (gives a buzz in the most sensitive people), then the NOEL dose would be non-alcohol beer. Divided by 100, you would be left with a reference dose of about 70 drops of non-alcohol beer.

cides. Yet dozens of people are killed every year by natural (some might even say "organic") bacteria such as *E. coli* O157:H7 and campylobacter.

If you are worried about possible health risks from these tiny traces of synthetic pesticides in our food, then you would probably also worry about the synthetic pesticides government testing found on organic apples, such as the 42 parts per billion (ppb) of thiabendazole, 32 ppb of azinphos methyl, or 29 ppb of carbaryl.

Or be worried about the natural toxins in our food. Dozens of natural chemicals that are toxic in lab animals at ultra-high doses are found in far higher natural concentrations in fruits and vegetables than the traces of synthetic pesticides.

Carrots contain carotoxin. Cucumbers contain curcurbitacin, which tastes bitter. Lettuce contains lactucopicrin. Most fruits and vegetables contain caffeic acid. All are carcinogenic when tested at high doses in rodents.

Chart #1, the Human Exposure/Rodent Potency

ACUTE TOXICITY

There are two types of toxicity: chronic and acute. Chronic toxicity refers to health problems caused by long-term exposures to low doses of a substance. Acute toxicity is the immediate impact of a high dose of a chemical or substance.

One way that acute toxicity is measured is the Lethal Dose 50% (LD50), the dose that kills half of the population of a test organism. The lower the LD50, the more toxic the substance.

Thiabendazole has an oral LD50 (if ingested by mouth) in rats of 3,100 to 3,600 milligrams per kilogram (mg/kg). There are 100,000 milligrams in a kilogram, so this is a 3% to 3.6 % of body weight dose. In mice, the LD50 is 1,400 to 3,800 mg/kg, or 1.4% to 3.8% of body weight. Using the conservative 1.4% LD50 from mice, this works out to over two pounds of thiabendazole for a 155 lb human male (equivalent to one kg in a 70 kilogram adult). Even if thiabendazole were toxic at half that dose, the 0.4 mg of thiabendazole in the pessimistically contaminated theoretical pound of apples is still less than 0.001% of an acutely toxic dose (1/112,500th). And even at high doses there aren't any long-term (chronic) toxicity concerns with thiabendazole, such as cancer.

For comparison, the organic insecticide pyrethrum has a mammalian LD50 ranging from 200 to 2,600 mg/kg. The minimum lethal dose in humans (yes, it has killed humans) is 750 mg/kg in children. Thus, organic pyrethrum is over twice as acutely toxic as thiabendazole.

The organic fungicide copper sulfate has a mammalian LD50 of 30 mg/kg, making copper sulfate at least 45 times more acutely toxic than thiabendazole.

(HERP) index, compares the theoretical cancer risk (based on dose) of just a few of the natural carcinogens in our foods to other cancer risks in our diet, including synthetic pesticide residues. The chart was compiled by Dr. Bruce Ames, who received the Presidential Science Medal from President Bill Clinton.

The HERP index indicates what percentage of the rodent carcinogenic potency (the daily dose in mg/kg/day resulting in tumors in 50% of test animals) a person receives from a given daily lifetime exposure.

As is clear, the theoretical rodent cancer risk from the average daily exposure to residues of these synthetic pesticides (in bold at lower end of HERP

Chart 1:

HERP (%)	Daily human exposure	Human dose of rodent carcinogen
14	Phenobarbital, 1 sleeping pill	Phenobarbital, 60 mg
1.8	Beer, 257 g	Ethyl alcohol, 13.1 ml
0.6	Wine, 28.0 g	Ethyl alcohol, 3.36 ml
0.1	Coffee, 13.3 g	Caffeic acid, 23.9 mg (natural)
0.04	Lettuce, 14.9 g	Caffeic acid, 7.90 mg (natural)
0.03	Orange juice, 138 g	d-Limonene, 4.28 mg (natural)
0.03	Pepper, black, 446 mg	d-Limonene, 3.57 mg (natural)
0.02	Mushroom (Agaricus bisporus, 2.55 g)	Mixture of hydrazines, etc. (whole mushroom) (natural)
0.02	Apple, 32.0 g	Caffeic acid, 3.40 mg (natural)
0.004	Celery, 7.95 g	Caffeic acid, 858 µg (natural)
0.004	White bread, 67.6 g	Furfural, 500 µg (natural)
0.0009	Brown mustard, 68.4 mg	Allyl isothiocyanate, 62.9 µg (natural)
0.0007	Bacon, 11.5 g	Diethylnitrosamine, 11.5 ng (natural)
0.0003	Tap water, 1 liter (1987-92)	Chloroform, 17 µg
0.00002	**Dicofol: daily U.S. avg (1990)**	**Dicofol, 544 ng**
0.000001	**Lindane: daily U.S. avg (1990)**	**Lindane, 32 ng**
0.00000008	**Captan: daily U.S. avg (1990)**	**Captan, 115 ng**
0.00000001	**Folpet: daily U.S. avg (1990)**	**Folpet, 12.8 ng**
<0.00000001	**Chlorothalonil: daily U.S. avg (1990)**	**Chlorothalonil, <6.4 ng**

index) is less than one one-thousandth the theoretical cancer risk of drinking a bottle of beer each day. The theoretical cancer risk from the natural d-Limonene in a daily glass of orange juice is 1,500 times greater than the theoretical cancer risk from the total average daily exposure to the synthetic pesticide dicofol. Neither of these is a realistic cancer risk, especially when eating five to seven servings of fresh fruits and vegetables per day containing all of these supposedly cancer-causing natural chemicals is believed to reduce overall cancer risk.[12]

Most of all, the pesticide residue data are a testament to our technical prowess in detecting incredibly tiny traces of specific chemicals in foods. Note that the synthetic pesticide residues in the HERP index are consumed in microgram quantities, or one-millionth of a gram. Remember, this is equivalent to one penny in $10 million, or one inch in 16,000 miles!

Misinformation Spread by Organic Materials Review Institute

The EPA reference doses for pesticides are the level of allowable pesticide residue on foods that the "EPA judges an individual could be exposed to on a daily basis for a lifetime with minimal probability of experiencing any adverse effect."[13] As discussed earlier in this chapter, they are based on a small fraction of doses deemed safe in animal or human testing — the No Observable Effect Level, or NOEL.

But some organic groups claim that the EPA reference dose is still harmful to your health.

One group that misleads consumers is the Organic Materials Review Institute (OMRI), a non-profit group that was "created to benefit the organic community." OMRI's Web site asks: "Isn't it true that the residues in conventionally grown foods don't pose any significant risks to health, so why does it matter if organically grown foods have fewer residues?" OMRI explains:

> Almost all pesticide residues detected in foods on the U.S. market are within legal limits, and essentially all of them are well below levels that are overtly harmful. That is, they would give a child a dose that is substantially lower than the dose that has had measurable adverse effects in studies with lab animals. However, there is a wide "gray area" between levels that are clearly harmful and the far lower

---

[12] http://potency.berkeley.edu/pdfs/herp.pdf
[13] EPA publication 735-F-98-034, "Protecting the Public From Pesticide Residues in Food," EPA Office of Pesticide Programs. http://www.epa.gov/pesticides/factsheets/protect.htm

levels that are "reasonably certain to cause no harm." Generally speaking, toxicologists apply a safety factor of 100- to 1,000-fold; i.e., presumed "safe" levels are 100 to 1,000 times lower than levels that cause detectable harm in lab animals. Many legal limits for residues and the doses resulting from exposures to residues in conventional foods fall in this "gray area" — they are higher than the "almost certainly safe" level, while below the "clearly harmful" level. (www.omri.org/FAC.html)

OMRI is essentially claiming that EPA reference doses for pesticides are higher than doses that are proven safe. This is a highly inaccurate and deliberately misleading statement. In fact, as is explained in "Establishing Reference Doses," EPA reference doses are required by law to be a small fraction of a proven safe dose: The No Observable Effect Level (NOEL) dose.

What OMRI is playing off is the requirement that lab animals be tested at the Maximum Tolerated Dose, or MTD. Lawmakers want food safety regulators to err on the side of caution and, thus, do their best to find possible adverse health effects of a pesticide or chemical. So they required that toxicity data be gathered by testing animals at the MTD so as not to miss more subtle health effects that might not occur at lower doses. Thus, the MTD and the NOEL are usually close to each other. But it is a massive stretch of intellectual honesty to call the NOEL dose a "clearly harmful" dose, as OMRI does. It is even more intellectually dishonest to then label the reference dose, calculated as one one-hundredth or one one-thousandth of the NOEL dose, as "higher than the 'almost certainly safe' level."

Again, the organic industry relies heavily on a carefully and deliberately crafted illusion and a twisted interpretation of the regulatory science. It will seemingly say just about anything to maintain that illusion, including trying to convince you that a fraction of a harmless dose is somehow harmful.

Unfortunately, they have been very successful at confusing enough people with technical doublespeak and complex non-explanations that they have perpetuated this lower-risk illusion for over 45 years.

Chapter 6:
___

Organic Pesticides? Yep!

Organic Faithful Say:

"The most effective way to reduce the risk [of pesticides] is not to use them — and this is precisely what organic agriculture successfully achieves on millions of hectares all over the world."

Bernward Geier, executive director of the International
Federation of Organic Farm Movements ($)[1]
From "Organic farming worldwide — A 100 percent pesticide risk reduction"
Keynote address to International Federation of Organic Agriculture Movements
(IFOAM) annual conference, Costa Rica, February 1998

"Although the [USDA's National Organic Program rules] prohibit pesticides ..."

OG Watchdog, *Organic Gardening Magazine*, April 2001, page 16 ($)

"There are no pesticides ... in organic farming."

Katherine DiMatteo, executive director of the Organic Trade Association ($)
From "U.S. Sets 'Organic' Standard," *Washington Post*, December 21, 2000

___

[1] ($) Indicates that the person quoted has a profit motive or other financial interest in promoting organic food.

"Organic food production is based on a system of farming ... without the use of toxic and persistent pesticides and fertilizers."

> Organic Trade Association Web site ($)
> http://www.ota.com/organic/faq.html
> March 2004

Reality Says:

"Under the [USDA's] National Organic Rule ... pesticides may be applied."

> Organic Farming Research Foundation Web site, "About Organic" ($)
> (http://www.ofrf.org/general/about_organic/)

"Organic farmers also rely on direct means to deal with pest problems ... when necessary, plant extract products or a rockdust are available to use." (Author's note: Plant extract products and rock dust are considered pesticides.)

> Bernward Geier, executive director of IFOAM ($)
> Keynote address to international conference, Costa Rica, February 1998

Organic farming is NOT pesticide-free farming, despite what the activists and organic foods companies would have you believe. The consumer myth that organic means pesticide-free and that organic farmers never use "toxic pesticides" is as old as the movement itself. After all, the organic movement was a backlash to the development of synthetic nitrogen fertilizers and other chemicals.

Organic farmers know that it's a myth because they use the organic pesticides. They read the warning labels and know how toxic some organic pesticides really are.

The organic industry merely pretends that its farmers don't use pesticides and has duped multitudes of otherwise savvy reporters into believing and repeating this misinformation. There have been literally thousands of newspaper and magazine articles incorrectly stating that organic farming prohibits the use of fertilizers and pesticides. And this myth feeds on itself, where a reporter reads it in several past reports and repeats the statement as if it were fact.

Often, organic activists flat out lie about their use of pesticides to perpetuate this all-important myth. (See quotes that start this chapter.) Other times they resort to verbal gymnastics to describe organic pesticides without actually using the term pesticide, lest the ruse be revealed. Instead, the organic industry calls their pesticides "extracts" and "rockdusts." Even the USDA's National Organic Rule — written by organic activists — uses the terms "input" and "substance" and "material" rather than the more technically accurate term "pesticide."

My favorite example comes from a booklet produced by Britain's Soil Association supposedly "debunking" the myths about organic food and farming. In a section on pesticides where the association cites one of my reports demonstrating organic growers use pesticides, the organization writes, "In certain circumstances, with severe restrictions, specific inputs with pesticidal properties may be used."[2]

Did you get that? Organic farmers don't use pesticides, they only use inputs with "pesticidal properties." But if something is sprayed to kill or ward off pests, especially if it has "pesticidal properties," it is by definition a pesticide. Period.

Many things are actually pesticides, including chemicals as innocuous as common dishwashing soap. In fact, potassium soap is a commonly used agricultural pesticide allowed for use by organic farmers. The USDA and EPA even track the use of pesticidal soap sprays.

NATURE'S WAY: EASY OR HARD?

Gardening Organically Is No More Complicated Than Following Nature's Way
by Dan Sullivan, *Organic Gardening* magazine, pp. 25-27, April 2001.

> "It's a curious urban myth that tells us it is easier to grow flowers and vegetables by applying poisons to them instead of simply taking our cues from nature. ... Organic gardeners believe there is a better way — a way to have beautiful, productive gardens without toxic chemicals. ... Organic gardeners acknowledge and observe a circle of life that predates agriculture by millennia. There's nothing mysterious or difficult about it. We simply follow and mimic the natural world. ... Life is like an organic garden — the key to success is finding the right balance. Gardening organically is about so much more than waging war with an arsenal of natural rather than synthetic weapons. It's about creating a living environment where the individual parts add up to a harmonious whole — a place where nature takes care of the details. It's no more complicated than that."

A Dream Called Meadowlark: One Couple's Fantasy of Farming the Earth Becomes a Reality — for Better and for Worse
by Doug Brown, *Organic Gardening* magazine, pp. 38-42, May/June 2000.

> "Watts has to admit that there are times when the day-to-day realities of being a small-scale organic farmer can be trying. He stops at the

---

[2] Organic Food and Farming: Myth and Reality. Soil Association 2001. http://www.sustainweb.org/pdf/myth_real.pdf

A pesticide is any "preparation for destroying plant, fungal, or animal pests." Some organic pesticides, however, are far more toxic than mere soap. The organic insecticide pyrethrum, for example, is literally a blend of nerve toxins, similar in some respects to the military nerve weapons Sarin and VX.

What's an Organic Pesticide?

First of all, what is an "organic pesticide"? What does it really mean? It doesn't mean "natural" because several approved "organic pesticides" are synthetic chemicals — meaning that the active ingredient was created by an industrial chemical process rather than extracted from plants or other biological organisms. Even many of the natural products approved as organic pesticides are heavily refined, processed, and toxic substances.

Moreover, the National Organic Standards Board (NOSB) here in the U.S. and other bodies outside of the U.S. continue to review and revise the list of pesticides allowed under organic rules. These include both natural and synthetic chemicals. So "organic pesticide" really means only what the organic community says it means.

"Organic pesticides" are often used by non-organic farmers, some of them widely.

There are also dozens, if not hundreds, of different organic-approved pesticide formulations — different combinations of chemical active ingredients mixed in water or a powder for applying to a crop. The exact number simply isn't known because there is no list of "officially approved" organic pesticide formulations.

Instead, the USDA has created the "National List" — a list of allowed syn-

---

long field of squash, the latest challenge in his battle to coax food from the earth. ... 'There's my nemesis,' he says, pointing to a thin, gray insect crawling along a vine, 'the squash bug.'

"He flips over a butternut with his sneaker. The ground swarms. Soft dimples decorate the skin of the gourd, which had once been as tight as a drum. 'There are thousands of them in here — thousands upon thousands,' he says, shaking his head. 'Look at it. It's ruined.' ... Had they known just how hard this vocation would be, they might never have pursued it. But it is their life now, and one thing is certain: There is no going back. 'We've put too much of ourselves into this to throw in the towel now,' Watts says. ...

"This season Meadowlark Farm will accept only 40 customers, even though that may mean more off-season work to make ends meet. (Tutlis waitresses; Watts works as a movie-theater projectionist.) So be it, the

thetic substances and prohibited natural substances. Any natural substance not listed in the USDA's National List is allowed, whereas all synthetic substances are banned unless they are on the National List.[3] This National List defines allowable active ingredients in pesticides but does not refer to specific brands or specific formulations.

The Organic Materials Review Institute (OMRI) maintains an up-to-date list of qualifying commercial formulations (products that pass NOSB/USDA requirements). However, you must pay OMRI a subscription fee to get access to this list. The main concern is not just whether the active ingredient in the pesticide has been approved, but also whether the other ingredients in the pesticide formulation comply. These other ingredients are things like surfactants that help disperse the pesticide on the waxy leaves of plants, the inert ingredients (like water), and chemical synergists that help make the toxins more effective at killing the target pests.

Active Ingredients

In practical terms there are seven major organic active ingredients. These are horticultural oils, sulfur, copper, pyrethrum, rotenone, Bt, and Spinosad. There are other approved organic pesticides, such as neem, sabadilla, and antibiotics. However, these appear to be used by a relatively small number of organic farmers or are used on fairly limited acreage.

• Horticultural oils are insecticides derived from highly refined crude

> couple says. *The more important consideration is to bring their farm —
> and their lives — back into balance. By cutting back they also hope to
> take control of the insect infestation of 1999. ... Watts, the inventor-tin-
> kerer of the team, has come up with a novel method for ridding the fields
> of pest bugs. With a shop vacuum powered by a generator in a wheelbar-
> row, he makes his way down the rows, inhaling insects the way an indoor
> vacuum sucks up dust motes."*
>
> Dan Sullivan says organic farmers "observe a circle of life" and "mimic the
> natural world." Who could argue? The whole natural circle of life right there in
> one field: Birth from the seed, growth, ripening, squash bugs feasting, nutrients
> returned back to the soil. (And who'd have guessed that an organic "living envi-
> ronment" would sprout a Hoover in a wheelbarrow as one of the parts adding
> up to a harmonious whole where nature takes care of the details?)

[3] http://www.ams.usda.gov/nop/NationalList/ListHome.html

petroleum oil. A few are derived from plant oils. Horticultural oils are mixed with water and an emulsifier (an ingredient to help the oil and water mix) and are then sprayed on crops. Horticultural oils work primarily by suffocating insects physically, although they can also disrupt insect feeding behavior and insect metabolism chemically. Horticultural oils are used widely by both organic and non-organic farmers.

• Sulfur is a contact poison used mainly as a fungicide, but also as an insecticide and rodenticide. Sulfur has a relatively low toxicity to humans, birds, fish, and bees, but is applied heavily. Because of its inherently heavy application rates, sulfur is believed to represent a greater environmental risk than many synthetic fungicides.[4] Sulfur is used heavily in the production of grapes and other soft fruits. Seventy percent of all sulfur used in California is applied to grapes.

• Copper compounds are used as fungicides and bactericides. Copper is a broadly toxic heavy metal. Various copper chemicals are allowed under the USDA National Organic Program standards. Copper "bioaccumulates," meaning it is concentrated in the tissues of animals, has a very high toxicity to fish, and is toxic to bees. Copper sulfate, one of the more widely used copper-based pesticides, is caustic and classified as Highly Toxic by the EPA. Vineyard workers have experienced liver disease after three to 15 years of exposure to copper sulfate in Bordeaux mixture. The European Union claims it will phase out the use of all copper pesticides in the near future because of environmental concerns. The ban was to have begun in 2003 but was delayed after organic farmers complained that without copper they had no effective way to control fungal diseases.

• Pyrethrins are a group of chemical nerve toxins produced in the flowers of the African chrysanthemum. The refined flower extract, a natural cocktail of pyrethrins, is called pyrethrum. Pyrethrum is obtained by either crushing the flowers or using a solvent. While pyrethrum breaks down rapidly in the environment, it is toxic to aquatic life and is classified as a Restricted Use Pesticide by the EPA. In 1999, the EPA reclassified pyrethrum as a "likely human carcinogen" after rodent testing showed that it caused tumors in rats. Pyrethrum has not even been tested for birth defects or genetic mutations.

---

[4] Kovach J., et al. A Method to Measure the Environmental Impact of Pesticides. *New York's Food and Life Sciences Bulletin* No.139, Cornell University, Ithaca, NY, 1992.

- Rotenone is a toxic plant extract obtained from the crushed roots of several tropical plant species. Amazonian natives were the first to discover rotenone's toxic properties. They poured rotenone into small pools and streams to kill fish for food. It is still one of the most effective fish killers (piscicides) known. Rotenone disrupts a key enzyme needed for respiration in cells and disturbs muscle coordination. Rotenone can cause long-term kidney and liver damage and is a suspected carcinogen (cancer), teratogen (birth defects), and fetotoxin (kills fetuses). Rotenone causes Parkinson's disease-like symptoms in rats. Rotenone breaks down fairly rapidly in the environment.

- *Bacillus thuringiensis* — commonly referred to as Bt — is a soil bacteria that produces a protein toxic to caterpillars. Solutions of the bacteria (either live or dead) and endotoxin protein in water have been registered for use as a pesticide on crops since 1961. Organic farmers use Bt extensively. Mammals, birds, and fish do not have the cellular receptor for the toxin, making them immune to its effects. However, the toxin kills the cells lining a caterpillar's gut, causing death. While Bt is considered safe for consumers, farm workers spraying Bt solutions have reported respiratory problems, and Bt bacteria have caused fatal lung infections in mice. Bt is commonly used by non-organic farmers as well, especially in the form of biotech insect-resistant crops that produce the Bt protein in the plants. This eliminates the need to spray a crop five to 15 times per season, thereby conserving fuel, eliminating spray drift, and reducing soil compaction and degradation.[5]

- Spinosad is a new class of biological pesticide that gained NOSB approval in 2002. Spinosad was developed by Dow AgroSciences, part of Dow Chemical Corporation. It is obtained from a natural fermentation bacteria found in soils (*Saccharopolyspora spinosad* — hence the name). The active ingredients (two similar chemicals: spinosyn A and spinosyn D) are insect nerve toxins that cause involuntary muscle contractions and paralysis in insects. It is both a contact and an ingestion poison, with high specificity for some insects and consequent low toxicity for mammals, birds, and even many non-target insects. Because of its safety and

---

[5] If one includes biotech crops, Bt has become one of the most widely used crop protection technologies in the world. You'd think that organic farmers and activists would laud their fellow farmers for using a natural protein they themselves deem safe, but instead they have attempted to have biotech Bt crops banned.

pest specificity, spinosad has been rapidly adopted by both non-organic and organic farmers for use on a wide array of fruit and vegetable crops.

- Neem extract, or azadirachtin, is a botanical insecticide/fungicide obtained primarily from the seeds of the neem tree. Little is known about the ways in which azadirachtin works to kill insects and fungi, although its toxicity to mammals appears to be relatively low. (It is interesting to note that while organic activists demand answers to every conceivable question regarding synthetic pesticides, they are content with using a natural toxin they know almost nothing about.)

- Sabadilla is an alkaloid toxin (like nicotine and cocaine) obtained from seeds of the South American lily. Sabadilla works by disrupting the nerve cells, leading to loss of nerve function, paralysis, and eventually death. Sabadilla is the least toxic of the botanical insecticides. However, the purified alkaloid is very toxic and is a severe skin irritant. Small amounts may cause headaches, nausea, vomiting, etc. Large doses may cause convulsions and cardiac and respiratory failure. It is used as a broad-spectrum contact and stomach poison. Sabadilla is effective against many insects, including honey bees.

How much of which "organic" pesticides organic farmers are using is a huge mystery, because nobody keeps track. When it comes to pesticide use by organic farmers the organic industry has essentially a "don't ask, don't tell" policy. That is, don't ask the farmers about the pesticides they're using, and don't tell consumers about them.

While a whole range of pesticide formulations are used routinely in organ-

IN DEFENSE OF SPRAYING:
TALE OF THE ENGLISH COUNTRY ORCHARD

I have been a general practitioner in the [U.K.'s] National Health Service for 16 years and have recently diversified into dermatology and medical education. [Julia and I are] originally from London. I've always loved apples, she's always wanted to be a farmer ... one day in 1992, after the property value collapse, I saw an advert for nine acres of pasture in Durley, Southern Hampshire, for a price that made me blink, rub my eyes, and look again. It was a little less than 4,000£ an acre. To spare you the boring detail, two months later in September 1992 we knelt in prayer and thanksgiving on OUR land and asked God to grant us success in planting up an orchard. ... Using information from books, we chose the varieties for our first planting. We planted 200 apples and 40 plums. ... We were really keen to be organic, to the extent that we tried to control

farming, no statistics are available indicating how much or how little these formulations are actually used on organic farms. There are no publicly available data from either private or government sources on pesticide use by organic farmers. This is particularly surprising given that organic farmers must submit detailed farm management plans (FMPs) to certification agents as part of the organic certification process. These FMPs include detailed disclosure of all chemicals and pesticides that might be used on the farm. The FMP must state what measures the farmers are taking to avoid using pesticides, as well as why, when, and how much organic pesticides will be used on the farm.

Despite all of this detailed farm-level information, not a single report or study of organic farm pesticide use has been issued by any organic industry or research group in the past 20 years. Annual certification reviews of organic farms have been occurring for decades, conducted by numerous independent and state-level organic certifiers that operated prior to the USDA program (such as Oregon Tilth, California Certified Organic, etc.). It would be easy to conduct a simple, anonymous survey of the farm management plans on file with these organizations.

Think about that for a minute. Here you have a sector of the food industry that arose in large part out of the supposed concerns over the use of farm chemicals and pesticides. Yet it hardly even acknowledges that its own farmers are allowed to use pesticides, let alone keeps track of its farmers' pesticide use.

No agency of the U.S. government (the USDA or EPA) has any immediate plans to compile statistics of pesticide use on organic farms.

In contrast, the USDA and the EPA compile exhaustive statistics on non organic farm pesticide use. While a couple of these "tracked" pesticides are

---

weeds by hoeing and did no spraying at all. We spent many an hour working up the rows squashing thousands of caterpillars that were eating our trees by hand. It took us about three years to realize the fact that this approach was totally unrealistic and wasn't working. We had severe infestations of winter moth caterpillars, apple scab, mildew, apple sawfly, and what not. Many trees died, others were stunted. When in the third year we had our first crop, 19 out of 20 apples had one or more codling moth maggots in [them]. There was clearly no future in this, so we decided to start spraying. The trees shot ahead, relieved of their heavy load of pests and diseases.

Of course we would strongly prefer not to spray, but even "organic" growers spray with total killer poisons like nicotine, which is OK by them as it comes from a plant. The customer will not accept a scabby, maggoty apple, let alone pay a premium price necessary for it since the crop yield is reduced by the pest

also approved for use by organic farmers, the USDA/EPA database lumps the pesticide use of all farms, not just organic. This makes the data useless for examining organic farm pesticide use.

Thus, we're stuck in an informational black hole. Nobody can claim to know specifically either how much or how little organic farmers use pesticides. And that is exactly the way the organic activists want it. In an information black hole, they can make any claims they want and there is no way to refute them.

However, we do know which pesticides organic farmers are allowed to use, the "effective use rates"[6] of these chemicals, and how farmers in general (organic and non-organic) use them. Using this information, we can get a rough idea of how some organic pesticides are used on organic farms.

History of Organic Pesticide Use

The first pesticides used by humans were "organic." Reports of the use of sulfur as a pesticide date back 3,000 years, to when Homer described how Odysseus "fumigated the hall, house, and court with burning sulfur to control pests." By 800 A.D., the Chinese were protecting crops with solutions of arsenic (a natural toxic element) mixed in water. Lead and mercury salts were used as agricultural pesticides as early as the 1400s. Nicotine from tobacco was first used as an agricultural insecticide in 1690 to protect pears from insects.

> load. Sorry about that. Of course we use an absolute minimum of pesticide, not least because it costs money and it's very uncomfortable to trudge up and down the orchard rows on a dry summer's day in protective clothing with a 15-liter knapsack sprayer on your back. Believe me, I would rather be writing poetry or making daisy chains. But don't be put off by this frankness, anything you eat from the shops is sprayed, and safety rules are stringent and enforced. We are the canaries, as not only do we eat massive amounts of our own fruit, to say nothing of the cider, but we are spraying them for hours. If anyone was going to have a problem it would be us. The last spray goes on by midsummer, so the dew, the wind, and the rain have been on the fruit for two months after the last application before it gets to you.
>
> Remember, and I speak as a medical man, that all the research (and there is a lot of it) that shows the health benefits of eating fruit, as opposed to not eating it, was done with sprayed fruit — there is no other kind in the shops.

---

[6] Use rates are like doses in medicine. Take too little and you won't effectively treat the condition. Take too much and you'll waste medicine or cause problems. Thus, farmers (organic and non-organic) tend to use pesticides at the same rates unless used in combination with other pesticides.

(Nicotine is a potent nerve poison.) Pyrethrum was first used to kill body lice on people in the early 1800s. Sulfur was first recommended as an agricultural fungicide in 1821.

There is a widespread misconception that the "pesticide era" of agriculture did not begin until after World War II. In practical terms, however, the pesticide era of agriculture began prior to the U.S. Civil War and accelerated with the rapid advances in chemistry through the turn of the 20th century. Pyrethrum was in regular use as an agricultural pesticide by the 1850s, and by 1886, the United States was importing over 600,000 pounds of pyrethrum annually for farm use. Farmers were widely using nicotine and arsenic-based pesticides by the late 1800s.

Bordeaux mixture, a copper sulfate-based fungicide, was invented in France in 1883 and its use spread rapidly around the world. Nicotine became far more widely used after 1909, when chemists discovered they could increase nicotine's lethality to insects (and people!) by chemically sulfating it into nicotine sulfate.

A home garden pest control handbook published in 1918 recommends gardeners protect their crops with lead arsenate, Bordeaux mixture (copper sulfate, lime, and water), nicotine sulfate, mercury bichloride, and formaldehyde.[7] All of these are broadly and highly toxic to people and wildlife.

By 1934, U.S. farmers were annually using 70 million pounds of sulfur, 10 million pounds of pyrethrum, 2 million pounds of nicotine sulfate, and 1.5 million pounds of rotenone. That's more than 80 million pounds of organic pesticides being used each year (in addition to over 100 million pounds of lead arsenate). Imports of organic pyrethrum to the United States peaked in 1939 at 13.5 million pounds.[8]

Nicotine sulfate use peaked in the 1940s and '50s at about 5 million pounds per year. Cheaper, safer, and more effective synthetic pesticides were developed during the 1930s, '40s, and '50s and quickly displaced nicotine sulfate. DDT, for example, was not only more effective against insects, but also far less toxic to humans. Nicotine sulfate is 40 times (4,000%) more toxic to humans than DDT! Scientists are still looking for evidence that DDT exposure is harmful to human health (it was dusted directly on soldiers and refugees during and after

---

[7] Merrill J.H. and Melchers L.E., Insects and Plant Diseases Attacking Garden Crops. Kansas State Agricultural College Agricultural Station Circular No. 65, April, 1918.
[8] Balandrin M.F., et al. Natural Plant Chemicals: Sources of Industrial and Medicinal Materials. Science 228:1154–60, 1985. http://www.ciesin.org/docs/002-266/002-266.html.

World War II to prevent outbreaks of deadly typhus).[9]

Organic farmers continued to use nicotine sulfate extensively through the 1970s, despite a large health risk to farm workers (including deaths), with many still using it into the 1990s. While legal nicotine sulfate sales in the U.S. ended in January 1993, the National Organic Standards Board — the group that decides the USDA's organic standards — didn't officially prohibit nicotine sulfate use by organic farmers until 1995, when the Board curiously ruled that nicotine sulfate was a "synthetic" substance.

Although organic farmers had been using nicotine sulfate since the very beginning of the organic movement, nicotine sulfate was suddenly a "synthetic" substance that could no longer be allowed. But the NOSB continues to allow the use of another compound sulfated with sulfuric acid: copper sulfate.

Why is a natural plant extract "synthetic" if it is chemically sulfated, yet a mined and heavily refined metal not synthetic when treated to the exact same chemical process? Clearly, there isn't any consistency in the NOSB's decisions regarding "organic" pesticides, either in the industrial processes used to make them or in the toxicity of the chemicals themselves.

How Much DO They Use Now?

It is no doubt true that most organic farmers want to use fewer pesticides. But desire and reality are two different things. The fact is that all farmers want to use the least amount of pesticide they can — pesticides cost money and require costly labor for application. However, pesticides are necessary tools for successfully growing many crops, especially fruits and vegetables. These crops are particularly susceptible to fungal diseases and are as appetizing to insects and pathogens as they are to people.

Organic farmers claim to use a combination of techniques to avoid having to "resort" to using pesticides, such as planting resistant crop varieties, using biocontrol organisms, rotating crops, keeping crops healthy, etc. In fact, all farmers use these techniques in varying degrees and combinations. But these techniques are only partially effective in preventing pest and/or disease outbreaks, which is why even organic farmers use pesticides.

Surprisingly, organic farmers may spray 10 times more pesticide per acre

---

[9] In occupied Japan, problems getting DDT powder from the U.S. to health authorities resulted in 31,141 typhus cases in Japan in 1946. But DDT reduced the epidemic to a mere 1,064 cases in 1947 and only 429 cases in 1948. No health effects from this or other uses of DDT have ever been detected, including the most recent major study on breast cancer in Long Island.

to grow some crops than their non-organic counterparts. Why? Because many organic pesticides break down so quickly in the environment that these chemicals must be sprayed more frequently to maintain effective pest control. Organic pesticides are also generally less effective at killing pests than their synthetic counterparts, so they have to be sprayed at higher concentrations (active ingredient rates) than most synthetic pesticides.

For example, natural pyrethrum breaks down into non-toxic byproducts mostly within hours after being sprayed on a crop. And while pyrethrum quickly affects the nervous system of insects, giving rapid "knockdown," many insects actually survive the natural pyrethrum sprays because their enzymes swiftly detoxify the natural pyrethrin toxins.

Synthetic versions of pyrethrins, called pyrethroids, were developed that are more effective at actually killing the insects and that protect crops longer in fields (days to weeks). Yet synthetic pyrethroids are often less toxic to mammals and (like natural pyrethrum) they, too, break down into non-toxic byproducts. Because of these characteristics, two sprays of synthetic pyrethroid insecticide will often do a better job than 10 sprays of natural pyrethrum while posing no greater threat to the environment and less risk to farm workers.

Pesticide costs are also substantially higher with natural pyrethrum for two reasons. First, because pyrethrum is an extract of flowers that are largely hand picked, it costs significantly more than synthetic pyrethroids. Second, the rapid breakdown of pyrethrum in fields requires that it be applied more frequently to crops. That means not only higher total pesticide costs, but also significantly greater fuel consumption and labor requirements.[10]

While we don't have reliable government or organic industry statistics on the use of pesticides specifically on organic farms, we do have some information.

The most heavily used pesticide on organic farms is Bt, the protein from the soil bacteria *Bacillus thuringiensis* that is toxic to caterpillars. Because Bt sprays are actually a formulation of living and dead bacteria, they cannot be measured in pounds of active chemical ingredient per acre like other pesticides. Therefore, there are no reliable or comparable statistics on how much Bt

---

[10] Pyrethrum costs considerably more than synthetic pyrethroids and other synthetic pesticides because it is a natural flower extract. Kenya is the world's largest producer, with more than 200 million pounds of dried pyrethrum flower petals produced each year. Literally billions of flowers are hand harvested by hundreds of thousands of women and children annually to supply pyrethrum to organic farmers and gardeners.

is used by organic farmers.

Organic farmers spray a solution of water containing Bt bacteria, bacterial spores, and toxic protein crystals. The bacteria do not proliferate on plants and the protein toxin rapidly degrades in sunlight, requiring frequent reapplications of Bt insectides. And as the Bt protein degrades, pests are exposed to a lower and lower toxin dose, promoting the development of pest resistance.

While organic farmers rely heavily on Bt pesticides, many non-organic farmers also use Bt insecticides. Some use the same spray formulations as organic farmers use, others grow biotech insect-resistant crops, where the plants have been genetically engineered to produce the Bt protein in their leaves. This eliminates the need to spray, saving labor, fuel, and equipment, as well as reducing soil compaction. (It also reduces worker exposure, but the risks from Bt sprays are fairly low.)

Biotech Bt crops have reduced pesticide spraying on many farms by 80 percent or more.[11] According to 2003 data, biotech crops have helped reduce overall pesticide use by nearly 50 million pounds, in significant part due to Bt insect-protected crops.

Moreover, because the Bt toxin protein is produced continually within the plant leaves, the crop is always protected, drastically reducing the likelihood of pest resistance to Bt due to a sub-lethal dose of the toxin.

It is interesting that organic activists have opposed biotech Bt crops mainly on the argument that pests are more likely to become resistant to Bt toxins if they are used by a large number of farmers. Organic activists want exclusive use of Bt technology for their tiny minority. However, even after a decade of widespread planting of biotech Bt crops on hundreds of millions of acres worldwide, scientists have yet to see any indication that pests are developing resistance to the biotech Bt crops. The only documented case of pest resistance to Bt was to Bt sprays like those used by organic farmers.

The irony is that if organic farming became the dominant way of farming, pests would likely become resistant to Bt sprays rapidly because so many farmers would be using them. There are too few alternative organic-approved pesticides available to prevent resistance development.

Another advantage of the biotech Bt approach is that the newest varieties of biotech crops are protected by more than one version of the Bt toxin pro-

---

[11] Huang J., et al. Insect-Resistant GM Rice in Farmers' Fields: Assessing Productivity and Health Effects in China. Science 308(5722):688-690, 2005; and Qaim M. and Zilberman D. Yield Effects of Genetically Modified Crops in Developing Countries. *Science* 299 (5608):900-902, 2003.

tein (There are dozens of Bt toxin protein variants available, even for organic farmers). This "stacking" of different Bt toxins presents a further barrier to the development of pest resistance because pests would have to simultaneously develop resistance to two or more toxins instead of just one.

Aside from Bt, we have statistics for three other organic-approved pesticides because of their wide use by non-organic farmers: Oil, sulfur, and copper.[12]

Oil and sulfur are the two most heavily used pesticides in the U.S. in terms of total pounds of active ingredient applied. In 1997, the last year for which we have reliable estimates, U.S. farmers applied 102 million pounds of oil on 22 different crops (ranging from almonds and walnuts to cotton and strawberries). Farmers applied an estimated 78 million pounds of sulfur on 49 different crops (from alfalfa to watermelons).[13] Copper is the second most heavily applied fungicide in the U.S., with over 13 million pounds applied to 54 crops (ranging from almonds and eggplant to peanuts and potatoes).

These three organic-approved pesticides accounted for a whopping 62% of the total pounds of insecticides and fungicides applied to U.S. crops in 1997. Copper and sulfur accounted for 69% of the total fungicides applied to U.S. crops, while oil accounted for 56% of the total pounds of insecticide applied to U.S. crops.

Why do these three organic pesticides account for such a huge percentage of the total applied to U.S. crops? Mainly because they are less effective than synthetics and thus must be applied at heavier rates to control pests. Copper is applied at up to 14 pounds per acre, with the average application at more than four pounds. Sulfur is applied at up to 144 pounds per acre, with the average at over 30 pounds.

In contrast, the average synthetic fungicide is applied at just over 1.5 pounds per acre.

Insecticidal oil is used at rates of up to 72 pounds per acre, with an average of just under 50 pounds. Synthetic insecticides are applied at average rates of only one to four pounds per acre — one-tenth to one-fiftieth the application rate for oil. And the newest synthetic insecticides, such as imidocloprid,

---

[12] Because organic farming is such a small percentage of the total farm acreage, these statistics reflect the use of these pesticides mostly by non-organic farmers. However, these pesticides are effective at relatively narrow application rates, so their use rates are essentially the same regardless of whether or not a farmer is "organic."

[13] National Center for Food and Agricultural Policy in Washington, D.C., 1999. The database quantifies the use of 235 active ingredients on 87 crops in the 48 contiguous states. [http://www.ncfap.org/database/default.htm].

have average per-acre application rates of less than 0.5 pound per acre, which is one one-hundredth the application rate of oil. (An acre is just less than a football field in area, so these are extremely low-rate pesticides.)

Some organic activists suggest that such statistics only prove how much more poisonous synthetic pesticides are compared to organic pesticides, a claim that is partially true. The question that should be asked, however, is toxic to what? Spinosad, the new bacteria-derived biopesticide now used widely by both organic and non-organic farmers, is highly toxic to certain insects yet has incredibly low toxicity to mammals. It has less than 5% of the toxicity of aspirin. Organic and non-organic farmers are protecting entire acres of crops with less spinosad than would be needed to make even one person feel nauseous, let alone be seriously harmed.

To a fungus, synthetic fungicides often are more toxic (effective) than the organic-approved copper and sulfur compounds. But to a human and for the environment in general, synthetic fungicides are often far less toxic.

Elemental copper has an LD50 score (lethal dose in 50% of animals tested, which is a measure of the immediate toxicity of a substance) in mammals of about 400 mg/kg. The synthetic fungicide thiabendazole has an LD50 of 1,300 to 3,800 mg/kg. That makes organic-approved copper 300% to 1,000% more toxic than the non-organic thiabendazole. And again, copper contaminates soil and poses a risk to aquatic organisms, whereas synthetic fungicides generally do not.

Copper sulfate has killed humans at doses as low as 11 mg/kg and caused liver disease in vineyard workers after only three years of exposure. When given to laboratory animals, copper sulfate caused reproductive effects, birth defects, mutagenic effects, and cancer-causing effects.

Nicotine sulfate has an LD50 in rats of 55 mg/kg. It is extremely acutely toxic. In fact, tobacco pickers occasionally fall ill (and some have died) from picking tobacco after a wet growing season when natural nicotine levels in tobacco plants skyrocket. Compare natural nicotine to imidocloprid, the recently developed synthetic insecticide that is similar in chemical structure to nicotine: Imidocloprid is only about one-tenth as acutely toxic to mammals (rat LD50 of 425 mg/kg) and has an ultra-low environmental impact risk.

This combination of extremely low health and environmental risk — yet high effectiveness against pests — explains why imidocloprid has quietly become one of the most widely used insecticides in non-organic fruit and vegetable production. Imidocloprid is so safe, it is the active ingredient used in once-per-month dog flea treatments.

I'm not suggesting that eating foods treated with copper-based or other organic pesticides will expose you to significant health risks or subject the planet to an irreparable eco-insult. The point is that organic pesticides pose exactly the same sort of environmental and health risks as do non-organic pesticides — and often pose more risk than synthetics. The fundamental difference between organic and synthetic pesticides is not their toxicity to pests, people, or the environment, but rather their origin.

This reality is changing in favor of non-organic methods. Organic farmers have gained one key new insecticide during the past 30 years — spinosad, the bacterial biopesticide developed by Dow AgroSciences and first used on crops in 1998. Spinosad was approved for organic farmer use in 2002. Meanwhile, non-organic farmers have gained not only spinosad, but also imidocloprid and many more highly effective pesticides that are safe for both the environment and human health. Non-organic farmers have also gained agricultural biotechnology, which is relegating organic farming methods to the Stone Age in terms of safety, effectiveness, and long-term sustainability.

What If the United States Went All Organic?

Obviously, because of the relatively high application rates of key organic pesticides as well as their rapid degradation, a switch to organic farming by a large number of farmers would result in a large increase in the pounds of pesticide applied to cropland and significantly increased soil contamination risks. This is contrary to the image that organic activists carefully cultivate, but it is nonetheless true. The alternative, of course, would be vastly higher crop losses from not protecting the crops at all.

We can roughly estimate the increase in fungicide use that could be expected if all U.S. agriculture converted to organic by replacing synthetic fungicides with copper or sulfur at the 1997 application rates (nominally based on their effective use rate).

Sulfur was applied to U.S. crops at an average rate of 34.8 lbs per acre in 1997. This rate is 22 times higher than the average application rate of synthetic fungicides of 1.6 lbs per acre. Thus, if all synthetic fungicides were replaced by sulfur, U.S. farmers would use an additional 840 million pounds of fungicide. This amounts to a 738% increase!

If copper were the organic replacement for synthetic fungicides, U.S. farmers would replace 40 million pounds of synthetics with 103 million pounds of copper, increasing total fungicide use by 63 million pounds. This would be a

50% increase in fungicide use. The environmental impacts from this increased copper use would be huge.[14] Yet crop losses from fungal diseases would be far higher because copper is significantly less effective than the synthetic fungicides it would replace.

What about insecticides? The only organic insecticides for which any statistics are available are oil and Bt. Under an all-organic scenario, the use of Bt sprays would increase considerably. However, Bt is effective against a relatively narrow range of insects. Therefore, the ability to use Bt as a replacement for synthetic insecticides is limited. Millions of additional pounds of oil, pyrethrum, neem, rotenone, and sabadilla would need to be used as replacements for the synthetic insecticides.

An additional factor ignored in these sorts of crude calculations is the effective suppression of pest populations by the overwhelming majority of non-organic farmers. If a majority of farmers in a region use more effective synthetic pesticides and/or advanced biotech pest-resistant crops, pest populations are suppressed and organic farmers in the region benefit from the "umbrella effect." It is extremely difficult to measure this "umbrella effect," although indirect evidence indicates that it is significant.

For example, many organic crops can only be produced economically in regions where pest populations are low. The advent of large-scale regional cotton boll weevil eradication programs in the 1990s — that use synthetic insecticides to suppress boll weevils over multi-state areas — has allowed the recent expansion of organic cotton production into areas of the U.S. South where it was previously uneconomical due to heavy pest pressure that organic methods simply couldn't cope with.[15]

It is also reasonable to conclude that overall insecticide use would increase even more than the above calculations imply under an all-organic scenario.

Organic farming proponents will argue that the above comparisons are invalid because they fail to incorporate the multitude of non-chemical strategies available to organic farmers, and overestimate the amount of pesticides used on organic farms. They will argue that the use rates of copper and sulfur are substantially lower on organic farms. Unfortunately, they simply have no data to support these assertions. The organic industry hasn't gathered or published any information on pesticide use on its industry's farms because the

---

[14] J. Kovach, C. Petzoldt, J. Degni, and J. Tette, A Method to Measure the Environmental Impact of Pesticides. *New York's Food and Life Sciences Bulletin* Number 139, New York State Agricultural Experiment Station, Cornell University, Ithaca, New York, 1992.

[15] Personal Communication, Frank Carter, National Cotton Council, Memphis, TN, 2001.

industry's proponents don't want to acknowledge that their farmers even use pesticides.

The biggest difference in pest management between organic and non-organic farmers is that organic farmers generally accept higher amounts of crop damage and crop loss before resorting to using pesticides. They can afford to absorb greater losses because they get a significant price premium from consumers.

Herbicides

The only category of pesticide use that would surely decrease under an all-organic scenario is herbicides. Organic farmers and researchers have yet to discover a natural herbicide acceptable to their ethical beliefs. They are looking very hard for an alternative to plowing and tilling against weeds because of the obvious advantages in terms of reduced soil erosion and improved soil structure.

Weeds are the biggest, oldest problem in agriculture. Weeds steal moisture and nutrients away from crops. They decrease crop yields and harbor crop pests. Until the advent of chemical herbicides, the only strategy for killing weeds was mechanical control — tilling, plowing, and hoeing the soil to kill the weeds and bury their seeds. But these "bare-earth" methods of weed con-

---

NATURAL INSECT REPELLENTS: DESPERATE TO GO ORGANIC?

One of the latest consumer fads is "herbal" or "botanical" insect repellents. Several major repellant manufacturers have come out recently with versions of "natural" repellents to compete with a plethora of smaller brand products.

Consumers automatically assume that these "natural" products are safer than DEET, the long-used industry standard.[16] But are they? The evidence to date isn't so encouraging.

First, despite widely held perceptions (and natural-product marketing) that it is poisonous, DEET is an extremely safe insect repellent. Invented in 1953, DEET is used hundreds of millions of times every year around the world, yet only about 50 cases of severe dermatitis or seizures have been reported over the last 50 years. Many of these reports are questionably connected to DEET and the ones that have been were caused by extreme over use.

Yet DEET does have its legitimate drawbacks, such as the sticky residue it leaves on the skin and its foul odor. Hence the booming market for DEET alternatives.

---

[16] DEET stands for N, N-diethyl-meta-toluamide

trol expose the soil to wind and rain erosion. Soil erosion is the biggest sustainability problem in agriculture.

That is why, in the early 1970s, innovative non-organic farmers devised what are now called "low-till" and "no-till" farming systems that kill the weeds without soil disturbance. This reduces soil erosion and decreases spring soil moisture loss — especially important in dry areas. The roots, stalks, and other residues of the weeds are left in the upper soil layers and on the soil surface, thereby increasing the organic matter content of the soil and protecting it from erosion.

As a result, soil erosion on no-till and low-till fields is a small fraction of the losses seen in conventional and organic fields. Instead of losing soil, these fields are actually creating topsoil and are fully sustainable for the first time in history.[17] Moreover, the structure of the soil in no-till fields becomes more conducive to crop production: Earthworm populations skyrocket, increasing soil porosity and water-holding capacity.[18]

But organic farmers refuse to use chemical herbicides to kill weeds. They are left with only inferior, less sustainable methods. As discussed, plowing and tilling invite erosion and loss of soil structure and organic matter. Extensive work has been done with cover crops that shade out weeds and that can be

> The problem with many alternatives is that they apparently don't last nearly as long or repel as well as DEET. A study published in 2003 found that citronella-based natural repellents (such as Avon's Skin-So-Soft) only repel insects for three to 20 minutes. This is because the repellent chemicals are so volatile and simply evaporate rapidly.
>
> Some natural products will last longer if distilled into nearly pure chemicals, but these are often smelly and toxic. USDA insect scientist Dr. Don Barnard said, "I know one lady who put 100% clove oil on her face and she got horribly burned; she must have been pretty desperate to go organic."
>
> But science is persistent and several "natural" repellents may work well and appear safe. The oil derived from the Australian lemon-scented gum tree can be distilled to yield para-menthane-3,8-diol (PMD), now sold under the brand name Repel. A beefed up version of Avon's Skin-So-Soft contains a derivative of a natural amino acid, beta-alanine, called IR3535. And Cutter Advanced contains a synthetic derivative of pepper called picaridin.
>
> But to call these refined and altered chemicals "natural" or "organic" is a stretch.

---

[17] Farming for a Better Environment, Soil and Water Conservation Society, Ankeny, IA, 1995.
[18] Clapperton M.J., Miller J.J., Larney F.J., and Lindwall C.W. Earthworm Populations as Affected by Long-Term Tillage Practices in Southern Alberta, Canada. Proceedings of the Fifth Symposium on Earthworm Ecology, *Journal of Soil Biology and Biochemistry*, 1995.

mowed or "flailed" to kill them before planting the next crop. Yet they continue to have problems and are therefore not widely used. Other organic farmers are using flame weeders, where weeds are fried at the soil surface. But this is both expensive and dangerous.

The irony is that herbicides are the class of pesticide least toxic to humans and wildlife, even as they offer the most environmental benefit. Herbicides are mostly compounds that narrowly target plant enzymes and are virtually harmless to insects and mammals. Yet the benefits from their use are enormous. An all-organic mandate would eliminate all of these benefits.

Organic's Dirty Little Secret: Child Labor in Poor Countries

What are the social and ecological costs of producing organic pesticides? Many organic insecticides are extracts of plants. Pyrethrum is extracted from the flowers of pyrethrum chrysanthemums, much of it produced in Kenya and Peru. In 1981, Levy estimated that global demand for pyrethrum flowers exceeded 25,000 tons annually, satisfied by an estimated 150 million flowers hand-harvested daily.[19] In 1995, USDA statistics indicated that Kenya produced over 100,000 tons of dry flower petals, indicating a significant increase in pyrethrum production since 1981. How much land is required to meet current pyrethrum production and how much land would be needed to increase organic pesticide production if all U.S. farmers went organic? What are the social costs of large populations of agricultural workers — most of them poor women and children in developing countries — hand-picking flowers for organic pesticide production? Is this not equivalent to a sweatshop?

Conclusion

In summary, organic farmers utilize an array of both natural and manmade substances to kill and discourage pests and protect their crops. That's what farmers do. The claims that organic farmers don't need to use pesticides because their crops are so "hardy" and because of the "balance" of nature on their farms is simply a marketing myth. It plays to consumers' fears and no doubt works on many consumers. But it isn't true.

Organic farming is not pesticide free. Organic farm practices pose as many (if not more) human health and environmental risks as the synthetic pesticides used by today's non-organic farmers. They even pose their own ethical quandaries, such as child labor in poor countries.

---

[19] L.W. Levy, *Environmental and Experimental Botany* 21:389, 1981.

In the future, biotech crops and even more advanced synthetic and biopesticides will make non-organic farming even safer for both people and the environment, as well as more sustainable. Whether or not the organic believers will acknowledge these positive achievements, or simply denigrate and mock them as they have with the recent biotechnology improvements, will remain to be seen.

Chapter 7:

Hormone Hype and Antibiotic Angst

Organic Believers Say:

"If you are eating dairy or farm produce then you are also eating the chemicals, drugs, and growth hormones given to the animals."

Organic Facts
http://www.organicfoodinfo.net/

"According to expert scientists appointed by the European Union, the use of growth hormones in food animals poses a potential risk to consumers' health. The scientists reported that hormone residues found in meat from these animals can disrupt the consumer's hormone balance, cause developmental problems, interfere with the reproductive system, and even lead to the development of cancer. Children and pregnant women are most susceptible to these negative health effects. Hormone residues in beef are also thought to cause the early onset of puberty in girls. This puts girls at greater risk of developing breast cancer and other forms of cancer."

Sustainable Table, a project of the Global Resource Action Center for the Environment
http://www.sustainabletable.org/issues/hormones/

125

"The use of antibiotics, synthetic hormones, and genetically modified organisms to intensify production in today's conventional agriculture practices ... have also been proven or suspected to play a role in numerous human health concerns including early puberty, allergies, and BSE (mad cow disease)."

Organic Valley dairy Web site
http://organicvalley.coop/why_organic/health/index.html

"By offering organic meat products from family farms we're protecting your family."

Organic Valley Cooperative
http://www.organicvalley.coop/products_recipes/products.html?cat=9

Reality Says:

"**Question:** Dr. Smith, do you at all worry about feeding non-organic meat and eggs to your family? **Answer:** Absolutely not! Not in the least. I have six children and 13 grandchildren and I happily and confidently feed them all regular, non-organic meat. My only dietary guilt is the amount of sugary baked goods I provide my grandkids on Sunday morning when they're at our house visiting."

Personal interview with Dr. Gary Smith, director of the Center for Red Meat Safety
Department of Animal Sciences, Colorado State University

According to organic marketers and activists, the majority of our meat, milk, and eggs is tainted by hormones and antibiotics that add up to a "potentially serious threat" to the health of you and your children. But what is the truth?

Non-organic meat, milk, and eggs are more than 99% free of residues of both antibiotics and artificial hormones and are safe according to the latest assessment from the National Research Council's Committee on Drug Use in Food Animals in 1999.[1]

Consider the following "bottom line" statistic from recent testing by the U.S. Department of Agriculture (USDA): Conventional milk in the U.S. is 100% free of artificial hormones and 99.999% free of antibiotics.[2]

---

[1] National Research Council Committee on Drug Use in Food Animals. The Use of Drugs in Food Animals: Benefits and Risks, page 141. National Academy Press, Washington, D.C. 1999.
[2] National Milk Drug Residue Data Base: Fiscal Year 2005 Annual Report. 2006. Food and Drug Administration Center for Food Safety and Applied Nutrition. Available at: http://www.cfsan.fda.gov/~ear/p-mis.html.

Contrast this with the incredible hype in organic milk marketing. Over the past decade, companies selling highly profitable organic milk have become shameless at scaring moms into believing that non-organic milk is full of artificial hormones and antibiotics. Their labeling practically screams, "No hormones, no antibiotics!" Often these claims are made in yellow and red, the colors traditionally reserved for danger warnings. Many parents pay nearly twice as much for organic milk, specifically because they fear conventional milk contains these contaminants after seeing the ominous labels on organic milk products. Consumers pay 50% to 100% more thinking they are buying protection from exposure to contaminants when the milk is identical.

First, if eating hormones scares you, then don't consume any milk, meat, eggs, or soy products, even if they are organic — they all naturally contain hormones or hormone-like substances. In fact, soy-based foods contain high levels of chemicals called phytoestrogens that act like estrogen in our bodies. Soy and other plant products contain estrogenic chemicals at levels often far higher than the natural levels of estrogen in meat, milk, and eggs. (See "The Breasty Boys").

Let's look at each food category in more detail, examining both the

THE BREASTY BOYS

Organic activists have stoked fears that synthetic hormones in meat and milk may contribute to early puberty in girls (they don't) or other "hormone disruptions." Other environmental scientists have worried publicly that synthetic chemicals in our environment are mimicking hormones and disrupting our "endocrine systems." Yet despite a decade of debate, no synthetic chemicals have been found "disrupting endocrine systems" in real people in the real world.

But scientists have now identified two substances commonly used in consumer products that upset the hormone balance and even cause breast development in young boys. Were they pesticides? Nope. Plasticizers? Nope. Synthetic chemicals? Nope. They were natural lavender and tea tree oil, both of them so-called "essential oils."[3]

That's right, personal hygiene products such as shampoos and soaps containing both of these natural plant oils caused breast development in young boys. The hormonal properties of the oils were discovered by a doctor who set out to explain why several of his young patients (all boys under age 10) developed breasts even though their blood hormone levels were normal, a condition called gynecomastia. The only common link in the boys' cases was personal hygiene products that contained lavender or tea tree oil.

[3] Henley D. Presentation to the annual meeting of the Endocrine Society meeting, Boston Massachusetts. 2006.

hormone and antibiotic worries.

Milk Hormones

There is only one hormone allowed for use in dairy cows, a biotech "nature-identical" copy of the cow's natural growth hormone (bGH). The biotech version, "recombinant" (rbGH), used in roughly a third of U.S. dairy cows, extends peak milk production and results in 15% to 20% higher total milk yield over the entire lactation cycle. (rbGH does not increase the size of a cow's udder or cause swollen, over-full udders.)

The urban myth is that if you feed your kids milk from cows supplemented with rbGH they will enter puberty at an early age or develop breast cancer. Or something like that. There is zero truth to these myths, but they have become "common knowledge."

The Web site www.babyreference.com stated in an article on early puberty and its causes: "Cow's milk (like mother's milk) is naturally full of estrogens, progesterone, testosterone, and growth hormones for the calf. More growth hormone is then added artificially. ... Cow's milk has a high fat content, high levels of biologically available hormones and growth factors, and other chem-

---

The pediatric endocrinologist, Dr. Clifford Bloch of Denver, Colorado, said that "a couple of patients were putting pure lavender oil on their skin."[4] He recommended that the boys stop using products containing lavender and tea tree oil and within a few months the problem had disappeared.

To confirm that the plant oils were the culprit, Bloch took his theory to scientists at the National Institute of Environmental Health Sciences. In the lab, the scientists exposed human breast cells to the oils and, sure enough, each oil turned on estrogen-regulated genes and inhibited male-hormone-associated genes.

Translation: They "disrupted" the boys' endocrine systems.

According to Tufts University endocrinologist Edward Reiter, the plant oils likely have similar effects in young girls. Some studies have found an apparent rise in incidence of early breast development in girls and Reiter postulates that this may at least partly explain why.[5]

Now imagine for a moment that a synthetic chemical in the hygiene products had caused abnormal breast enlargement in young boys. Instead of an

---

[4] Harder B. Lavender Revolution: Plant Essences Linked to Enlarged Breasts in Boys. *Science News*, vol. 170:6. 2006.
[5] Ibid.

ical contaminants from highly medicated cows fed environmental trash ... all linked to early puberty and proliferation of cancer cells in human reproductive organs."[6]

Dairy farmers do not add hormones to milk and cow's milk is not full of chemical contaminants from "highly medicated cows fed environmental trash." rbGH is injected into a cow's muscle, not the udder. Its use does not alter the levels of natural hormones in milk or add any "artificial hormones" to the milk. The milk remains indistinguishable. The reason is that the biotech hormone is essentially identical to the cow's own natural bGH.

But the science continues to be misreported and hyped.

Time magazine jumped on the fear bandwagon in 2003 with an article on organic milk. The article stated, "Retail sales of organic dairy products are growing about 20% a year, even though a gallon of organic milk typically costs more than twice as much as regular milk. Its fans believe that organic milk is healthier because it comes from cows that aren't treated with antibiotics (which some researchers warn can be passed on in the milk and can increase the incidence of antibiotic-resistant bacteria) and synthetic growth hormones (which are believed to accelerate development in children). Studies are not conclusive, and nonorganic milk producers insist that their products are safe."[7]

The studies *are* conclusive. The FDA would not have approved the use of

interesting feature-story in your daily papers about the wonders and curiosities of nature, it would be front-page news. The tag line would be that the chemical companies had "threatened society's future."

Who knows what the long-term health impacts from this hormonal havoc might be. The calls for the strict regulation, if not outright bans, of the substance would be loud and immediate. The U.S. Food and Drug Administration (FDA) would likely call emergency regulatory meetings. Congress would hold hearings. There would be lawsuits. Trial lawyers would be trolling for "class-action" victims, running ads on TV about careless corporations threatening your children's health and sexual development. Every remotely similar synthetic chemical would be under renewed scientific scrutiny and increased regulatory burden, lest there be an epidemic of "boys with breasts."

Ironically, natural products and exposures to natural hormones have been nearly ignored by the environmental health community in the hype over "endocrine disruptors," even though they pose a larger theoretical and now-proven risk.

---

[6] http://www.babyreference.com/EarlyPuberty.htm
[7] Organic is Saving Family-Sized Dairy Farms. *Time*, July 14, 2003.

rbGH if it wasn't safe and did not result in wholesome milk.[8] (The meat from dairy cows given rbGH is also safe for consumption for this reason.) Extensive testing was conducted before farmers were allowed to use this hormone to boost milk production efficiency in 1993. All studies were conducted by independent third-party scientists and the results were extensively reviewed by FDA scientists. All said it was safe and none of the studies indicated that the hormone appeared in or altered the natural hormonal composition of the milk or meat.

To understand how much of a non-issue this is, you need to understand the nature of bGH and how it works. First, bGH (and rbGH) is a protein hormone, as opposed to a "steroid hormone" like testosterone. Because rbGH is a protein, it has no effect on cows (or people) if it is eaten. Our digestive system breaks it down as food like any other protein. Cows must be injected with rbGH for it to have any effect on maintaining peak milk production.

Second, organic activists call rbGH a "synthetic growth hormone." It is not synthetic, it is a biologically created "nature-identical" hormone made using the DNA sequence from cows. What's the difference? Synthetic hormones are "synthesized" using chemical reactions in test tubes; biologically created molecules are made in living systems. Because rbGH is made in bacteria (a living biological system) using the DNA blueprint from cows, it is 99.5% identical to the cow's natural bGH protein and acts just like the natural hormone.[9] The same exact bacteria-based biosynthesis process is used to make replacement human insulin, human growth hormone, and other biotech human medicines.

For the sake of argument, however, let's assume that the supplemental hormone did appear in the milk and made it past digestion to appear in our blood stream. What would the consequences be? Nothing. Humans simply do not respond to bGH from cows — even when it is injected!

Here's how we know this. In the 1950s, doctors discovered that dwarfism is caused by a lack of human growth hormone (hGH) production in the pituitary gland. They immediately began searching for a source of replacement growth hormones to treat the condition. One of the first places they looked was cows' pituitary glands because the beef industry would have been an inexpensive and abundant source of therapeutic hormone. But after purifying bGH

---

[8] Juskevich J.C., Guyer C.G. Bovine Growth Hormone: Human Food Safety Evaluation. *Science* vol. 249, pg. 875-884. (Both authors were FDA scientists). 1990.
[9] Of the 191 amino acids that make up the bGH protein, the approved biotech version is different in one amino acid.

and injecting it into children suffering from dwarfism, they were disappointed to find no effect whatsoever. Zip. Zero. Nada.

It turns out that while bGH is in many ways similar to human growth hormone, it is still different enough (about 35% different) that human cells don't recognize or respond to it. Because of that, children with dwarfism had to be treated with human growth hormone purified from human cadavers until the 1980s, when biotechnology made making recombinant human growth hormone (rHGH) possible. Today, rHGH not only is used to treat dwarfism, but also is a key therapy against the physical wasting seen in AIDS patients.

Despite all of these overlapping facts, 15 years after the approval of rbGH in dairy cows and a perfect safety record (including the health of the cows), organic activists and the willing media continue to perpetuate fears and supposed "uncertainties" about its safety to consumers. A few organic activists are still trying to get the FDA to ban use of rbGH. (See Scaremongering: The Never-Ending Crusade.)

I don't expect that the controversy (or fear-oriented marketing) over this "artificial hormone" will end anytime soon because too many are making too much money on the perception that the cows are "juiced up" with something that taints the milk. They'll work to prolong the fear for as long as there are consumers willing (literally) to buy into it.

SCAREMONGERING: THE NEVER-ENDING CRUSADE TO BAN rbGH

Having failed to produce any scientific evidence indicating use of rbGH in dairy cows is in any way a human health threat, organic activists have since turned their focus on another protein hormone present in milk (and also digested when consumed by people), called Insulin-like Growth Factor-1 (IGF-1). IGF-1 is present at low levels in all milk, including organic milk.

Organic activists have mischaracterized research on IGF-1 levels as they relate to cancer, claiming that a slight statistical increase in the average levels of IGF-1 in milk from rbGH-supplemented cows means the milk poses a cancer risk. Based on this mischaracterization, one activist petitioned the FDA in 1999 to rescind approval of rbGH.

The FDA concluded that the activist's "arguments do not demonstrate any human food safety issue related to the use of [rbGH]. Therefore, the petition requesting withdrawal of the approval of [rbGH] was denied."[10] The FDA's

[10] FDA Responds to Citizen Petition on BST. Federal Food and Drug Administration. http://www.fda.gov/cvm/CVM_Updates/cpetup.html. 2000.

Milk Antibiotics

Antibiotics are used in dairy cows to treat bacterial infections, just as they are used in people. Current laws require that the milk from a cow receiving antibiotics must be discarded or diverted from the human food chain until the residues of antibiotics are absent from the milk. The length of time that the milk must be discarded or diverted following treatment of a cow with antibiotics is called a "withdrawal period" and these periods are specified by the FDA for each antibiotic approved for use in dairy cows. But the safety system goes much further.

There is really a triple-plus layer of purity verification protecting consumers. First, there are FDA-specified withdrawal periods. Second, every single delivery of milk to a milk bottling and processing plant in the U.S. is tested for antibiotics. Any shipment that tests positive is discarded or diverted from the human food chain (it can still be fed to livestock). Third, processors often test milk in their storage tanks because a mistake there could cost them hundreds of thousands of dollars in lost profits. Finally, the milk leaving the bottling plant gets randomly tested. Of 170 billion pounds of milk processed in the U.S. in 2005, 52.7 million pounds (0.3%) tested by both private companies and the government tested positive for antibiotic traces and were discarded or safely blended into livestock feed. That's one out of every 3,000 pounds of milk. And because this milk never entered the food chain, the likelihood of purchasing a carton of milk with antibiotic traces is far less than one in 3,000.

Even this is an overestimate because many samples that test "positive" aren't really contaminated by antibiotic traces. The National Research Council's expert committee recommended in 1999 "increasing the specifici-

reasoning is quite simple and compelling: Humans naturally produce far more IGF-1 in their own bodies than could be consumed in milk, and the IGF-1 in milk (also present at the same levels in organic milk) is digested by people because it is a protein.

Here's a key quote from the FDA's response to the activist's petition, published in 2000:

> FDA has previously maintained and continues to maintain that levels of IGF-1 in milk, whether or not from rbGH supplemented cows, are not significant when evaluated against levels of IGF-1 [internally] produced and present in humans. IGF-1 is normally found in human plasma at concentrations much higher than those found in cow's milk. Reported percentage increases in IGF-1 concentrations in milk of rbGH supplemented cows

ty of certain tests to reduce the inordinate number of false-positive results, particularly in the inspection of milk. The high false-positive rate can cause unnecessary dumping of large quantities of milk and it causes unnecessary concern among consumers about the safety of the milk supply."[11]

According to the scientist contracted by the FDA to compile and analyze its milk testing data, the U.S. milk supply is more than 99.999% free of antibiotic residues. In short, there simply isn't a food sold that is assured of being more pure.

Meat Hormones

No artificial or supplemental natural hormones are allowed or sold for use in pigs or poultry, so right off the bat we can say that 75% of the total U.S. meat supply is 100% free of "artificial hormones." (Though remember, all meat, milk, eggs, and many plant-based foods contain natural hormones or hormone-like chemicals.)

That leaves beef, which makes up nearly 25% of all meat consumed in the U.S. About 2% of beef has detectable traces of synthetic hormones.

Currently, there are six hormones allowed for use in U.S. and Canadian beef production. Three of the six approved hormones are natural (estradiol, progesterone, and testosterone) and are produced naturally in all humans

---

can be misleading because the levels of IGF-1 in milk are so low prior to any increase. IGF-1 is a normal, but highly variable, constituent of bovine milk with the concentration depending on the animal's stage of lactation, nutritional status, and age.

While some studies indicate that levels of IGF-1 may statistically increase in the milk of rbGH supplemented cows relative to unsupplemented cows, reported increases are still within the normal variation of IGF-1 levels in milk.

The Agency pointed out that even if all of the IGF-1 in milk was absorbed, and there is insufficient evidence that it would be, the levels of IGF-I in human plasma would not rise by 1%. ... Like most dietary proteins, rbGH is degraded by digestive enzymes in the gastrointestinal tract and not absorbed intact (end FDA statement).[12]

---

[11] National Research Council Committee on Drug Use in Food Animals. 1999. Page 141.
[12] FDA Responds to Citizen Petition on BST. Federal Food and Drug Administration. http://www.fda.gov/cvm/CVM_Updates/cpetup.html. 2000.

throughout our lifetimes (including children) at levels considerably higher than the levels naturally found in beef or in beef from hormone-treated cattle. The other three hormones allowed in beef production (melengestrol acetate, trenbolone acetate, and zeranol) are synthetic chemicals that mimic the activity of natural hormones. Melengestrol acetate (MGA) mimics progesterone, trenbolone acetate (TBA) mimics testosterone, and zeranol mimics estradiol.

These hormones are allowed to be used because they are safe, improve beef quality, and improve growth rates and feed conversion efficiency (5% to 15% more meat from the same amount of feed). All of this lowers costs to consumers as well as conserving natural resources and reducing pollution. It is estimated that the use of hormone implants increases annual U.S. beef production by more than 700 million pounds while saving over 6 billion pounds of feed.[13]

How Do Hormones Work?

Supplemental hormones mimic the natural hormone levels in bulls that more efficiently produce the leaner beef desired by many consumers. A bull produces about 1,000 times more testosterone and estrogen than a steer (a castrated male bovine). This higher amount of hormone directs the bull's body to convert more of the feed energy into muscle rather than fat. However, the very high testosterone levels in bulls naturally make them aggressive, which can make them dangerous to people and other steers. The natural aggressiveness of bulls is why cattle producers castrate them; steers are safer and easier to handle.

Without supplemental hormones, castration means lower hormone production more like that of non-pregnant cows (who put on fat to support potential future pregnancies). In the past, this meant much higher fat content in the meat from steers. Steers produced 30 years ago often had 2 to 3 inches of back fat and the meat was heavily marbled with fat. As consumers became more concerned with heart health, beef producers responded by using leaner breeding stock and supplemental hormones.

In the 1950s, livestock scientists discovered that replacing a very small

---

[13] Anderson P.T., Crooker B.A., Pullen M.M. Animal Products: Contributors to a Safe Food Supply. University of Minnesota Extension Service. http://www.extension.umn.edu/distribution/nutrition/DJ5513.html. 1991.

amount of the natural hormone lost through castration resulted in leaner beef without bringing back the aggressive tendencies of bulls. Young females (heifers) respond similarly to added hormones, putting on lean muscle faster and more efficiently (i.e., with less feed, water, waste, etc.).

The first supplemental hormone implants were approved by the FDA for use in cattle production in 1956. Since that time, additional compounds and combinations have been approved in more than 30 countries. The European Union (EU), the pan-European regulatory and trade authority for Europe, continues to ban the use of beef hormones, though it is widely known that EU farmers illegally use supplemental hormones in beef production (with many well-documented "contamination" scandals).

Ironically, because European beef is predominantly bull-sourced (which produce roughly 10 times more testosterone than steers), whereas American and Canadian beef is primarily steer-sourced, American and Canadian "hormone-treated" beef generally contains lower levels of hormones than most European beef.

Are Beef Hormones Safe?

The $60 billion question, of course, is whether beef produced with supplemental hormones is safe.

Yes. Here is the science.

First, one safety factor is the way hormones are given to cattle. Except for MGA,[14] FDA regulations only allow hormones to be administered through time-release implants placed under the skin of the animals' ear at about six months of age. Each implant contains a specific, legally authorized dose of hormones. The implant ensures that the hormone is released into the animals' bloodstream very slowly so that the concentration of the hormone in the animal remains relatively constant and low. Because the ear is discarded at slaughter, the implant does not enter the food chain.

Second, there is no incentive for farmers to "overdose" an animal on hormones. Each implant contains the optimal dose for maximum economic return, and implanting a second implant would have little impact on further weight gain and would only waste money. This economic reality, coupled with the USDA's annual monitoring program, safeguards the system and ensures

---

[14] MGA is given via feed at a dose of 0.25 to 0.5 mg/day, or about 2 to 3 micrograms/kg body weight.

that hormones are used properly and safely.

The science indicates that use of supplemental hormones in cattle has only a minor impact on hormone levels in meat — well below the natural variability in hormone levels in cattle or the amounts produced naturally in our own bodies. Consider that the amount of estradiol-equivalent hormone in hormone-implanted beef is far less than the amount found in eggs. According to the USDA, a person would need to eat over 13 pounds of beef from an implanted steer in order to equal the amount of estradiol found in a single egg![15] One glass of milk contains about nine times as much estradiol as a half-pound of beef from an implanted steer. And remember, it's not just animal products that contain hormonally active chemicals. A half-pound potato has 245 nanograms (ng, or 1 billionth of a gram) of estrogen equivalent compared with 1.3 ng for a quarter pound of untreated beef and 1.9 ng for beef from an implanted steer.[16]

And it's not just the United States and Canadian food safety authorities who say beef hormones are safe. So do the World Health Organization (WHO) and other European scientific bodies.

The Joint Expert Committee on Food Additives of the World Health Organization and United Nations' Food and Agriculture Organization (WHO/FAO Expert Committee) calculated that even assuming the highest residue levels found in beef, a person consuming one pound (~500 g) of beef from an implanted steer would ingest only 50 ng of additional estradiol compared to non-implanted beef.[17] That's less than one-thirtieth of the Acceptable Daily Intake (ADI) of estradiol for a 75 pound child established by the WHO/FAO Expert Committee. (See ADIs Explained)

The use of the natural hormones is so safe that the WHO/FAO Expert Committee didn't even establish a Maximum Residue Limit (MRL) for them because the committee concluded that residues occurring from proper use were so low that they are unlikely to pose any health hazard. The FDA made the same decision.

And don't forget that our own bodies produce these same hormones every day in amounts a hundred times or more higher. A pound of beef raised using estradiol contains approximately 15,000 times less of this hormone than the

---

[15] Foreign Agricultural Service, USDA. A Primer on Beef Hormones. Available at: http://stockholm.usembassy.gov/Agriculture/hormone.html. 1999.
[16] Ibid.
[17] Joint FAO/WHO Expert Committee on Food Additives. Summary and Conclusions of the Fifty-second Meeting. 1999.

amount produced daily by the average man and about 9 million times less than the amount produced by a pregnant woman.

Do residues of the synthetic hormones TBA, MGA, and zeranol appear in beef? Yes, but only rarely and only in inconsequentially small amounts.

The most common synthetic residue is MGA, a synthetic hormone which mimics progesterone. It is given to heifers at doses between 0.25 and 0.5 mg

---

ADIs EXPLAINED

Acceptable Daily Intakes (ADIs) are the dose of a substance experts believe is totally safe to consume each day for a lifetime. They are established by taking a safe, no-effect dose and then applying a suitable "uncertainty" or "safety factor" to ensure against any health impacts, ranging from 100- to 1,000-fold less than the no-effect dose. ADIs are listed as a dose per pound or kilogram of a person's body weight.

For example, the ADI for estradiol is 50 ng per kilogram of body weight, based on a no-effect dose in women of 300 micrograms (µg, millionths of a gram) per 60 kg person per day and an uncertainty factor of 100. (Here's the math: 300 µg ÷ 60 kg = 5 µg/kg. 5 µg ÷ 100 uncertainty factor = 0.05 µg/kg, or 50 ng/kg.)

Here is a chart listing the ADIs, the corresponding dose for a 75 pound child and 150 pound adult, and the percentage of the ADI for a 150 pound adult in an average pound of beef from a treated animal (based on values reported by USDA and in the 1999 WHO/FAO Expert Committee report).

Hormone	WHO/FAO Acceptable Daily Intake (per kg body weight)	ADI for 75 lb person	ADI for 150 lb person	Maximum theoretical percent of ADI (150 lb person) in a pound of implanted beef	
Estradiol	0.05 µg	1.75 µg	3.5 µg	(50 ng/lb)	1.50%
Progesterone	30 µg	1,050 µg	2,100 µg	(100 µg/lb)	5.25%
Testosterone	2 µg	70 µg	140 µg	(46 ng/lb)	0.03%
MGA	0.03 µg	1.05 µg	2.1 µg	(50 ng/lb)	2.30%
TBA	0.02 µg	0.7 µg	1.4 µg	(8 ng)	0.57%
Zeranol	0.5 µg	17.5 µg	35 µg	(0.09 µg)	0.25%

As is readily apparent, one pound of beef from implanted animals never exceeds or even approaches the ADI. The closest they come is 5.25% of the ADI for progesterone. Even if a 75 pound child ate an entire pound of implanted beef (or four large hamburgers), that child wouldn't be exposed to even one quarter of the ADI.

per day in their feed. According to annual testing by the USDA, MGA residues show up at non-violative levels in between 4% and 8% of fat samples from heifers. For example, in 2004 MGA was found in 20 samples out of 238 tested at levels "less than 0.1 μg per kg." In 2003, USDA found it in seven out of 187 fat samples at just over 5 μg (millionths of a gram) per kilogram, well below the maximum residue limit (MRL) set by the FDA of 25 μg per kilogram of beef.

If you pooled all 27 contaminated samples together, one pound of this beef would still not contain enough MGA to exceed the ADI for a 75 pound child of 1 μg. For comparison, prepubertal boys produce an estimated 150 μg of progesterone per day, or 150 times more hormone-equivalent than found in this theoretical "highly contaminated" pound of beef.[18]

But that is an absolute worst case scenario. Actual consumer exposure to MGA is far less because hamburger contains less MGA than is measured in the fat and over 90% of fat samples tested by the USDA contained no MGA at all. Scientists at the USDA can detect MGA at levels as low as 10 parts per trillion. Based on the combined 2003 and 2004 USDA monitoring data, the average pound of U.S.-produced heifer beef contains less than 0.05 μg of MGA. To begin to exceed the ADI set by the WHO/FAO Expert Committee, a child would have to eat more than 20 pounds of beef specifically from heifers per day.

The WHO/FAO Expert Committee extensively modeled theoretical consumer exposures to hormone residues based on worst-case exposure estimates and also found no indication of appreciable risk. This issue is at the heart of the EU's justifications for not allowing the sale of U.S. beef to European consumers since 1989, the subject of a long-running and bitter trade dispute. The only way that the EU has been able to manufacture enough theoretical risk to even remotely justify to the World Trade Organization (WTO) the ban on the sale of U.S. beef in Europe has been to give cattle three- and 10-fold doses of the synthetic hormones and then declare that U.S. regulators cannot guarantee that the hormones aren't being misused in such a way. Yet even then, hormone residues exceed the ADIs set by the WHO/FAO Expert Committee only in cow livers and not the other edible tissues.

The British government's Sub-Group of the Veterinary Products Committee estimated a "worst-case" exposure to residues of TBA (the synthetic hormone that mimics testosterone) based on the maximum amount the Sub-Group could extract from tissues following TBA's proper use. Even that didn't exceed

---

[18] World Health Organization. Toxicological Evaluation of Certain Veterinary Drug Residues in Food. WHO Food Additives Series vol. 23. 1988.

half of the conservative ADI for children set by the WHO/FAO Expert Committee. The highest TBA residue they found in muscle and fat translates into a pound of hamburger containing only 2.5% of the WHO/FAO Expert Committee's ADI for children.

So why has Europe banned the use of these hormones? Mainly to reduce farm output and, therefore, expensive government subsidy payments to European farmers, but also to placate misinformed European consumers. More than 30 other countries currently allow use of these hormones in beef production, and even European scientific groups have deemed hormones safe for use. Here is just a partial list of the high-powered expert groups that have declared the use of supplemental hormones in beef production safe:

- **U.S. Food and Drug Administration,** which has approved nearly a dozen different formulations since the late 1980s;

- **European Economic Community Scientific Working Group on Anabolic Agents,** chaired by Dr. G. E. Lamming in 1987;

- **International Codex Alimentarius Committee on Residues of Veterinary Drugs in Foods,** in 1987; The Codex sets safety standards for international trade under the WTO.

- **European Agriculture Commission Scientific Conference on Growth Promotion in Meat Production,** in 1995;

- **FAO/WHO Joint Expert Committee on Food Additives (JECFA),** 1981, 1983, 1988, 1999;

- **Sub-Group of the Veterinary Products Committee of the British Ministry of Agriculture, Fisheries, and Food,** 1999.

No matter who or how many groups have examined this issue, no realistic health threats have been found from the use of hormones, natural or synthetic, in beef production. But that won't stop the marketing and fearmongering because the story is too juicy for reporters and the profits are too high for those selling so-called "hormone-free" meat.

Meat Antibiotics

Given the media and product labeling hype, one would think that a sizable percentage of our meat was contaminated with antibiotic traces. But in reality antibiotic residues are found in less than 2% of the U.S. meat supply and less than 0.1% has antibiotic residues above FDA limits.

Here are the statistics by meat category from USDA monitoring for antibiotic residues in kidney tissue in 2002, 2003, and 2004 (the latest years for which data exist at the time of this writing):

	% of samples that have positive antibiotic residue detection	% of samples with antibiotic residue above FDA limit
Beef	0.32	0.09
Pork	4.75	0.13
Chicken	0.90	0.03

As the table shows, pork has the highest antibiotic residue detection rate at nearly 5%. But only one out of 35 detections in pork kidney (the "target tissue" examined by the USDA) was above the maximum residue limit established by the FDA. This means you have only a one in 20 chance of finding any antibiotic residues in conventional pork and only a one in 1,000 chance of there being antibiotic residues above the FDA limit.

Beef and chicken are even more "antibiotic-free" than pork, with less than 1% detection and less than 0.1% residue violation rates.

Moreover, antibiotic traces above the FDA's maximum residue limit do not mean the residues pose a health risk. After all, we all use antibiotics whenever we get a bacterial infection at doses hundreds of thousands of times higher than the levels found in even the "violative" samples. Even the vast majority of those allergic to antibiotics are not threatened by the traces occasionally found in food.

A European expert group noted that only a tiny few — "less than 10 cases reported in the last 25 years" — were at risk of allergic reactions to antibiotic traces in food.[19] All 10 individuals were "hypersensitive" to the penicillin class of antibiotics because of previous medical exposures, and most suffered only a rash. Only one person was hospitalized from food-antibiotic exposure, and no deaths were reported. The number of people hypersensitive to penicillin-type antibiotics is extremely low, estimated at fewer than two dozen individuals worldwide.

Nor is anyone becoming allergic to antibiotics because of food residues. The world's health experts agree that not a single person has become allergic to antibiotics from food exposures. As one group of European experts noted, "No

---

[19] Dewdney J.M., et al. Risk Assessment of Antibiotic Residues of Beta-Lactams and Macrolides in Food Products With Regard to Their Immuno-Allergic Potential. *Food Chemistry and Toxicology* 29:477-483. 1991.

evidence has been found that any individual has become sensitized by [antibiotic residues in meat and other foods]. Furthermore, the oral [exposure route] is much less sensitizing than [injections or other methods of] administration."[20]

Organic proponents will no doubt proclaim, "We don't have ANY antibiotic traces in our meat, so there is no risk even for those folks." Of course, if I were one of the world's dozen or so penicillin-hypersensitive individuals, I might well buy organic meat and dairy products. But I'm not, so I don't. How much lower risk can you get than a rash in 10 people worldwide over 25 years? For perspective, an estimated 30 children drown in buckets each year in the U.S. and more than 8,000 adults and children die each year from accidental poisonings (from common household chemicals, shellfish, mushrooms, etc.). Should we ban buckets and cleaning supplies?

Among the real risks in our world, antibiotic residues in meat are as close to zero as is possible. Yet the use of antibiotics in animal agriculture is enormously controversial and scary to so many consumers.

Why do farmers use them? For the same reasons you give them to your kids when they get sick. In fact, organic farmers are prohibited by humane animal treatment laws in most countries (including the U.S.) from withholding antibiotics from farm animals if they are needed to treat a life threatening illness.

The dirty secret about organic farming is that organic farmers either (a) don't use the antibiotics and allow their animals to remain sick or die from treatable illnesses or (b) administer antibiotics to the animals and then sell them as non-organic. It's an open secret in farm policy circles that nearly all organic dairies have a non-organic side to their operations so they have someplace to send the animals that eventually require treatment with antibiotics (usually for mild infections of the udder, which reduce milk quality and productivity).

In Europe, organic farmers are allowed to use antibiotics. They merely have to double the standard "withholding" period following antibiotic use.

The marketing hype is that organic farmers don't need to use antibiotics because they don't "cram the animals in crowded cages and pens" and because their animals are so "naturally healthy." Phooey. Every animal farm has to deal with microbial diseases and infections and virtually no evidence has been brought forth by organic proponents to support their claims of superior health and disease resistance in their farm animals. Extensive outdoor livestock rear-

---

[20] Ibid.

ing systems suffer greater losses of animals to predators and exposure to harsh weather (and resulting diseases), which is one reason indoor hog and poultry houses were devised in the first place.

The Truth About "Factory Farms" and Antibiotics

Contrary to the popular myth that non-organic livestock and poultry farms cage and crowd their animals inhumanely, the only animals raised in actual cages are egg-laying hens (usually three to five hens per cage) and mother sows. Mother sows aren't really kept in cages. When they don't have piglets, they are kept in pens just like any other hog. But after they give birth to piglets,

---

THE FLU-IEST FLOCKS: FREE-RANGE OR CONFINEMENT?

Free Range Chickens and Ducks Dangerous to Humanity
Friday April 7, 2006
by Dennis Avery and Alex Avery

The evidence is now clear: Free-range chickens and ducks are a major, direct threat to humans worldwide.

Fortunately, we can prevent a massive, global replay of the Spanish flu epidemic that killed perhaps 25 million people in 1918-19 simply by putting the world's poultry into confinement houses.

Despite the protests of the "natural and organic" movement, letting our chickens be outdoors encourages the bird flu virus to evolve. That could trigger millions of human deaths if the new H5N1 bird flu virus morphs again into an airborne form that can be transmitted directly between people. Half of the recent Asian victims of H5N1 have died.

Free-range chicken enthusiasts claim — loudly and without evidence — that "factory chicken farms" produced the new bird flu virus. In Thailand, however, officials found that none of that nation's modern, indoor chicken flocks had bird flu. In dramatic contrast, 56% of the backyard chickens and 47% of the backyard and free-range ducks had the disease.

Historically, modern flu epidemics have come from Asia, apparently for two reasons:

First, Asia still has millions of chickens and ducks raised outdoors, in backyards and village streets where they interact with wild birds and people. That lets the virus pass back and forth among birds and humans — and even among pigs and cats. Second, Asia has a huge population of free-range ducks that graze in its rice paddies. Thai officials have recently discovered that ducks can transmit the virus without showing symptoms themselves.

they are kept in "farrowing crates" that prevent them from rolling on top of and crushing the little ones. Egg laying hens are caged to prevent cannibalism, reduce disease incidence, and ease timely egg collection. Other than these two instances, no cages are used.

The EU had passed a future ban on caging laying hens in Europe but is now reconsidering it before it goes into effect because of now well-documented increases in disease and cannibalism among non-caged hens and demonstrably higher food safety risks to consumers.

In confinement dairy farming, cows are allowed to roam within the barn (where it is both cooler in summer and warmer in winter) and eat and drink at will. Each cow has her own "stall" she can relax in, complete with a padded

---

Thai officials initially culled all sick birds and banned outdoor duck grazing. That produced a one-year lull in the epidemic. Unfortunately, several thousand ducks illegally grazing in rice fields quickly produced a surge of dying chickens across a whole region, even without any known contact between the ducks and chicken flocks. One person died who worked directly with the chickens.

The flu was first discovered in Chinese geese. Wild birds, especially waterfowl, have now spread the bird flu virus from China, Thailand, and Vietnam to Russia, Turkey, India, and Europe. It's likely to spread worldwide. The solution to the bird flu danger? We must put our poultry flocks indoors, where the birds are more comfortable, commit less cannibalism, and have less interaction with people and wild birds.

This obvious precaution has drawn screeches of protest from free range poultry advocates. In Germany, officials rescinded a ban on allowing chickens outdoors after such protests — so long as the birds are covered by a net. What a strange ruling. Nets characteristically have holes. What if droppings from wild birds fall through the net? In Thailand, a quarter of the chicken flocks in net-walled open houses were infected.

What possible benefits can outdoor poultry offer that would override the risk of another 25 million human deaths from Spanish flu? There are absolutely no nutritional differences. Free-range birds have also been found to carry more illness-causing bacteria, such as Campylobacter and Salmonella. Spread to our kitchen counters, these bacteria are themselves potentially deadly to our kids.

Oddly, many of the advocates who demand that their chicken be raised outdoors spend the vast majority of their own hours inside air-conditioned homes, offices, schools, and cars.

It's time to step around the free-range chicken cult and eliminate the pandemic threat of bird flu. It's time to put the world's poultry flocks indoors.

bed of sawdust, thick rubber mat, or a literal water bed! Pigs are raised in groups of five to 10 in open pens in a climate-controlled hog house, with more than enough room to move around. Turkeys and chickens are raised in houses where the interior is wide open to all the birds and with plenty of room. Again, these animals are raised indoors because the birds are more comfortable, there is less loss of birds to predators and severe weather, and the resulting poultry is safer for human consumption.

Raising poultry "free-range" has repeatedly been shown to lead to higher bacterial contamination rates of eggs and meat and increased disease risk to the birds. (See Flu-iest Flocks). Even when the birds are nearly full-grown, there is plenty of room in the poultry house for the birds to run, jump, flap their wings, and otherwise do what poultry do.

Infection and disease rates are very low in confinement livestock rearing systems unless the farmer is doing something wrong. If disease and infection losses were consistently high, farmers would stop raising animals that way. But all over the world, farmers are moving to confinement rearing systems because of better animal health, comfort, and growth efficiency.

What about the increasing ability of microbes to resist the killing power of antibiotics? This is where the controversy heats up, but there is almost no evidence that use of antibiotics in animals has contributed at all to the antibiotic resistance problem in people. If the evidence were clear, the debate would be over.

The big debate is about the low-dose (sub-therapeutic) use of antibiotic feed additives to promote growth, rather than uses of antibiotics to treat disease or infection (therapeutic). Organic activists and others claim that the sub-therapeutic use of antibiotics has increased the prevalence of antibiotic-resistant microbes on our food. This is true. However, these bacteria rarely cause human infections. Of the 20 most serious bacterial infections associated with antimicrobial resistance in humans, 12 cannot be acquired via food. The remaining eight each account for 1% or less of all cases of antibiotic-resistant illness in people.[21]

The EU banned the sub-therapeutic use of antimicrobial feed additives against the advice of its own Scientific Committee for Animal Nutrition and saw a huge jump in the number of diseases in the animals. This surge in disease was then followed by a surge in the use of therapeutic antibiotics, many

---

[21] Bywater R.J. and Casewell M.W. An Assessment of the Impact of Antibiotic Resistance in Different Bacterial Species and of Contribution of Animal Sources to Resistance in Human Infections. *Journal of Antimicrobial Chemotherapy* 46:1052. 2000.

of which are in the same classes as the antibiotics used to treat people (whereas sub-therapeutic antibiotics are mostly not used to treat people). Banning the sub-therapeutic use of antibiotics may have unintentionally increased the risk of antibiotic resistance in people.

Following a ban on sub-therapeutic antibiotics in Denmark, the use of antibiotics to treat illness in farm animals more than doubled from 105,000 lbs of antibiotics used in 1997 to 250,000 lbs in 2004. This is clear evidence that sub-therapeutic antibiotics were preventing disease and promoting animal health.

None of the bans on sub-therapeutic antimicrobials have measurably reduced the antibiotic resistance problem in human medicine. In fact, while the U.S. has not banned sub-therapeutic use of antimicrobials in animal agriculture and has seen the incidence of foodborne illness decrease in recent years, Europe has banned sub-therapeutic use of antimicrobials and seen its incidence of foodborne illness increase. There may or may not be any real connection in these numbers, but clearly the controversy has been blown far out of reasonable proportion to the science.

Conclusion

All in all, our food supply is amazingly safe and healthy. More than 99% of meat, milk, and eggs is completely free of any detectable traces of supplemental hormones and antibiotics. None of the residues detected in the food supply remotely constitutes a health threat. Use of these inputs helps to produce meat, milk, and eggs more efficiently, using less feed and water, and producing less waste per pound of meat produced. Data collected by neutral government agencies and examined by independent international food safety authorities have led those authorities overwhelmingly to conclude that it is safe to use these inputs.

The only groups to determine otherwise are European entities attempting to justify a two-decade-old trade restriction designed to eliminate foreign competition and protect government coffers. Even they could not come up with a realistic scenario indicating appreciable risk, even after grossly overdosing animals with hormones.

So the next time you see the milk carton or beef label on the supermarket shelf declaring that product to be "Hormone-Free" and proclaiming "NO Antibiotics," chuckle to yourself at how gullible some people are and buy with confidence based on taste and quality.

Chapter 8:

If It's Better, Buy It!

Organic Faithful Say:

"Do organic foods taste better? We think so, and hundreds of gourmet chefs across the country agree. It's common sense — well balanced soils grow strong, healthy plants that taste great."
Statement on Web site of for-profit organic foods retailer Whole Foods Market, May 2004 ($)[1]
http://www.wholefoods.com/issues/org_questions.html

"Organic produce simply tastes so much better. Fruit and vegetables full of juice and flavour, and so many different varieties to try!"
10 Top Reasons to Go Organic, Web site of for-profit Organicfood U.K., May 2004 ($)
http://www.organicfood.co.uk/topten.html

"As a chef, using organic fruits and vegetables is a matter of taste. The flavor is better than conventionally grown produce, so I'm not surprised that more chefs and home cooks are preparing dishes with fresh organic ingredients. I even see it with children, including my own. Kids who grimace at frozen green

---

[1] ($) Indicates that the person quoted has a profit motive or other financial interest in promoting organic food.

beans are eager to try organic beans picked fresh from our restaurant's garden."

ORGANIC: It's All in Good Taste, by Chef Cal Stamenov
Article on Web site of for-profit ($) Earthbound Farm, May 2004
http://www.ebfarm.com/why_organic/chef_cal_goodtaste.html

"Organic farming delivers the highest quality, best-tasting food."

Prince Charles, owner of for-profit Duchy Originals organic food brand ($)
http://observer.guardian.co.uk/foodmonthly/story/0,9950,1078139,00.html (Web published
May, 2004)

Reality Says:

"There were minor differences between the farming systems in food quality."

Soil Fertility and Biodiversity in Organic Farming, Report on 21 years of research on seven
different crops
Science, May 2002, pages 1694–1697

"Taste tests … found no differences among organic, conventional, and integrated apples in texture or overall acceptance."

Sustainability of three apple production systems
Nature, vol. 410, 2001, pages 926–930

"In June 2000, around 40 CHOICE staff munched on carrots, cucumbers, bananas, and Pink Lady apples … to find out whether you can pick organic fruit and vegetables by taste alone, and whether those we bought tasted better … only 38% preferred the taste of the organic apples. There was generally no huge preference for organic or conventional … larger taste tests have shown no significant taste differences."

Australian Consumers' Association, CHOICE
http://www.choice.com.au/viewArticle.aspx?id=101575&catId=100406&tid=100008&p=8

Organic foods can be better. There is no question about that. In fact, my wife and I occasionally buy some organic products. For example, we regularly buy organic bread from our local food supermarket. When we are having friends and family over for a special dinner, the organic bread is what we serve. Why? Because it is simply the best bread in the store.

The bread is great because the bread company uses a good bread recipe, uses an appropriate wheat flour (See Wheat Flours), bakes the loaves in a European-style, stone hearth oven, and delivers the bread to the store in a timely manner. (The company has to because it uses no preservatives.) These simple measures are what make the bread great, not whether the wheat for the flour was protected in the field by an organic-approved pesticide instead of a non-approved synthetic pesticide. (Even some organic pesticides are synthetic; see Chapters 4 and 5.)

The organic bread loaves are actually the only European-style bread in the entire store. This bread has a wonderful crisp crust and chewy inside, and thus was made with flour from a higher-protein hard winter wheat variety. The rest of the bread available at the store is a softer, American-style bread. That kind of bread is fine for a peanut butter and jelly sandwich, but it's hardly something to serve with a gourmet meal. Yet nothing about the good organic bread loaves requires organically grown ingredients. It could just as easily be made using non-organically grown ingredients. If it were available in a non-organic version at a cheaper price, we'd buy that instead.

The bread is a high-quality specialty product. The targeted consumer happens to significantly overlap with organically minded consumers, who are mostly from the more affluent sector of society. Plus, buying this specialty

---

WHEAT FLOURS

According to Molly Stevens of *Fine Cooking* magazine, "A stroll down the supermarket's baking aisle reminds me that there are more than a few kinds of flour to choose from. To decide which type is best for the kind of baking you do, it helps to understand that flour is made up of carbohydrates (or starch), proteins, and in the case of whole-wheat flour, a bit of fat. Of these three nutrients, protein matters most to the baker. The proteins in wheat are called gluten-forming proteins, and the quantity and quality of these proteins determine how a flour will perform in the kitchen."

A high percentage of protein means a harder (stronger) flour best suited to chewy, crusty breads and other yeast-risen products. Less protein means a softer flour, best for tender and chemically leavened baked goods, like pie crusts, cakes, cookies, and biscuits.

Since the protein content of wheat can range from 5% to 15%, the flour industry has established labeling standards that help us find the right flour for our needs. Whole wheat from hard red spring wheat has a protein content of 14%. Most bread wheat flours contain between 13% and 14% protein. All-purpose flours contain about 12% protein, whereas Southern all-purpose cake and pastry flours contain 9% to 10% protein.

Bread flour is used in bread recipes because there is enough gluten protein to form a strong network that traps the CO_2 released by the yeast, making the voids in the body of the bread, while also creating the strong, hard crust.

bread says to people, "I'm unique" and plays into the current societal fad of "natural is better" and "natural luxury." It is the same phenomenon that has led to "organic" ingredients in so many things, including shampoo.

My family also occasionally buys organic vegetables when they happen to be the best quality in the store on that particular day. The organic vegetables may be better because they were sourced from a local farmer, and therefore had a short trip to the store and may have been allowed to ripen longer on the vine or stalk. Perhaps the organic farmer planted a variety of that vegetable with better taste and/or texture qualities that make it more appealing.

In short, we buy organic foods based on their culinary qualities, not organic ideology. Yet to a certain extent, preference is all in the eye of the beholder. If you ask believers in organic foods and farming, many if not most will tell you they can taste the difference and organic is better. I've done my own taste tests at home and I simply don't agree. Sometimes the organic product is better, but in my opinion that's the exception rather than the rule. Mostly I don't find the organic products worth their higher prices, even when marginally better in quality or taste.

Why and When Are Organic Foods Better?

Here are some basic guidelines for examining whether or not a particular organic product might be better or worth the higher price. The first important distinction is between fresh produce and processed products. When I say processed products, I'm talking about everything from bread and breakfast cereal to soups and tortilla chips.

Processed organic foods have no inherent superiority to non-organic processed foods. But they may be excellent products, and even ones you prefer. It all depends on the recipe and ingredients used in making the product. I prefer some brands of canned soup over others because they contain more and larger chunks of meat and vegetables. But given identical recipes and using ingredients of equal quality, soups made with either organic or non-organic ingredients are of equal quality.

Consider some real-world taste and quality testing conducted by *Cook's Illustrated* magazine. *Cook's Illustrated* runs a taste kitchen where it conducts comparisons of various foods. In several testings, the magazine has included organic products in the tests. In these blind tastings organic products have compared both well and poorly to non-organic products.

In a comparison of canned beans, for example, the organic products ended up at the bottom of CI's "not recommended" list. Non-organic Green Giant and

Goya brands of kidney beans (both 59 cents per can) came out ahead of Westbrae Natural Organic ($1.59) and Eden Organic kidney beans ($1.99). Same exact story with the navy beans. Despite costing 2½ to 3½ times more per can, the organic beans rated the lowest in taste and texture.

Cook's Illustrated's comparison of tortilla chips was kinder to organic brands, with two organic brands (Newman's Own Organics™ and Bearitos Stone-ground Organic™) making it to the "highly recommended" list. Yet both of these organic brands came in behind first-place Doritos™ yellow corn chips and second-place Miquel's Stowe Away White Corn™ tortilla chips. The third organic brand in the test (out of a total of 10) came in last, at the bottom of the "not recommended" list.

There are multiple ways in which food processors can ensure the quality of their products and this explains why so many processed food products have consistently excellent quality.

For example, bread makers need high-protein wheat flour to make good hard-crusted breads (like the one we prefer to serve our dinner guests). Yet growing wheat organically (i.e., with organic nitrogen fertilizer) results in a lower protein content in the wheat flour. Bread makers compensate for this simply by pur-

---

ORGANIC BEEF SCAM: CAVEAT EMPTOR
BUT HOW TO TELL IT'S REALLY ORGANIC?

In November of 2002, the *New York Post* ran several articles exposing a scam run by the supposedly organic Manhattan meat retailer Healthy Pleasures. (Note that the name implies that organic foods are healthier for you.) The *Post's* reporters uncovered evidence and testimony from former employees that the chain had been purchasing non-organic meat from a major nationwide supplier and then repackaging it as natural and organic meat. The supplier, IBP, does not handle any natural or organic meat products. According to one employee:

"We would open the boxes, take the meat from the bulk bags and carry it upstairs on a lug. Then we would put it in the case and stick the natural and organic signs on it. We were told never to take IBP boxes up to the selling floor, where customers might see them."

The manager of the meat department at the [University Place Healthy Pleasures] store said the store buys its entire supply of organic and natural meat from E&S, a top Meat Packing District distributor. But E&S owner Evan Wexler said he sells 'a small amount' of organic meat to Healthy Pleasures and that its most recent delivery was Oct. 8. E&S does not carry natural beef.

Chain manager Omar Bashar refuted his manager's account, saying the

chasing high-protein varieties, such as hard red wheat, and testing the wheat to ensure it has a high enough protein level to meet their requirements.

The last word about organic processed products is that it is entirely within the rules to create an organic Twinkie. This was even the topic of a discussion at an organic food conference I attended.

Michael Jacobson, head of the Center for Science in the Public Interest notes that "just because foods are organically grown, they still could be loaded with organic fat and organic sugar, and they still could be contaminated with dangerous bacteria."

Consider organic pancake syrups. There are now several brands of organic pancake syrup being marketed nationally in the U.S. You might think that organic syrups would be made from maple syrup tapped from wild maple trees. You'd be wrong. Like most other so-called "pancake syrups," they are made almost entirely from plain old sugar (from organic sugar beets and organic sugar cane) along with a small percentage of maple syrup or maple flavoring.

Only 100% pure maple syrup can call itself maple syrup. The advent of these organic syrups[2] has angered some natural maple syrup makers, who tap

> chain bought all its beef from Alberts Organic and Green Circle, not mentioning IBP. 'Some of my employees are new and don't know the product,' he said.
>
> Less than an hour after speaking with the Post Wednesday, Bashar called in large orders for organic and natural meat from Alberts Organic and Green Circle, the organic meat producer used by many of the city's top restaurants and food stores.
>
> Reps for both firms confirmed that Bashar placed calls late Wednesday asking for large quantities of organic and natural beef to be delivered the next day. 'They were scrambling to get their house in order,' one insider said.
>
> Organic and natural beef fetches top dollar from health-conscious food shoppers, but prices for such meat at Healthy Pleasures are significantly lower than at competing stores.
>
> For example, organic rib-eye steaks at Healthy Pleasures were being sold for $10.99 per pound last Tuesday.
>
> At Citarella, they were $23.99 per pound. At Gourmet Garage, natural rib-eyes sold for $14.99 per pound. Conventional rib-eyes at supermarkets ranged from $8.99 to $10.99.
>
> "They are selling their organic and natural beef often for less than most of us can buy it for," said one competitor.

[2] Two prominent brands are Shady Maple Farms Certified Organic Pancake Syrup™ and Sorrell Ridge Organic Syrup™.

natural maple trees and painstakingly boil the sap down to make the concentrated syrup. They rightly ask, what could be more natural and organic than syrup obtained from wild trees from basically a wild forest setting. If the natural maple syrup makers want to also label it as organic, however, they'll have to get their maple farms certified according to the USDA's rules.

Yet the manufactured sugar syrups fit all the requirements to be called organic: They are made entirely of ingredients from organically grown crops. As I said, it is entirely possible to create an organic Twinkie!

What About Fruits and Vegetables?

We all have stories of juicy and delicious homegrown tomatoes that make many store-bought tomatoes seem like cardboard in comparison. Why are they so much better, so often? It isn't rocket science.

First, our homegrown garden tomato varieties have been selected for totally different criteria than commercially grown tomato varieties. Whereas the home gardener is most interested in taste, texture, color, novelty, and such, the commercial farmer is interested in yields, pest resistance, shipping tolerance, storage tolerance, and other factors. In short, there is a completely different set of priorities applied to crop varieties grown by commercial farmers than for the home gardener. So, too, the needs of many organic farmers, who cater to a different market niche, have a shorter marketing chain (few to no middlemen between them and retailer), garner higher prices, but have a shorter season.

Second, the homegrown tomatoes have been picked from the vine at their peak ripeness (when they're red!), and prepared and eaten soon after. It simply doesn't get any better than homegrown stuff when it comes to vine ripening and freshness. Note what Chef Stamenov said in the quote at the beginning of this chapter: "Kids who grimace at frozen green beans are eager to try organic beans picked fresh from our restaurant's garden."

Is it a really a big revelation that kids prefer fresh, just-picked beans over frozen?

But for how much of the year does the typical home garden deliver those awesome, fresh tomatoes and other just-picked veggies? Not for very long. That's why 50 and 100 years ago nearly every household canned foods from a home garden for winter, spring, and early summer. Not long ago in our rural area of western Virginia, seasonal canneries operated in every small community. Often they were run by the local FFA or 4-H club or other such community group as modest fundraisers. Families would bring in their garden harvest and the cannery would help process the goods (snap the beans, shell the peas, peel the peaches, etc.), put them in quart or pint-size metal cans, and then steam-sterilize them after they were sealed tight. As the canned foods emerged from the steamer, family members would mark each one with the date and contents using a permanent marker.

Thanks to today's low-cost transportation, we have access to an incredible selection of relatively fresh vegetables and fruits the year round. But compromises must be made to make non-canned tomatoes or peaches possible in February. They must be grown where it's still warm (often California or Central America), picked when they are still green, shipped hundreds of miles and several days away in refrigerated containers on ships, trucks, or rail cars, and then distributed to retail stores. This is true even of most off-season organic products, too.

Bananas, for instance, are often brought by ship from Central America or Brazil. They are picked green, shipped under refrigeration, and ripened before sale by exposure to ethylene gas. (This gas-ripening process sounds "chemical," but ethylene is actually a natural plant hormone and humans have been doing this for millennia.)[3] If the fruits and vegetables were picked at their peak ripeness, like at home, they'd spoil before they ever arrived at the store — let alone your home kitchen.

Some products, like apples, must be stored for up to several months in refrigerated and other long-term storage because a harvest occurs only two times per year, once in the Northern and once in the Southern hemisphere.

All of these realities impact what crop varieties are grown and the resulting taste, texture, and other qualities of the produce when it finally reaches consumers. Because of the long-distance shipping and handling, firmer and tougher fruit/vegetable varieties are chosen so they'll survive the trip to consumers in a marketable condition. Who wants to buy bruised tomatoes?

Substance, Not Sentiment

So the advice is to assess your food purchases based on perceivable quality and taste differences, not on the philosophy of the grower or marketing company.

---

[3] Ethylene, C_2H_4, is created by the burning of natural gas and other combustibles. Ethylene is also produced by plants as a natural hormone. Ethylene has been used to purposefully ripen fruits for millennia. The ancient Egyptians would stimulate ripening of figs by burning fires in closed fig storage rooms. The ancient Chinese burned incense to enhance the ripening of pears. The common practice of placing a tomato, avocado, or banana in a paper bag to hasten ripening works via the action of ethylene released by the fruit. The bag traps ethylene, stimulating the production of more ethylene and hastening ripening.

When you see a product that you feel is superior and priced right, buy it. When the bread is better, buy it. When the fruits and vegetables look better or fresher, buy them. If the fruit is more fragrant and enticing, buy it.

But don't believe the marketing hype that just because something was grown organically it is automatically better, tastier, or of higher quality. There are great, high-quality foods of all kinds, both organic and non-organic.

Chapter 9:

A Few Bushels Shy

Organic faithful say:

"Since less than 1% of agricultural research dollars are spent on organic practices, I assumed it would be difficult for organic methods to compete with conventional practices in the yield category, in particular since yield is an over-arching objective of conventional research. But that is not what I found. ... In summary, for a total of 154 growing seasons for different crops, grown in different parts of this country on both rain-fed and irrigated lands, organic production yielded 95% of crops grown under conventional high-input conditions."

Bill Leibhardt, sustainable agriculture specialist, University of California, Davis
"Get the Facts Straight: Organic Agriculture Yields Are Good" *Organic Farming Research Foundation Information Bulletin*, Summer 2001, Number 10

Reality Says:

"We found crop yields to be 20% lower in the organic farming systems ... cereal crop yields under organic management in Europe typically are 60% to 70% of those under conventional management, whereas grassland yields are in the range of 70% to 100%."

Mader, et al. Research Institute of Organic Agriculture
"Soil Fertility and Biodiversity in Organic Farming"
Science 296:1694-1697, May 31, 2002

"On average, Lundberg concludes, organic rice growers produce a yield of about half that of a conventional grower, so there is a need to receive a significant premium for the organic rice just to stay competitive on the bottom line."

"Long-Haul Organic: Higher Price, Lower Cost? Watch Out for the End of the Honeymoon" by Mary Ann Rood, *Rice Journal,* March 25, 2002, www.ricejournal.com

The reality that organic farming is less productive than non-organic farming is apparently a hard pill for many organic believers to accept. They continually deny it, even though many of their own studies show it to be true. Maybe it is just ego and good, old-fashioned bragging rights: "Organic methods are better, so organic yields should be at least as good." Perhaps it is because the organic faithful realize that if, in fact, organic methods are less productive, it poses a problem for feeding humanity without undue harm to wildlife.

The fact remains that organic methods get lower yields. Direct yield comparisons show that organic methods almost always produce less per acre than non-organic methods. (See Figures 4 through 7.)

For hardy crops, the yield differences can be minor. For other crops, such as potatoes, where diseases and pests are a continual threat, the yield differences can be large.

But beyond the direct field-to-field yield comparisons, it's important to remember that organic farming requires far more than just the land directly involved in growing a crop. Organic farming systems — "the whole farm," so to speak — must devote land to producing organic nitrogen to grow crops that can't fix their own nitrogen.

Not only is there the land needed to produce the organic fertility, but organic farms must also rotate fields into other crops to break pest cycles, and these alternative crops are often less profitable and/or less in demand by consumers.

Direct field-to-field yield comparisons show that non-organic farming methods achieve 10% to 50% higher yields than organic methods when using identical varieties grown side by side.

These graphs show the results of published yield comparison studies conducted at universities, organic research institutes, and government agencies. Each pair of bars in the graphs represents the cumulative average results of a single study, with conventional crop yields represented as a percentage of the organic crop yields (represented as 100%). Thus, if a conventional crop yield was 40% higher than the organic crop yield in that study, the conventional crop yield is represented as 140%.

Most studies were conducted over several years, and therefore the results represent multi-year yield averages. Several of these studies were conducted over periods of 10 years or more.

These studies were conducted at various universities and institutions, including Iowa State University, South Dakota State University, the University of Nebraska, University of Maine, University of California (Davis), the Swiss Research Institute of Organic Agriculture, the Michael Fields Agriculture Institute, the U.K. Agriculture Development Advisory Service (ADAS), the U.K. Department of Environment, Food, and Rural Affairs (DEFRA), and Aventis Corporation. (See Table 2, page 166 for a complete list of the studies and their results.)

Only two studies, one in soybeans and one in wheat, found organic methods averaging higher yields than non-organic methods. Both studies were conducted by researchers at South Dakota State University. Collectively, however, the studies show an overall 20 to 40 per-

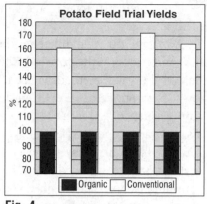

Fig. 4

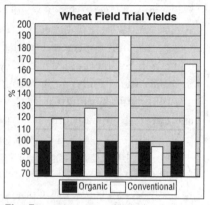

Fig. 5

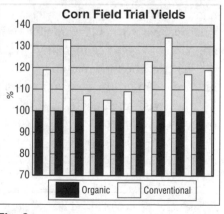

Fig. 6

cent yield deficit using organic farming methods.

Averaging the yield differences for all the studies for each crop individually finds that organic methods yielded 12% lower soybean yields, 15 percent lower corn yields, 20% lower wheat yields, and 40% lower potato yields.

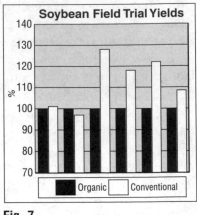

Fig. 7

Put the other way: Conventional soybean yields averaged 14% higher, conventional corn 18% higher, conventional wheat 25% higher, and conventional potatoes 65% higher.

The most recent direct yield comparison data were published in *Science* in 2002, reporting the results of 21 years of research conducted by the Research Institute of Organic Agriculture in Therwil, Switzerland.[1] The 21-year experiment compared organic, conventional, and "biodynamic" cropping systems. Biodynamic is the extreme form of organic agriculture that evolved from Rudolf Steiner's radical teachings. For more insight into biodynamic farming, see Appendix A.

According to the Swiss researchers, organic crop yields averaged "only 20% lower" than non-organic yields. Specifically, organic wheat yielded an average of 15% less than non-organic wheat while organic potatoes yielded "58% to 66% of those in the conventional plots."

Stating these same yield numbers relative to organic crop yields (rather than relative to conventional crop yields), conventional yields averaged 25% higher. Conventional wheat yields were 18% higher than organic, and conventional potato yields were 50% to 70% higher. When most crop scientists are happy to get incremental yield gains of 2% to 3%, these are enormous differences. The biodynamic fields fared as poorly as the organic fields; significantly behind the conventional yields.

The Swiss researchers have refused requests to share any data from the other five crops grown over the course of 21 years of research. Why?

The Swiss researchers readily admit that conventional cereal crop yields are typically 40% to 65% higher than organic and that conventional grass-

[1] Mader, et al. Soil Fertility and Biodiversity in Organic Farming. *Science* 296:1694-1697, 2002.

land yields are up to 40% higher than organic.

The U.K.'s Department for Environment, Food, and Rural Affairs (DEFRA) reviewed the findings from years of scientific studies it conducted or sponsored and found that conventional crop yields average 65% higher than organic.[2] (See Figure 8).

So, the available scientific studies indicate pretty convincingly that organic farming methods are lower yielding, on average, than conventional.

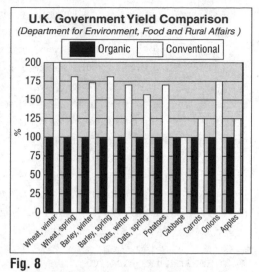

Fig. 8

Organic farming supporters often criticize these types of university field studies on the grounds that they don't represent real-world farming conditions on working farms. They often cite the fact that the university research plots have only been under organic management practices for a limited time and that organic farming relies on the long-term buildup of soil properties for its benefits. However, the data from farm-based research and surveys of organic farmers' experience show essentially the same yield deficits as the experimental field studies show.

A review of 28 farms from the Midwestern United States (half organic, half non-organic) conducted in the mid-1970s found that conventional farmers produced 30% higher wheat yields (organic 23% lower), 7.8% higher corn yields, 6.5% higher soybean yields, and 2% higher oat yields. Without price premiums the average market value of the crops produced on the organic farms would have been 11% less than the value of the crops produced on the conventional farms.[3]

Another study comparing 42 organic farms to all similar conventional farms in their respective counties found that organic corn yields were 8% to 17% lower than the county average. (County average was 10% to 20% high-

[2] Shepard M., et al. An Assessment of the Environmental Impacts of Organic Farming: A Review forDepartment of Environment Farming and Rural Affairs (DEFRA)-funded project OF0405. DEFRA, 2003. www.defra.gov.uk/science/project_data/DocumentLibrary/OF0405/OF0405_909_ TRP.doc
[3] Lockeretz W., et al. *Journal of Soil and Water Conservation* 33(3):130–134, 1978.

er than the organic farms.) Organic soybean yields ranged from "nearly equal" to 7% lower than the county average.

There was one bright spot: Organic oat yields beat the county averages by 6% to 10%.[4] Unfortunately, the market for oats is very limited. Organic farmers grow them primarily as "break crops," so named because they "break" pest cycles, as well as to provide forage for livestock, provide straw for livestock bedding, and increase the carbon content of manure compost that is used heavily as fertilizer for organic crops. While oats are useful in these ways, they add little to farm income.

Another study of on-farm yields, conducted by South Dakota State University from 1985 to 1992, found that conventional corn yields were over 5% higher and conventional soybean yields were 28% higher than organic.[5]

Whole-Farm Perspective

The only truly valid way to look at the productivity of organic farming is by looking at the entire system, not just a single crop from a single field. Field-to-field comparisons examine only half of the productivity picture. The other half is the extra land needed to produce the organic fertilizer, discussed in Chapter 1.

When you combine the lower crop yields in organic fields with the additional land requirements needed to produce organic nitrogen, the total system productivity of organic farms drops to roughly half to two-thirds that of non-organic farming systems. When considered in this light, debates about the relative productivity of specific crops or crop rotations between organic and non-organic farming become irrelevant. The overall productivity gap of organic farming is simply so large and so inherent that it's useless at some point to argue about it.

I should clarify that many organic farmers are excellent farmers and get good yields from their crops. Sometimes their yields are even higher than their non-organic farming neighbors', especially in drier years. The reliance on organic nitrogen fertilizers often adds more organic matter (bits of partially degraded plants, a term used for both organic and conventional farms) to the soil than on the typical equivalent conventional crop field. The higher levels of soil organic matter increase the water infiltration and storage capacity of the

---

[4] Shearer, Lockeretz, et al. *American Journal of Agricultural Economics* 63(2):264–269, 1981.
[5] Dobbs and Smolik. *Journal of Sustainable Agriculture* 9(1):63–79, 1996.

soil, which makes the fields more drought resistant.

However, there is ample evidence that organic crop yields are, on average, considerably lower than non-organic crop yields. Conventional crops currently out-yield organic by 10% to 80% in direct field-to-field and farm-level comparisons. Moreover, organic farming requires far larger areas of legume break and forage crops, and more animal pasture area to support non-legume crops.

CROP YIELDS — THE DEVIL IS IN THE DETAILS

Organic Faithful Say:

DiMatteo noted a study published by the Organic Farming Research Foundation (www.ofrf.org), which found that organic production yielded 95% of crops grown under conventional high-input conditions for a total of 154 growing seasons for different crops in different parts of the U.S. and on both rain-fed and irrigated land. Study highlights included: Organic corn yields were 94% of conventional corn yields, organic soybean yields were 97% of conventional soybean yields, and there were no differences between organic and conventional tomato yields.

Organic Trade Association Press (OTA) release, May 1, 2002

When comparing different farming systems, it is important to know the details of the farming methods used and of the research findings. This is illustrated by the claims of Dr. Bill Leibhardt, who is quoted at the opening of this chapter claiming his review of available research shows there are "no yield differences between conventionally and organically grown crops."

The OTA cites Leibhardt's newsletter article in its press release, but it wasn't really a study in the scientific sense. In his newsletter article, Leibhardt resorts to an age-old set of tricks: citing only the data that support his contention and comparing apples to oranges.

For example, Leibhardt compares the yields of organic corn grown following a soybean crop with the yields of conventional corn grown year after year, called "continuous corn." What's the big deal? Corn yields are always higher when planted after a soybean crop because of the additional nitrogen from the soybeans (which is a nitrogen-fixing legume) and the pest and weed suppression that results from rotating different crops.

According to the exact same research study cited by Leibhardt, conventional corn grown in rotation with soybeans out-yields organic corn following soybeans by 10% to 30%. Instead of presenting the yield differences from comparable crop rotations, Leibhardt deliberately cited the yields of different crop rotations — comparisons that Leibhardt knew would favor the organic system

— so he could falsely claim that organic corn yields were "94% of conventional corn yields." It was almost literally an apples-to-oranges comparison, though in this case it was a continuous versus rotation comparison.

Many conventional farmers rotate corn with soybeans because of this well-known yield gain. However, when corn prices are high, they may grow corn for several years straight to take advantage of the higher prices. Using synthetic fertilizers affords greater flexibility so farmers have more opportunity to take advantage of high commodity prices and market demands. Thus, research studies often compare corn-soybean rotations with continuous corn to gauge the yield penalty.

Regarding tomato yields, Leibhardt erroneously combined yield data from two separate research projects at the University of California-Davis to arrive at his conclusion that there are no yield differences between organic and non-organic. One was the Sustainable Agriculture Farming Systems (SAFS) Project directed by Dr. Steve Temple. The other was the Long-Term Research into Agricultural Systems (LTRAS) project.

Both the SAFS and LTRAS studies clearly demonstrate that organic methods achieve substantially lower yields. This is what Dr. Temple and his research team wrote about the SAFS results in 1999 in the heavily pro-organic publication *The American Journal of Alternative Agriculture*:

> "Tomato yields in the [conventional] system tended to be the highest among the four farming systems, averaging 83 tons/hectare while those of the organic system tended to be the lowest. Organic tomato yields were significantly lower in five of eight years, three in the first rotation and two in the second, and averaged 16.5% less than those of the [conventional] system over the eight-year period."

Conventional tomato yields therefore averaged fully 20% higher than organic tomato yields over the last eight years of the 11 years of research. But Leibhardt ignored the conclusions of the researchers themselves and instead selectively cites only part of their yield data.

Why were the yield data for only the last eight years of the project given? Because during the first three years of research, conventional tomato yields beat organic yields by a whopping 66%. The researchers excluded the first three years of yield data from their research reports, claiming that this was a period of "transition" for the organic plots.

Why the big change in organic tomato yields after the first three years? Was it the often talked about "organic transition period"? No, starting in the fourth year the researchers switched from planting tomato seeds in the organic plots to planting tomato transplants because of the abysmally low organic tomato yields. The non-organic fields, however, continued to be planted with un-germinated tomato seeds, giving the organic tomatoes a literal head start on the growing season. So of course the organic tomato yields went up, along with planting and labor costs.

But this still wasn't enough to raise organic tomato yields on par with the conventional tomatoes. The conventional tomato fields continued to outperform the organic by an average of 20% in the four years following the switch to transplants. So in 1996, after testing indicated the organic tomato plants weren't getting enough nitrogen, the researchers once again altered the experiment to advantage the organic by tripling the amount of poultry manure applied to the organic plots. This meant that starting in 1996, the organic tomatoes received three to four times more total nitrogen each year than the conventional tomatoes.

The result of these drastic changes isn't surprising: In the last three years of the project the organic tomatoes averaged 9% higher yields than the conventional tomatoes. Prior to this last change in 1996, the conventional tomatoes outperformed the organic by an average of 28%.

Some might argue that the researchers were "cheating" when they kept tweaking the organic treatment to raise the yields. I won't go that far. The UC Davis researchers were professionally forthright about the methods involved in their research and the changes made to their experiment. As the UC Davis researchers explained, they were attempting to find a "sustainable" and financially viable "alternative" tomato farming system. Fair enough. Organic farmers will certainly adapt and compensate in their efforts to achieve economically viable yields and productivity. But the changes necessary to get organic tomato yields on par with non-organic methods demonstrate quite clearly how much lower yielding organic farming methods really are.

They also cost a lot more. The use of tomato transplants, for example, added over $300 per acre to the organic system's production costs. This, combined with higher cost from using animal manure, severely lowered the profitability of the organic system. Without high price premiums, the organic system simply loses money. As the researchers noted in their final report for 2000, "While the organic system with premium prices has performed better than [one of the two non-organic systems], large increases in organic production within the region would likely result in a depression of the premium prices."

The SAFS researchers offered some other illuminating observations in the 2000 final report:

• Fruit quality was lower in the organic.

• The organic system used more irrigation water.

• Weeds were a much greater problem in the organic system.

So, after the researchers had given the organic system two huge advantages at significantly higher production cost, the organic system finally matched non-organic tomato yields, used more irrigation water, resulted in significantly more weeds, and produced tomatoes of lower quality.

Table 2:

SOURCE OF YIELD DATA IN YIELD GRAPHS
CORN FIELD STUDIES

University or Institute	Publication	Conventional yields (% vs. organic)
Michael Fields Agriculture Institute	Lakeland farm data from 1992-1999 published in "Comparing Upper Midwestern Farming Systems: Results From the First 10 Years of the Wisconsin Integrated Cropping Systems Trial (WICST)"	119
Michael Fields Agriculture Institute	Arlington farm data from 1992-1999	133
University of California, Davis	Sustainable Agriculture Farming Systems, data 1989-1999, SAFS project Final Report	107
South Dakota State University	Dobbs T.L. and Smolik J.D. *Journal of Sustainable Agriculture,* Vol 9(1): 63-79. 1996	105
Iowa State University	Delate K., Duffy M., Chase C., Holste A., Friedrich H., and Wantate N. Long-Term Agroecological Research (LTAR) in Iowa: An Economic Comparison of Organic and Conventional Grain Crops, data for 1998-2001	109
Iowa State University	Duffy, Michael research at Northeast Research Center in Floyd County, IA — data for 1988-1997	123
Iowa State University	Duffy, Michael research at Northeast Research Center in Floyd County, IA — data for 1978-1997	134
University of Nebraska	Helmers G.A., Langemeier M.R., Atwood J. An Economic Analysis of Alternative Cropping Systems for East-Central Nebraska, *American Journal of Alternative Agriculture (AJAA),* Vol. 1(4):153-158. 1986	117
South Dakota State University	Smolik J.D., Dobbs T.L., Rickerl D.H., Wrage L.J., Buchenau G.W., Machacek T.A. Agronomic, Economic, and Ecological Relationships in Alternative (organic), Conventional, and Reduced-Till Farming Systems. Bulletin 718. South Dakota Ag Exp Sta., Brookings. 1993.	119
	SOYBEAN FIELD STUDIES	
Iowa State University	Delate K., Duffy M., Chase C., Holste A., Friedrich H., and Wantate N. Long-Term Agroecological Research (LTAR) in Iowa: An Economic Comparison of Organic and Conventional Grain Crops, data for 1998-2001	101
South Dakota State University	Smolik J.D., Dobbs T.L., Rickerl D.H., Wrage L.J., Buchenau G.W., Machacek T.A. Agronomic, Economic, and Ecological Relationships in Alternative (organic), Conventional, and Reduced-Till Farming Systems. Bulletin 718. South Dakota Ag Exp Sta., Brookings. 1993.	97

SOYBEAN FIELD STUDIES (Continued)

South Dakota State University	Smolik J.D., Dobbs T.L. Productivity and Profitability of Conventional and Alternative Farming Systems: A Long-Term On-Farm Paired Comparison. *Journal of Sustainable Agriculture*, vol 9(1) 1996.	128
University of Nebraska	Helmers G.A., Langemeier M.R., Atwood J. An Economic Analysis of Alternative Cropping Systems for East-Central Nebraska, *AJAA* Vol. 1(4):153-158. 1986	118
Michael Fields Agriculture Institute	Michael Fields Agriculture Institute, Lakeland data from 1992-1999 from "Comparing Upper Midwestern Farming Systems: Results From the First 10 Years of the Wisconsin Integrated Cropping Systems Trial (WICST)"	122
Michael Fields Agriculture Institute	Michael Fields Agriculture Institute, Arlington data from 1992-1999 from "Comparing Upper Midwestern Farming Systems: Results From the First 10 Years of the Wisconsin Integrated Cropping Systems Trial (WICST)"	108.5

POTATO FIELD STUDIES

Swiss Research Institute of Organic Agriculture	P. Mader, A. FleiBbach, D. Dubois, L. Gunst, P. Fried, U. Niggli. Soil Fertility and Biodiversity in Organic Farming. *Science* 296, 5573:1694-1697, 2002. (Total 21-year average)	161
University of Maine	Gallandt E.R., Mallory E.B., Alford A.R., Drummond F.A., Groden E., Liebman M., Marra M.C., McBurnie J.C., Porter G.A.. Comparison of Alternative Pest and Soil Management Strategies for Maine Potato Production Systems. *AJAA* 13(4): 146-161. 1998.	133
U.K. Ag Development Advisory Service	ADAS Terrington (DEFRA-funded study) yields from 1993-2003	172
U.K. Department of Environment Food and Rural Affairs	DEFRA Environ Impacts review study under DEFRA Organic Farming Scheme, 2003	164

BARLEY FIELD TRIALS

Swiss Research Institute of Organic Agriculture	P. Mader, A. FleiBbach, D. Dubois, L. Gunst, P. Fried, U. Niggli. Soil Fertility and Biodiversity in Organic Farming. *Science* 296, 5573:1694-1697, 2002. total 21-year average	133
Swiss Research Institute of Organic Agriculture	P. Mader, A. FleiBbach, D. Dubois, L. Gunst, P. Fried, U. Niggli. Soil Fertility and Biodiversity in Organic Farming. *Science* 296, 5573:1694-1697, 2002. Rotation 2 average	138

WHEAT FIELD TRIALS

Swiss Research Institute of Organic Agriculture	P. Mader, A. FleiBbach, D. Dubois, L. Gunst, P Fried, U. Niggli. Soil Fertility and Biodiversity in Organic Farming. *Science* 296, 5573:1694-1697, 2002. 1985-1998 average	119

WHEAT FIELD TRIALS (Continued)

U.K. Ag Development Advisory Service	DEFRA research from ADAS Terrington, U.K. organic yields 1993-2003	128
U.K. Department of Environment, Food, and Rural Affairs	DEFRA Environ Impacts review study under DEFRA Organic Farming Scheme, 2003	190
South Dakota State	Smolik J.D., Dobbs T.L., Rickerl D.H., Wrage L.J., Buchenau G.W., Machacek T.A. Agronomic, Economic, and Ecological Relationships in Alternative (organic), Conventional, and Reduced-Till Farming Systems. Bulletin 718. South Dakota Ag Exp Sta., Brookings. 1993.	95.5
Aventis Corporation	Aventis 10-year Farm Study results [www.aventis.co.uk/farm_study/farm_mngmnt.asp]	166

TOMATO FIELD TRIALS

University of California, Davis	UC Davis Sustainable Agriculture Farming Systems project Final Report	115

Chapter 10:

Biocontrol or Out of Control?

Organic Faithful Claim:

"Cuba, with 2% of Latin America's population, has 11% of the region's scientists, and many of them had been studying methods of natural pest control. Now the nation has 218 biocontrol centers, spread throughout farming regions. They monitor pest outbreaks and breed and release natural enemies. Against all odds, with almost no chemical fertilizers or pesticides, Cuba's food supply is slowly rising to what it was before the [crisis of 1990 when imports of fertilizer and pesticides abruptly ended with the collapse of the Soviet Union]."

Donella Meadows, Organic Gardening magazine, May 2000

"In ecologically balanced farm production systems, insect pests are always present, but massive outbreaks resulting in severe economic damage are minimized. This results in good part from the presence of natural control agents — especially predatory and parasitic insects, mites, and spiders — that keep pest populations in check."

Making the Transition to Sustainable Farming: Fundamentals of Sustainable Agriculture
Bart Hall & George Kuepper, Appropriate Technology Transfer for Rurual Areas (ATTRA)
Technical Specialists, December 1997

169

Die-hard organic believers maintain that by "working with nature" using biocontrols, instead of "against nature" using synthetic chemicals, Mother Nature's hordes of yield-robbing insects and other pests will largely leave organic crop fields unmolested. Instead of having to fight off the multi-legged marauders with bad chemical pesticides, armies of friendly "beneficial" insects, fungi, and bacteria will do the fighting for us and thereby deliver organic paradise.

Technically, biocontrol is defined as using one organism to control or suppress another organism. Biocontrol agents can theoretically be insects, fungi, viruses, or protozoa. They can be predators, parasites, or diseases and be used against insects, weeds, fungi, or bacteria. Put most simply, biocontrol involves manipulating nature to reduce pest and disease pressures on our crops and livestock.

Have we "fooled" ourselves into believing that we "had" to use pesticides because we upset the balance of nature and caused the pests to become a problem in the first place, as some proclaim? As one biocontrol Web site notes: "Natural biocontrol is an extremely common phenomenon, both in natural and agricultural ecosystems. There are more than 300,000 plant species and 1,000,000 insect species. Very few of these species dominate their habitats or are pests, so it is clear that most populations of most species are suppressed most of the time."

Unfortunately, biocontrol has only limited potential in reducing pest damage to our crops. Where biocontrol works, it works for all farmers — not just the organic "believers." Moreover, even when successful, biocontrol programs only reduce, rather than eliminate, the need to use pesticides.

The notion that nature — in its ideal form — is in a state of perfect balance is one that animates many in the organic movement. This is why they call themselves "ecological farmers" and speak not of farms, but "agroecosystems." But farms cannot be ecosystems; they are inevitably managed human systems. Farmers and humanity need stable supplies of food and fiber, so farms are managed for stable, high production. This not only allows farmers to earn a living, but also conserves farm resources (land, water, etc.) so they aren't lost to pests and disease.

In contrast, natural ecosystems are dynamic, ever-changing systems. Perfect balance never exists. Ecologists call this "dynamic equilibrium." This is an important concept to understanding the limitations of biocontrol and why farmers will likely never be able to completely abandon chemical or biochemical pesticides (or biotechnological pest control strategies within crops).

Consider the following dynamic. When prey populations increase, predator populations will eventually increase too as they benefit from the abundance of food. However, as the predator population increases, the pressure on the prey population increases accordingly. Eventually, when the predator population is large enough, the predators begin taking prey faster than it is replaced via reproduction and the prey populations begin to decline. The dwindling prey population eventually causes the predator population to decline. When the level of predators reaches a low enough density, the prey population begins to rebound. Thus, the cycle begins anew. Figure 9 is an excellent illustration of this cyclical predator-prey dynamic in the abundance of Canadian lynx and snowshoe hares.

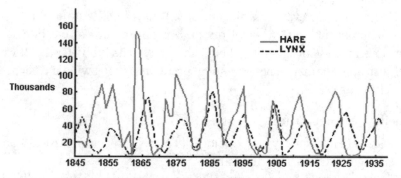

Fig. 9: Canadian lynx and snowshoe hare pelt trading records of the Hudson Bay Company indicating the relative population size (and population dynamics) of this predator and prey.

This is the essence of dynamic equilibrium — an ever-changing, cyclical, and competitive "balance," or seesawing, that really isn't balanced. The only balance is that one side of the equation never completely "wins" the war.

How big the prey (or crop pest) population gets depends on how much food (crops) is available for the prey and how quickly the predator populations (or disease agent numbers) can respond to the abundance of prey. These dynamics are extremely complex. Not only is food availability a factor, but also temperature, moisture, sunlight, diseases, other predators, and so on.

Crop pests have a long and well-documented history of rapid population surges because of short generation times and the inherent food abundance of farm fields. Insects, fungi, and bacteria can multiply at extraordinary rates. Antoni van Leeuwenhoek, the 17th century Dutch tailor and amateur biologist, calculated in 1687 that in the absence of limiting factors, a single pair of blowflies could give rise to 3.87 billion flies in only six generations. This explains why pest outbreaks often develop so suddenly, outpacing the biocontrol predators that normally keep insect populations in check. Add to this the incredible amount of food available to pests in a high-yield modern field and it is clear why farmers need to use pest controls — even organic farmers.

Let me be clear: Biocontrol, in the classic sense, can be an extremely useful addition to a well-designed integrated pest management (IPM) system. There is absolutely nothing wrong with working "with nature" as much as is practicable to minimize pest pressures and reduce the need to use additional inputs to combat pests. That's just smart farming. In fact, one of the advantages of newer, "softer" pesticides and pest-resistant biotech crops is that they leave many beneficial insects unmolested in the fields to assist us in keeping bad bug numbers as low as possible.

The fact is, however, that biocontrol will never take care of most — or even a significant portion — of our pest problems unless we pursue the enormous promise of agricultural biotechnology to its full potential. If we do that, instead of farmers having to spray pesticides, crops will be designed to protect themselves.

Specifics of Biocontrol

There are generally four types of biological control strategies: classical, conservation, augmentation, and inundative.

Classical biocontrol involves introducing the natural enemies to an introduced, or "exotic," pest species. Over the past few centuries, many organisms have been intentionally or accidentally released into new ecosystems, mostly by human actions. When these insects and plants encounter favorable conditions, they can flourish in the absence of the natural enemies that keep their populations in check in their original environment. By going to these organisms' native areas, researchers attempt to find natural enemies of the introduced pest for release into the new environment. After they are screened for undesirable characteristics, such as damage to non-target and native flora and fauna, the natural enemies are released into the new environment with the hope that they will also establish themselves and permanently lower the density of a pest population.

Conservation biocontrol involves increasing the populations of existing natural pest enemies. This may be accomplished by tailoring farming systems to favor the existence of natural pest enemies in fields. Factors that hinder natural enemies may be altered, and factors that favor the presence of natural enemies may be enhanced. This often means using specific, low-impact pesticides or no pesticides at all. Farmers can also encourage pest enemies by planting rows of "nursery crops" within fields or planting alternative host plants on field edges.

Augmentation biocontrol involves releasing natural pest enemies each year or several times per season to control pests. This approach is used when natural pest enemies are present at concentrations too low to suppress pest populations or when a non-native biocontrol agent won't establish itself in a region because of unfavorable environmental conditions (such as a cold winter climate). Then the natural enemies are mass-produced in laboratories and are released either early in the season (say, after the last frost), before pest pressures are high, or after pests become a problem. Releasing the enemies early gives the beneficials time to build up with seasonal pest population surges and to keep them in check. If releases are made too late in the season, the natural enemies may not reproduce fast enough to catch up with fast-growing pest populations.

Inundative biocontrol is used when conditions may not be favorable to the biocontrol agent. In these instances, mass release (or inundative biocontrol) can be used. This method relies on sheer numbers and periodic releases within a season to immediately and quickly knock down pest populations, much the way that chemical insecticides work. Augmentation and inundation biocontrol rely on constant human management and do not provide a long-term solution in the way that importation or conservation approaches sometimes can.

Obviously, biocontrol is extremely complex. It requires an understanding of the physiology, population biology, and ecology of both the target organism and the biocontrol organism, as well as a good understanding of the surrounding environment and its constituent organisms.

Biocontrol's Ecological Costs

Biocontrol often means introducing new species into an ecosystem. In these instances, knowledge and testing of the biocontrol agents against a wide array of non-target organisms is imperative lest a bigger problem be created from the introduced biocontrol species. This work is extremely expensive and uncertain. Who is to say whether the biocontrol organism has been tested against enough plants and species to know its true potential ecological impact? Even if one did test against hundreds of species with no major ill effects observed, who could say whether it was tested against all vulnerable species?

There is no question that there are serious ecological risks with releasing biocontrol organisms. Biocontrol agents aren't like chemical pesticides, which have known environmental half-lives and are limited mostly to the fields in which they're sprayed. Biocontrol agents breed, multiply, and can migrate far away from their release points. They can eat or infect non-target organisms and plants, and can have unknown ecological consequences far beyond those of chemical pesticides.

After all, if we'd wanted to rid North America of the chestnut tree, we could hardly have developed a chemical herbicide more complete in its lethality than the unintended "biocontrol" agent of chestnut blight, a natural fungus. *Cryphonectria parasitica* was accidentally introduced into North America from Asia via plant imports in the late 1800s. By the 1930s, less than 50 years after its accidental introduction, chestnut blight had wiped out virtually every single chestnut tree within the North American range, even in the deepest forests untouched by human hands.

There are, in fact, many instances of biocontrol agents becoming serious ecological problems. In the fragile island ecology of Hawaii, for instance, ecologists have documented significant impacts on native moth species from parasitoid wasps introduced to help control sugarcane pests. Parasitoids are distinct from parasites in that parasitoids usually kill their hosts, whereas parasites don't. Parasitoid wasps lay their eggs within or on caterpillars. The larvae kill the caterpillar, feed on it, and then pupate into wasps within the body of the dead caterpillar.

Two ecologists recently went to the remote Alakai swamp in the highlands of the Hawaiian island Kauai, which is much cooler and wetter than the lowland Hawaiian sugarcane fields. More than 120 different species of parasitic wasps have been released over the last 100 years in the lowland sugarcane fields. Because of the Alakai swamp's extreme environment, the researchers figured this would give them a minimum estimate of the impacts of the biocontrol wasps on the rest of the island's natural ecology. They captured more than 2,000 native Hawaiian moth caterpillars and incubated them in the lab to see if any introduced, non-native wasp parasites hatched out of the caterpillars.

Lo and behold, they found that wasps had parasitized roughly 20% of the moth caterpillars. Of this 20%, only 3% were parasitized by native wasp species; 14% were parasitized by wasp species accidentally introduced into Hawaii, while a whopping 83% were parasitized by wasp species intentionally released as agricultural biocontrol organisms. All of this last group were of wasp species first released into Hawaii on purpose more than 50 years ago. Some biologists hope this means that biocontrol scientists have been more careful in picking parasite species for more recent releases. However, others speculate that more recently released species simply haven't yet reached these more remote environments. Only time will tell who is right.

How much native biodiversity ("native" being a relative term for an ever-changing island ecosystem) has been lost and what changes have occurred in the Alakai swamp because of the presence of the new wasps? Ecologists simply don't know because no detailed survey of the swamp's biodiversity has ever been done. Vulnerable moth species could have been wiped out decades ago, soon after the exotic wasps were released, and we'd never know it.

The impacts from the loss of this biodiversity might be ecologically significant. Consider that there are 24 native silk moth species east of the Mississippi River, yet the caterpillars from these species support close to 100 native parasitiod insect species. How is it they can support so many? Because in addition to the various parasitic flies and wasps that prey on the moth caterpillars, there are also "hyperparasitoids," insects that specialize in killing other parasitoids, and even one hyper-hyperparasitoid that specializes in killing only hyperparasitoids. In Maine potatoes, 22 species of aphid parasitoids were identified, yet these aphid parasites were in turn attacked by 18 additional species of hyperparasitoid insects.[1] The web of life is incredibly tangled, especially with insects.

On an interesting side note, scientists discovered in the 1970s that many parasitoid wasps have co-evolved with viruses that co-infect the host when the wasps lay their eggs. These viruses wipe out the host caterpillar's immune system and prevent it from destroying the wasp's eggs. These viruses are so specialized that they are only made inside the wasp's ovaries, so they're entirely dependent on the wasp and vice versa. In fact, the virus' DNA has become part of the wasp's genome and is inherited by each new wasp generation.

The introduced wasps in Hawaii are now a part of that ecosystem and are intertwined into the web of life there. In fact, so is another intentionally released biocontrol agent, a caterpillar introduced to control a non-native blackberry. A large population of these blackberry-eating caterpillars apparently exists in the Alakai swamp, impacting the native ecology to an unknown extent. Ironically and unfortunately, none of the introduced parasitic wasps prey on these particular alien caterpillars.

---

[1] Amazingly, there may be as many as 500,000 different species of parasitic wasp (chalcidoids), although "only" about 22,000 species have been documented. This includes the world's smallest known adult insect, the male of Dicopomorpha echmepterygis, which is only 4 thousandths of an inch long (0.11mm)!

Casualties in the Gypsy Moth Campaign

The gypsy moth is an exotic pest introduced to North America accidentally in 1869 by an amateur scientist in Massachusetts. Ever since, gypsy moths have been ravaging forests in North America, with occasional outbreaks of millions of caterpillars per acre. Starting in 1906 and continuing on through the mid-1980s, government and university scientists in 30 states have deliberately released a parasitic fly (*Compsilura*) in an attempt to control the gypsy moths.

As early as 1919 scientists noted that one North American silk moth, the Promethean moth, was becoming rare in areas where the fly had been released. North America's largest moth (*Hyalophora cecropia*) with a wingspan of 15 centimeters, once common in eastern and central forests, is also now rare. Why? While some have blamed pesticides such as DDT and habitat loss, many ecologists now believe that the evidence points to the Compsilura fly. We now know that *Compsilura* attacks not only gypsy moths, but at least 180 other moth species, including native silk moths.

In a recent experiment, a team of ecologists set out Promethean moth caterpillars at varying densities on trees in Massachusetts. Flies killed 50% to 100% of the caterpillars. Coauthor Joseph Elkington says while this isn't proof, "there's a fairly strong likelihood that *Compsilura* is the reason for the [silk moth] decline." "When you see that kind of mortality, it's a wake-up call," said lead researcher Dr. George Boettner of the University of Massachusetts, Amherst.

Introduced species can also impact native plants. There are a number of examples of damage to native plants from introduced species in addition to the widely known example of chestnut blight. A weevil first introduced accidentally in the U.S. Northeast has since been purposely released into western states and Canada to control Canada thistle (an invasive plant accidentally introduced from Europe, despite its name).

The weevil was authorized for deliberate introduction into these states as a biocontrol agent because a 1990 greenhouse study indicated it preferred Canada thistle to native ones. Thus it was believed to pose little threat to native plants. It now appears that the weevil actually prefers native Tracy's thistle, a relatively rare thistle species found only in western Colorado and eastern Utah. The weevil reduces seed production on these rare thistles by two-thirds. Ecologists are now worried that the introduced flowerhead weevil could wipe out native Tracy's thistle completely.

These and other problems have caused a massive rethink of biological control programs in recent years. Ecologists are divided between the promise of reducing the use of "toxic" pesticides — a concern greatly overstated by some activists — and the reality of negative impacts on native plants and animals from supposedly "eco-friendly" biocontrols. As one prominent biocontrol scientist, Frank Howarth, has noted, when we make a mistake with a pesticide, we're dealing with "half-lives" (the time it takes for half of the chemical to degrade), whereas, when we make a mistake with a biological control agent, we are dealing with "doubling times" (the time it takes for the population to double).

Of course, not exerting *any* control of exotic introduced pests, either biocontrol or chemical, is still a decision with impacts on the native ecology. For example, if we decided not to treat an area infested with gypsy moths to bring populations down (biologically or chemically), native caterpillars will have to compete for leaves with the gypsy moth caterpillars. Multi-year gypsy moth outbreaks can kill trees, pressure tree species (oaks), and wipe out whole sections of forest, further changing the ecology.

Biocontrol: Effective or Not?

Aside from possible ecological impacts from biological control efforts, how effective has biocontrol been for farmers? The short answer is: moderately successful. However, it varies widely depending on the pest, the region, the crop, and whether we are discussing regional biocontrol of introduced pests or field-level biocontrol of native or endemic pests.

As yet, there simply aren't any effective biocontrols against weeds in farmers' fields, so we can set weed control aside. And except for a couple of preventative inoculations against bacterial diseases using "good" bacteria in a few orchard crops (used by both organic and non-organic farmers), there aren't any effective biocontrols against crop diseases. That leaves biocontrol of insect pests, and the rest of this chapter will focus on this area.

The best measure of success of any pest control method is cost/benefit analysis, weighing the research and implementation costs against the benefits to farmers and comparing these to the costs of other pest control approaches. Where cost/benefit analysis has been done, biocontrol shows only modest success.

Regional Biocontrol

Arguably the most successful agricultural biocontrol program in the United States is a classic biocontrol program against the alfalfa weevil. This program now saves Northeastern U.S. farmers an estimated $90 million per year in pesticide costs and lost harvests, a significant savings. Alfalfa is the fourth largest crop grown in the U.S., with 24 million acres planted for livestock feed. The alfalfa weevil, a European insect, began devastating alfalfa fields in North America in the 1930s.

Researchers began looking for an effective biocontrol agent against the alfalfa weevil in the late 1950s, and since then, they have released 12 different parasitic wasp species. Six of these wasp species have established themselves in the U.S. Northeast, where they have achieved roughly 90% control of the alfalfa weevil. Where 90% of fields used to need spraying each year, only 10% need spraying now. Outbreaks that do occur are often thought to be the result of poor farming practices, such as not harvesting the alfalfa in the fall and thereby giving the weevils a place to survive over the winter.

There is one problem with the alfalfa weevil biocontrol program, and it is apparently common to successful regional biocontrol programs: The alfalfa weevil population has been reduced so low that the parasitic wasps are having a hard time surviving for lack of hosts and food. Populations of the wasps are way down for four of the six established wasp species. It's dynamic equilibrium again. These low wasp populations are leaving openings for the weevil population to explode and cause crop damage.

In fact, the compatibility of biocontrol with crops genetically modified to resist pests, such as Bt crops that incorporate a bacterial protein toxic to caterpillars,[2] is under question because these crops are so effective against pests that there are too few prey insects for the biocontrol insects to survive. Not surprisingly, it is only biocontrol scientists who are raising this concern — not the farmers growing the pest resistant crops.

All Northeastern farmers, not just organic ones, have benefited from the alfalfa weevil biocontrol program. However, organic farmers also gain further protection from the occasional use of chemical pesticides on conventional alfalfa fields. These help prevent larger, region-wide weevil outbreaks from occurring that could devastate organic alfalfa fields.

Moreover, the alfalfa weevil biocontrol program has only been successful in a relatively limited area, the U.S. Northeast, where conditions are favorable for the parasitic wasps. None of the wasp species has established itself south of New Jersey or northern Pennsylvania, or farther west than Pennsylvania.

Non-organic farmers use pesticides to deal with the inevitable alfalfa weevil outbreaks. What do organic farmers do? Organic farmers grow alfalfa some-

---

[2] The Bt protein is toxic only in the alkaline gut of caterpillars. In the acidic gut of mammals, birds, fish, etc., the protein is harmless and digested as food. As such, organic farmers have been using aqueous solutions of Bt bacteria as a "soft" crop insecticide for decades.

what differently trying to make up for their limited, less effective, more expensive pesticide options. Some harvest their alfalfa in strips to maintain a refuge for beneficial insects and hopefully increase their survival, thereby preventing weevil population surges. Others have livestock graze the alfalfa down in the early spring to reduce weevil numbers.

These efforts are only marginally effective, however, so some organic farmers resort to "flaming" alfalfa fields. In flaming, liquid propane field flamers are pulled across the field after harvest with the flames directed at the ground to burn up the alfalfa crop residue and alfalfa weevils and their eggs. (Flaming is considered "organic" because propane is derived from petroleum extracted from the earth.) Flaming is certainly a dramatic approach to pest problems. But flaming is also very expensive and extremely dangerous. Field flamers blow up. As a result, no farm equipment company will sell field flamers commercially because of the obvious insurance liabilities. Organic farmers must make their own flaming rigs.

Mostly, as they do for many pest problems, organic farmers simply accept any alfalfa losses they incur and hope to make up for the losses with price premiums on the crops they successfully harvest. A USDA-supported Web site giving advice to organic farmers notes that alfalfa is a good crop for biocontrol because "although protein content of alfalfa hay is important, cosmetics is not as important as for fresh vegetable and fruit crops."

Another successful agricultural biocontrol program targets the tarnish plant bug (TPB), a pest of alfalfa and high-value fruit and vegetable crops. Biocontrol wasps were released against the TPB in the late 1980s and early 1990s, and have established themselves in the U.S. Northeast much like the alfalfa weevil. The wasps have reduced the economic damage from TPBs in this region by roughly two-thirds, saving American farmers an estimated $15 million annually in lost harvests and increased pesticide costs. Apple crop damage from the TPB in New Hampshire, for example, has fallen by 60% since the wasps were released.

Farm-Level Biocontrol

Aside from these few examples of successful ecosystem-wide biocontrol of exotic insect pests, how well does biocontrol work at the field/farm level? The answer is not very well and usually at high cost. For most pests on most crops, no cost-effective field-level biocontrol strategies have been developed.

Research studies have shown that while it is possible to reduce crop damage from specific pests using field-level biocontrols, the costs are often far higher than using pesticides and are rarely as effective. (If they were cheaper or as effective, non-organic farmers would use them.) Leonard Gianessi at the National Center for Food and Agriculture Policy noted, "Growers don't care whether [a] product is chemical or non-chemical, just that it work well and be cost effective. The deciding factors are always likely to be when choosing among pest control alternatives: How much does it cost and how well does it work?"

Compared to using pesticides or biotechnology approaches, biocontrol requires more planning, more pest scouting, more record keeping, more patience, more education, more training, and more tolerance for crop damage and economic losses. All of these are reasons why no farmers rely solely on biocontrol and why pesticides are so popular with farmers — even organic farmers.

For example, biocontrol organisms must be released well before a pest or disease becomes an actual problem. In contrast, pesticides don't have to be used until pests reach economic thresholds. If they never reach problem levels, nothing is sprayed. With biotech pest control, pests are suppressed throughout the season and pesticide use is reduced even further. Some biotech crops never have to be sprayed with a pesticide at all. (And remember that biotech pest controls are still in their infancy — they'll get far better very quickly.)

Biocontrol organisms are extremely narrowly targeted, usually attacking only one pest. Therefore, multiple biocontrol organisms have to be released to deal with multiple pests, drastically increasing labor and costs. In contrast, most insecticides kill an array of different pests. While biocontrol activists tout the narrow range of biocontrols as good ecologically, farmers usually see that as a negative.

The University of Massachusetts' floriculture Web site notes: "Correct diagnosis of the pest problem is essential. ... It is not enough to merely know the broad category of pest. Rather than 'whitefly,' it is necessary to know that an infestation is silverleaf whitefly or greenhouse whitefly. Rather than 'aphid,' it is necessary to know if it is green peach aphid, chrysanthemum aphid, or any of 30 or so other aphids commonly found in greenhouses." Thus for biocontrol to work, farmers need to be semi-professional entomologists — then hope that a commercially available biocontrol organism exists for the identified pest.

Greenhouse Biocontrol

Practical farm-level biocontrol of insect pests has been most successful in greenhouse crops. The greenhouse contains any biocontrol insects that are released, so it is easier to reach effective numbers of predators. Maintaining an environment favorable to biocontrol agents is also easier inside the protection of a greenhouse. And finally, pests have a harder time getting into greenhouses to attack crops, so predatory insects can more effectively reduce pest populations.

The actual use of biocontrol techniques in greenhouse crops varies widely. In Canada, it has been reported that more than 90% of greenhouse tomatoes and peppers, and 50% of greenhouse cucumbers are grown using some biocontrols. This is due in part to consumer concerns over pesticide residues and in part to the high value of these particular crops, which justifies greater spending on pest control.

In contrast, only 12% of greenhouse ornamental crops are protected using biocontrols because of a more complex array of pests and a general lack of consumer concern.

When fungal or viral diseases are a problem, biocontrols are almost never cost effective because even a few insect "escapes" can transmit enough disease to decimate a crop. For example in Spain, biocontrol of sucking aphids in greenhouse tomatoes is reasonably effective. But biocontrols cannot be used in areas where the tomato yellow leaf curl virus exists, because even a few aphids will transmit the devastating virus and cause crop failure.

Biocontrol is costly even in greenhouses. Whiteflies are one of the biggest pest problems for greenhouse vegetable and flower growers. A study comparing biocontrol versus conventional control of whiteflies in greenhouse poinsettias found that overall, biocontrol systems cost at least 300% more than using pesticides.[3] Assuming that labor for pest scouting was the same (a dubious assumption), the researchers found that the material costs of using biocontrol wasps were 10 to 14 times higher (1,000% to 1,400%) than the material costs of controlling whiteflies with a modern, "soft" chemical pesticide.

The authors noted that "if, as is strongly suspected, biological control strategies require greater monitoring efforts, then total labor costs also increase significantly. Consequently, an order of magnitude reduction in the costs of [the parasitic wasp] may still not be a sufficient incentive to motivate producers to adopt" biocontrol methods.

Nor did the wasps control whiteflies as well as the soft pesticide. The scientists wrote, "These cost estimates for biological control are conservatively

---

[3] Ramakers and Maaswinkel. Pest Occurrence and Control in Organic Year-Round Production of Chrysanthemums. *International Organization for Biological and Integrated Control of Noxious Animals and Plants West Palaearctic Regional Section Bulletin* 25(1):221-224, 2002.

predicated on the assumption that [the system using biocontrol wasps] is, or can be, as effective in controlling whiteflies as conventional chemical pesticides. At the time the field trials for this study were conducted, it did not appear certain that this was the case."

Finally, using biocontrol wasps didn't even eliminate the need to use pesticides and chemicals. In addition to 13 releases of parasitic wasps throughout the poinsettia growing cycle, the biocontrol system also included eight treatments with two different chemical insect growth regulators, two treatments with a pyrethroid insecticide, and one treatment with a long-residual organophosphate insecticide to protect the poinsettias during shipping.

So, the total costs, which charitably low-balled at 300% to 360% higher per poinsettia than the "conventional" system, didn't control whiteflies as well as a soft, safety-tested pesticide with minimal human health or ecological concerns, and didn't eliminate pesticide use.

The need for pesticides, even when biocontrols are being used, is demonstrated by the comments of these poinsettia researchers. "A complex of four aphid species and western flower thrips were the prevailing problems. The lack of natural insecticides for controlling these pests was the bottleneck for compiling a biological control program. Available botanical insecticides are not selective enough for being used in combination with natural enemies."

In other words, the available organic pesticides killed too many of the biocontrol organisms, yet the biocontrol organisms were not enough on their own to keep the pests at bay. The researcher further stated, "Accepting new microbial insecticides would make organic production feasible for organic growers."

The pesticide they are referring to is spinosad, discussed in Chapter 5. Organic farmers begged for spinosad to be approved for organic farming, and it eventually was. The point here is that the poinsettia greenhouse biocontrol system wasn't viable until the certification of this new chemical pesticide that allowed the growers to kill insects not controlled with biocontrol organisms. How this is better than just using spinosad to control pests is highly debatable — especially given the higher costs of the biocontrol system.

Biocontrol in Open Fields

In open fields, biocontrols are even less successful than in greenhouses because the biocontrol organisms fly away and die more quickly, and more pests fly in from other areas.

Consider the experience in trying to come up with a field-level biocontrol approach for artichoke plume moths (APM). The APM is a significant pest of artichokes in California. Yield losses from the moth can reach 70% or more if left untreated. In an experiment sponsored by the Organic Farming Research Foundation, APM was controlled on conventional fields with two sprays of insecticide at a cost of roughly $100 per acre. In the experimental "biorational" field, APM was kept under control by (1) releasing parasitic wasps, (2) placing pheromone strips or emitters in the fields to disrupt mating, and (3) using adult APM traps.

Nine to 13 releases of parasitic wasps were made in the "organic-like" artichoke fields during the crop cycle. Cost: $20 per acre for monitoring, $800 per acre for wasps, and undisclosed costs for the pheromone mating disruption and APM traps. Estimating the pheromone and trap costs at a conservative $50 per acre gives a total cost of $870 per acre, compared to less than $100 per acre for conventional control.

These experiments were conducted away from the main artichoke growing area of California, so pest pressures were lower than average. (Total artichoke area is estimated at only about 8,000 acres nationwide.[4])

In areas of California where artichokes are commonly grown, annual pesticide costs run higher because of higher pest pressure — between $500 and $600 per acre. However, this would be true of a biocontrol system as well. Only about 50 to 100 acres of organic artichokes are grown in the United States because of the high costs of production.

Because of these high costs, some organic farmers are experimenting with growing annual artichokes. Artichokes are normally a perennial crop that grows in the same fields year after year. Annual artichokes with other crops grown in alternate years would prevent pests like the APM from establishing themselves in those fields. The problem is that while annual artichokes suffer less from insect pests, other costs are significantly higher. Annual artichokes are more susceptible to fungal diseases, so organic farmers end up spraying annual artichokes multiple times per season with expensive copper and sulfur-based "organic" fungicides, defeating the cost savings from lower insect pressures. Ironically, the organic fungicides are more toxic and more environmentally contaminating compared to short-residue synthetic fungicides.

---

[4] Personal communication, Dr. Mohamed Bari, 2004.

Compatibility of Modern Farming With Biocontrol

Some biocontrol advocates criticize modern farming techniques as being incompatible with biocontrol strategies. One Web site run cooperatively by the Universities of Nebraska, Wyoming, Colorado, and Montana states, "Modern cropping systems often lack adequate resources for natural enemies. These resources include food such as nectar, pollen, and honeydew; alternate prey or hosts; overwintering sites; and other types of refugia. Management practices that can conserve natural enemies by providing these resources include cover cropping, intercropping, strip harvesting, proper crop residue management, maintenance of diverse plant communities at crop borders, and the direct provisioning of missing or deficient resources (e.g. food supplements)."[5]

Yet one of the reasons why modern farming systems are as productive as they are is that crops are grown in monocultures, where weeds and other competition for resources are eliminated or drastically reduced. Refugia for beneficial insects usually mean tolerating more weeds that reduce crop yields. Refugia for beneficial insects mean possible refuge for pests. Farmers have learned that keeping fields as weed free as possible reduces weed pressures in following years. Farmers have learned that many plants are alternate hosts for pests and disease and have made conscious efforts to eliminate them from their fields. While this may reduce the populations of beneficial insects, they know that those insects likely aren't going to protect their crops enough to benefit them appreciably anyway.

Note the recommendations from University of California's Small Farm Program in the publication "Plant Disease Management for Organic Crops":

> *"Pastures, foothills, riverbanks, grasslands, and other areas that support weeds and natural vegetation often are reservoirs of pathogens that cause virus and viruslike diseases. The vectors that carry such pathogens also can be found in these high-risk areas and often migrate into production fields. For example, the aster yellows phytoplasma and its leafhopper vector can be found in weedy grasslands in coastal California. Once the grassland vegetation dries up in*

---

the summer, the leafhoppers migrate into nearby lettuce or celery fields, resulting in aster yellows disease in these fields."

Conclusion

Although biocontrol has definite good uses and is something that most farmers shouldn't completely ignore, it has only very limited potential for protecting humanity's food and fiber supply. Without effective pesticides (or effectively biotech-protected crops) as a backstop against pest population explosions, biocontrol is too risky and ineffective.

The most successful biocontrol programs have targeted non-native species imported from other continents, where introduction of the pests' native predators or control agents has a comparatively large impact. The other area where biocontrol has had the most success is in greenhouses protecting high-value crops. Yet even here, the success and use of biocontrols are highly limited.

Remember that even organic farmers do not rely very heavily on biocontrol and continue to rely on pesticides as their main line of defense. Or they simply accept the damage and losses to pests and make up for them in the significantly higher price premiums they have been able to get the public to pay for their products.

Either way, while biocontrol has its uses, it isn't utopia and it isn't cheap. When it works, it relies on pesticides as the backup. If farmers were left to only biocontrol, we'd all go hungry. The activist wing of the organic movement would have the public believe that we don't need pesticides, biotechnologies, and other modern pest control technologies based on the illusion that there are effective alternatives such as biocontrol. But there aren't. We should use all of these approaches where and when they work best. But don't bet the farm on biocontrol.

Chapter 11:

Dismantling Capitalism and Other Fun Ideas

Organic Faithful Say:

"Growing the market for organic or 'local' food relative to other food is not equivalent to dismantling the current food system, nor is finding technical solutions to specific agronomic problems. Widespread change in the way we grow, distribute and eat food can only be achieved with major social and political reform."

Julie Guthman, treasurer, Ecological Farming Association
Taking on the Sacred (Grass-Fed) Cows, *Organic Matters* magazine, 2005

"The draw of the market already has brought into organic production some farmers and business people who are marginally committed, if not oblivious to the broader social agenda of the organic community."

Dr. Charles Benbrook
Sharing the Lessons of Organic Farming Conference
University of Guelph, January 31, 1998

"The critical problem facing organic agriculture today is how to produce food in sufficient quantity to feed modern populations without adopting an industrial system of production and distribution."

Peter Reynolds
Fearless Foods, LLC, 2000($)[1]

"[Small community-supported organic farms] could afford to pay a living wage if Americans realized that in most of the world people pay 20% to 30% to 40% to 50% of their income for their food, and we pay an average of 11%."

Anonymous speaker
The Inaugural Assembly of the Scientific Congress on Organic Agricultural Research, Breakout session on Economics, Marketing and Communities
January 23-24, 2001

I f you buy most of your family's food at a supermarket; if you enjoy the freedom to shop at different stores competing with each other to offer you food at low prices; if you like the incredible array of fresh and ethnically diverse foods available to you today year round, including off-season fruits and vegetables, understand that the ultimate goal of the organic farming movement is to take all of this away from you.

They'll deny it, but the policies and "food system" that they envision is absolutely antithetical to all that we currently take for granted in our food system, including choice, convenience, low prices, and off-season fresh fruits and vegetables.

Through their writings, speeches, and proposed policies, it is clear that the organic movement would like to deconstruct our free-market, capitalist food system and severely restrict our food choices regionally and seasonally.

Free Markets

It is undeniable that a major aspect of the "organic movement" is an antagonism toward market-driven capitalism and affinity for socialist and communist ideals. The movement has a palpable disdain for free markets and corporations. This is a broad characterization, but organic activists generally see open markets and economic institutions (and the technologies they have nurtured)

---

[1] ($) Indicates that the person quoted has a profit motive or other financial interest in promoting organic food.

as inherently destructive to the idealized agrarian communities they wish to bring back as the dominant organizing paradigm for human society.

Instead of the current free-market system, organic activists envision an unrealistic food system based on far more direct relationships between consumers and local farmers. "Know your farmer, that was one of the keys of the organic mission that has been lost," says organic farm certifier David Gould, who now complains that the mass market is turning organically grown food into just another brand, rather than an alternative social, economic, and ecological paradigm.

Peter Reynolds is a Yale-trained anthropologist and co-founder of a company that sells software to help manage organic Community Supported Agriculture (CSA) farms. CSAs are farms supported by consumers who pay an annual subscription fee in exchange for a "share" of whatever is harvested. Reynolds writes that "industrial models of mass production and distribution threaten the future of sustainable farming and its vision of community. ... organic farming cannot feed the population of the planet by being 'scaled up' on an industrial model. Any radically new system of production requires a system of distribution appropriate to it."[2] To Reynolds, community seems more important than food.

Reynolds argues instead for a network of "optimally sized" CSA farms allied with each other to provide subscribers with a larger range of food products than they could provide on their own. "Unlike the capitalist farm, the goal is not to make each CSA as large as possible, but to bring it to an optimal size and maintain it there." What is optimal? Reynolds defines it as "big enough to handle inter-farm transactions and to provide diversified [subscriber food baskets] but not so big that the social relations of big business are required to manage it."

Yet imagine trying to effectively feed the city of Seoul, South Korea (10.3 million people) or the New York metropolitan area (21 million people) without large supermarkets and food companies. These companies (private and corporate) effectively deliver tens of millions of meals each and every day to the residents of these urban/suburban areas. Nor could this gargantuan task be accomplished without large food processors that take the raw commodities and crops produced on farms and transform them into ingredients for cooking products and ready-to-eat foods. Food processors, much maligned by "whole food" activists, convert mountains of grains into flour, breakfast

---

[2] Peter C. Reynolds. Social Sustainability: Organic Food at the Crossroads. Fearless Foods, LLC, 2000.

cereals, noodles, and breads. They create the rows of canned soups, frozen piz-
zas, and all flavors of cheeses and other dairy products. They help to preserve
our food and prevent waste and spoilage, thereby conserving natural
resources. None of this could be done via farmers' markets and CSAs. How
many among us wants to devote most of our free time to making our own
pasta and bread, canning our own vegetables, etc.?

And forget about urban and suburban regions producing even a fraction of
their own food. These areas don't have nearly enough unpaved or undevel-
oped land to provide more than a tiny proportion of what they consume each
day, let alone be able to grow diverse foods like oranges, bananas, and such.
Like it or not, large, efficient, and adaptable agribusinesses, food processors,
and retail food stores are an essential part of today's highly populous world and
global food economy.

More fundamentally, what are corporations? Corporations are simply business democracies that allow many owners (shareholders) to make collective
decisions (through the elected board) and to systematize and streamline the
actions of very large groups of people (employees). Today, many corporate
employees are also shareholders. Corporations exist because lots of products
can't be produced by the village blacksmith and lots of tasks are simply too large
to be handled in the one-to-one fashion advocated by organic social engineers.

So many of the technologies, products, and services we all take for granted simply would not exist without an efficient way to organize and coordinate
the actions of the large number of people needed to produce and deliver them.
As but one example, none of the electronic devices in use today, from cell
phones to iPODs, would exist without corporations.

Members of the organic hard core don't see it that way. They argue that fos-
tering a consumer-to-farmer connection is essential and that market-driven
intentions are destructive to communities. It's a decidedly communist agro-
utopian philosophy, similar to that of the ruthless Cambodian dictator Pol Pot
in the 1970s.

Within days of winning a civil war in 1975, Pol Pot and his communist
rebel group, the Khmer Rouge, forced all city dwellers from their homes and
into the countryside onto communal organic farms. According to a 1999 *Time*
magazine article, Pol Pot was on a "quest to create a rural Utopia," and he
wanted to do it without synthetic fertilizers or other modern inputs.[3] Within

---

[3] Time 100. *Time Asia*, August 23-30, vol. 154(7/8), 1999.
http://www.time.com/time/asia/asia/magazine/1999/990823/pol_pot1.html

three years, an estimated 2 million to 3 million Cambodians had died of malnutrition, illness, and forced farm labor.

It is certainly true that large human institutions tend to be impersonal, as anyone who has experience with the post office or Department of Motor Vehicles can attest. But this does not make these institutions corrupt, immoral, or unjust. Nor does it mean that they are automatically socially destructive or insensitive to environmental concerns, as is so often stated or implied by organic activists.

In fact, larger organizations that maximize the resource-use efficiency of land, water, and equipment can be argued to serve environmental protection better. Too often, smaller farms and operations are less efficient and use more resources per unit of good or service delivered.

As a rural resident who loves the countryside, I share the organic activists' nostalgia for small farms. But I also know that theirs is a wish-dream of what never was and reveals a fundamental misunderstanding of what their proposed policies would actually reap for humanity and nature.

A resurgence of 18th century American farm community structure — complete with tens of thousands of small rural towns, each surrounded by hundreds of 50-acre diversified farms raising their own food staples and selling/trading/bartering a modest surplus of grains, meats, and dairy products — is unrealistic. It's unrealistic primarily because we must feed and clothe 9 billion human beings in the year 2050 from a decidedly limited land and resource base. It's also unrealistic because few people in the modern world want the hard physical labor, the long hours, and the harsh outdoor working conditions of a small farm.

Nor is it possible or just in a free society to limit people's creative abilities to improve their production efficiency, productivity, or profitability — either through specialization in producing one crop or livestock product, through designing or implementing new technologies, or through novel human institutions such as corporations. To our credit, humans have always strived to build better mousetraps, just as they have also strived to improve food production efficiency.

Two thousand years ago, a farmer who devised more productive grain growing methods could feed his family better and produce a larger surplus to trade/sell to improve the life of his family. This is no less true today. It is somewhat ironic that organic farmers and activists, who pride themselves on being individualistic and innovative, would decry and oppose the fruits of innovation and free association.

The same can be argued for technologies, which often allow greater productivity or efficiency at the price of interdependency with the complex groups, companies, or corporations that developed and manufacture them. Tractors, combines, sophisticated hybrid seeds, fertilizers, improved dairy genetics, global positioning satellites that enable precise applications of crop inputs — all of these technologies require large and complex human institutions for their development, manufacture, and distribution. Yet all of them allow us to produce more from fewer resources and man-hours — and usually do it more environmentally responsibly in terms of eco-impact per unit of production.

Wendell Berry, the poet-laureate of the organic movement, provides an example of the modern cultural self-loathing and anti-technology world view espoused by many in the organic movement in his new book *The Way of Ignorance*. In it, Berry decries the social impact of the adoption of tractors and mechanization (a.k.a. "industrialization") in farming during the middle and second half of the 20th century:

> *I remember well a summer morning in about 1950 when my father sent a hired man with a McCormick High Gear No. 9 mowing machine and a team of mules to the field I was mowing with our nearly new Farmall A [tractor]. That memory is a landmark in my mind and my history. I had been born into the way of farming represented by the mule team, and I loved it. ... But now I saw them suddenly from the vantage point of the tractor, and I remember how fiercely I resented their slowness. I saw them as "in my way." ... Year after year, agriculture would be adapted more and more to the technology and the processes of industry and to the rule of industrial economics. ...*
>
> *In 1964 my family and I returned to Kentucky and settled on a hillside farm in my native community, where we have continued to live. ... it was evident at once that the human life of the place, the life of the farms and the farming community, was in decline. The old self-sufficient way of farming was passing away. The economic prosperity that had visited the farmers briefly during World War II and for a few years afterward had ended. The little towns that once had been social and economic centers, thronged with country people on Saturdays and Saturday nights, were losing out to the bigger towns and the cities. The rural neighborhoods, once held together by common memories, common work, and the sharing of help, had begun to dissolve. There were*

no longer local markets for chickens or eggs or cream. The spring lamb industry, once a staple of the region, was gone. The tractors and other mechanical devices certainly were saving the labor of the farmers and farmhands who had moved away, but those who had stayed were working harder and longer than ever. [4]

Berry apparently forgets that most Kentucky farms of his childhood were not the self-sufficient type that he describes, growing all of their own food crops and livestock, but rather cash-crop farms growing tobacco to sell to city people. Without tobacco, many Kentucky farmers would likely have left long before. Even today, with a federally funded tobacco buyout program, we still don't know how many Kentucky farmers will choose to remain.

Berry also conveniently ignores one of the biggest reasons for rural depopulation over the past 50 years: rural isolation and the nature of farm work compared to other employment options available to young people. Whereas farm life in rural Kentucky in the 1950s and '60s was comparatively simple, it was also extremely hard and tedious work for comparatively small monetary rewards. After World War II, during which many rural men and women were sent overseas to fight or to big cities to help staff manufacturing facilities, younger people had gained a taste for life beyond the farm. They saw a world with five-day workweeks instead of seven, and leisure time to fritter away however one wished. They saw a world that included an array of entertainment simply unavailable to rural residents, including museums, theaters, nightclubs, and amusement parks.

Today's organic elites see poetry and beauty in the simplicity of rural, small-farm life, but do so within the context of today's modern communications and entertainment networks such as satellite television and high-speed Internet. But rural life on a small farm is still hard work, seven days a week, 365 days a year. As the occasional overseer of my family's cattle and horses, I can attest that livestock are a 24-7-365 responsibility. Dairy cows must be milked at least twice a day, period. Farm animals don't know what a Christmas vacation is or observe three-day weekends. If we want to take a vacation, we must coordinate with our fellow livestock-owning friends for their daily care and maintenance. While this certainly creates stronger community bonds, it is far more limiting than most would tolerate. There aren't any "cattle kennels" to which we can deliver our animals while we're away.

---

[4] Berry W. Renewing Husbandry. *Orion Magazine*, September/October 2005. http://www.oriononline.org/pages/om/05-5om/Berry.html

Ask young people whether they would prefer to earn a meager income from constant seven-day-a-week hard work and little or no vacation or whether they would prefer to earn a larger income from a job that ends at 5 p.m. and affords weekends off and two to three weeks of paid vacation every year. Given this choice, most will choose the city job. The reality is that farmers today do it for the independence and rugged, rural lifestyle rather than monetary rewards. But they are a decided minority of our overall society.

Even worse is the organic movement's denial of the aspirations of human beings outside the small farm and traditional, self-sufficient rural community. In the late 1990s, the wife of a Swiss chemical company executive said all Swiss should be either farmers or shopkeepers. But what of the would-be actors, poets, math geniuses, astronauts, physicians, scientists, and medical researchers?

Philosopher Berry continues in his denunciation of farming "industrialization":

> The tractor's arrival had signaled, among other things, agriculture's shift from an almost exclusive dependence on free solar energy to a total dependence on costly fossil fuel. But in 1950, like most people at that time, I was years away from the first inkling of the limits of the supply of cheap fuel.
>
> We had entered an era of limitlessness, or the illusion thereof, and this in itself is a sort of wonder. ... Mechanical farming makes it easy to think mechanically about the land and its creatures. It makes it easy to think mechanically even about oneself, and the tirelessness of tractors brought a new depth of weariness into human experience, at a cost to health and family life that has not been fully accounted.
>
> Once one's farm and one's thoughts have been sufficiently mechanized, industrial agriculture's focus on production, as opposed to maintenance or stewardship, becomes merely logical. ... The farm and all concerns not immediately associated with production have in effect disappeared from sight. The farmer too in effect has vanished. He is no longer working as an independent and loyal agent of his place, his family, and his community, but instead as the agent of an economy that is fundamentally adverse to him and to all that he ought to stand for.

It's a rather amazing philosophy that any farmer who buys a tractor or any other machine or input to successfully farm more land than could be farmed with a mule team is suddenly an "agent" working against all he ought to stand for. It is even more telling that Berry and his fellow philosophers see farmers' primary role not as feeding and clothing humanity, but maintaining the land. What are they "maintaining" the land for if not to feed and clothe humanity? By all means we should be good stewards of the land in order that we may continue to successfully feed and clothe humanity, but this focuses on the horse and not the cart when society needs both. The farm is without purpose if it doesn't feed and clothe humanity.

Yet this farm-centeredness illustrates exactly the social agenda of organic activists, to one degree or another. Larger is bad, smaller is better. Total farm independence is ideal while being interdependent with others and focusing on providing food for others (the market) makes one an immoral capitalist sell-out. Berry writes:

> Through World War II, farm life in my region (and, I think, near-ly everywhere) rested solidly upon the garden, dairy, poultry flock, and meat animals that fed the farm's family. Especially in hard times farm families, and their farms, survived by means of their subsistence economy. The industrial program, on the contrary, suggested that it was "uneconomic" for a farm family to produce its own food; the effort and the land would be better applied to commercial production. The result is utterly strange in human experience: farm families that buy everything they eat at the store.

Berry goes even further to decry the "scientization" of agriculture; that is, the dissection of farming into scientific disciplines and the demystification of agriculture via science. According to Berry, "'Science' is too simple a word to name the complex of relationships and connections that compose a healthy farm — a farm that is a full membership of the soil community." But science is simply a tool to observe the real world. Science will just as accurately document and detail the yield or soil quality benefits of organic farming techniques as it will non-organic farming techniques.

I believe that the widespread anti-science attitude within the organic community is a reaction to science's unvarnished examination of organic farming, which hasn't been very flattering. Science has shown that there aren't any yield benefits from organic techniques, that there aren't any nutritional benefits from organic foods, and that organic methods aren't better at warding off pests and diseases — though the advocates constantly claim superiority in all three areas.

Science also shows that organic fertilizers pose just as great a nutrient pollution risk as non-organic fertilizers[5] and may pose greater food safety risks.[6]

But the organic's anti-science attitude is more than just sour grapes over an unflattering review. Berry and many in the organic movement seem to resent the reality that small farmers have lost the top spot in the social hierarchy of those who contribute to the feeding and clothing of humanity. Science and scientists have joined farmers as part of an enormous interdependent team of farmers, crop and livestock breeders, geneticists, nutritionists, veterinarians, chemical engineers, soil scientists, plant pathologists, mechanical engineers, and many more.

The result of all of this specialization and knowledge is a more competitive market in which it certainly is more difficult for small farmers to earn a living. Undeniably, specialization and the economies of scale have put the squeeze on small farmers of all stripes. This loss of perceived independence, revered social status, and cultural significance is what drives the organic farmer's social agenda perhaps more than any other single factor.

Berry articulates well the organic farmers' resentment of science and their vision of a return to primacy of the small, diversified farms of his pre-WWII remembrance. He even advocates forcing agricultural scientists to become small farmers, too:

> An intention to replace husbandry with science was made explicit in the renaming of disciplines in the colleges of agriculture. "Soil husbandry" became "soil science," and "animal husbandry" became "animal science." This change is worth lingering over because of what it tells us about our susceptibility to poppycock. Purporting to increase the sophistication of the humble art of farming, this change in fact brutally oversimplifies it. ... During the half-century and more of our neglect of local adaptation, we have subjected our farms to a radical oversimplification of form. The diversified and reasonably self-sufficient farms of my region and of many other regions have been conglomerated into larger farms with larger fields, increasingly specialized, and subjected increasingly to the strict, unnatural linearity of

---

[5] Pimentel D., et al. Environmental, Energetic, and Economic Comparisons of Organic and Conventional Farming Systems. *BioScience* 55:573-582, 2005.
[6] Mukhergee A., et al. Preharvest Evaluation of Coliforms, *Escherichia coli, Salmonella,* and *Escherichia coli* O157:H7 in Organic and Conventional Produce Grown by Minnesota Farmers. *Journal of Food Protection* 67(5):894-900, 2004.

the production line. ...

The effort of husbandry is partly scientific but it is entirely cul-
tural; and a cultural initiative can exist only by becoming personal.
It will become increasingly clear, I believe, that agricultural scientists
will need to work as indwelling members of agricultural communi-
ties or of consumer communities. It is not irrational to propose that
a significant number of these scientists should be farmers, and so
subject their scientific work, and that of their colleagues, to the influ-
ence of a farmer's practical circumstances. Along with the rest of us,
they will need to accept all the imperatives of husbandry as the con-
text of their work.

Rural Agenda vs. Urban Rationale

Berry and his organic followers have an incredibly narrow perspective that
indulges them in the fantasy that they are the center of humanity, which is
why Berry is perhaps one of the most popular speakers at organic farming
conferences. This is an audience distinct from the vast majority of organic
consumers.

Most organic consumers are affluent urbanites that have become chemo-
phobic after years of newspaper and media misinformation claiming there are
hidden dangers lurking in the food supply. They want to support small farms,
but mainly to preserve the "Old McDonald" landscape that they like to drive
through while "antiquing" on weekends. They have little desire to reshape
society. Urban organic consumers don't want to live in a small farm town, at
least one any farther than an hour or two's drive from the good shopping and
abundant entertainment of the big cities.

In contrast, organic social activists have a strong distaste for urban/subur-
ban areas. They see densely populated urban areas as an affront to nature and
the natural order, an environmentally and socially destructive force that needs
to be opposed. They would like to see the cities depopulated and the countryside re-filled with small, mixed farms. Those of us who don't farm are supposed to get to know our own organic food suppliers and interact with them
on a weekly or monthly basis. We are supposed to devote considerable time to
them, visit their farms (or at least their farm stands at the farmers' market), and
allow them to teach us their rural values and environmental ethics.

Most urgently, the ethic the whole organic movement would like to teach
us is "limits." They believe that we have already taken the earth beyond its
limits. We eat too much, drive too much, desire too much, and demand too

much. As Berry writes, "in this world limits are not only inescapable but indispensable."

And that brings me to the point made at the beginning of this chapter: They don't want you to eat so well. They don't like it that you have access to foods from far off lands. They don't like it that you can buy fresh fruits and vegetables during the winter. They believe that shipping food long distances is an unnecessary waste of resources and unnecessarily contributes to air pollution. Never mind that overall, the bulk transport of food adds comparatively little to our society's consumption of fossil fuels. Ship and rail transport are incredibly efficient. It is more important to them that you've "lost the connection to the land" and the relationship with the farmer.

They believe that it would be desirable for consumers to pay considerably more for a regionally and seasonally confined diet. They even argue that we should all individually earn less so that we consume less. This was openly discussed during a roundtable at a 2002 conference hosted by the Organic Farming Research Foundation:

> *Speaker A:* "... we're making the assumption that today's standard wage is the preferred choice, and I would beg to differ that the union scale wage that everyone strives for is the unsustainable wage model that promotes mass consumerism or consumption of the environment. And that, in reality, the sustainable wage is the smaller wage with lowering the consumption of the status quo. I mean, we are in this country 6 percent of the world's population and consume 30 percent of the world's resources. So I'm more of a proponent of saying we're 6 percent of the population, let's take the consumerism down to 6 percent of the world's resources and go to that economic level as the preferred economic model to promote to the future."
>
> *Speaker B:* "I think your principle is OK. But let's keep working and keep our organic price up there because we, ... it's our own incomes."
>
> *Speaker A:* ... I think, from what I know about the farmers I've worked with who were doing CSA — particularly on a small scale — they're always grappling with the issue of labor, because they're not making sufficient money from sale of their product really to be able to deal with paying. Vegetable production is very intense, labor intensive. ... The answer is not subsidization, the answer is to teach the American population what food really costs. You could afford to pay

a living wage if Americans realized that in most of the world people pay 20 to 30 to 40 to 50 percent of their income for their food, and we pay an average of 11 percent.

Never mind that the reason why people in so much of the world pay such a large percentage of their incomes for food is because their incomes are so low. Organic activists would like for us to simply pay vastly more for our food so that the small, inefficient, labor-intensive organic farms can prosper and their employees can be paid a "living wage" for producing comparatively little.

Recall the essay in the introduction of this book, where the utopian vision was for everyone to sew their own clothes on communal sewing machines, out of cloth made on local looms, using locally sourced material. The envisioned ideal economy reaches no farther than the next county over. It's a sentimentalized vision of 18th century America, conveniently ignoring the amount of worldly goods available even to our 18th century forefathers — whale oil, steel, salt, sugar, spices, tea, gunpowder, glass, china, cotton, wool, and silk. They're really talking about a return of the feudal society of the 10th century where the "lord" in the manor house owned the only horses.

How far can this self-sufficiency philosophy go? It reminds me of the question I ask every time I see an Amish horse-drawn carriage or "Mennonite car" (invariably black with all the chrome removed or painted over) on a local road in my Shenandoah Valley. Just who draws the line at how much technology is enough and what is their rationale? The total self-sufficiency philosophy falls apart when one realizes how interdependent and global our economy has become. No person or community can truly be an island in the 21st century unless they live an incredibly meager and isolated existence.

Judging by their prolific Web sites, Internet postings, travel to conferences, and constant agitating, even hard-core organic activists enjoy being worldly folk and fully utilize the technologies they would deny the rest of humanity. They celebrate exotic cultures and cuisine, even as they advocate bottling everyone up into regional, self-contained fiefdoms. The paradoxes and contradicting messages from organic activists — earn less, pay more — make little if any sense for a 21st century world.

We cannot put the human population or technology genie back in the bottle. People, especially those in developing countries that have yet to share in the technological abundance, simply won't settle for forced poverty. The answer isn't to deprive, but to thrive and innovate. We cannot turn the clock back to a time that never existed. We must look forward.

We have the technologies, resources, and know-how to feed and clothe humanity well and without fulfilling the dire predictions of the organic doom-sayers — but only if we get over our crisis in confidence in technology, science, and social/economic structure. Free-market democracies are the most adaptable and humane of any system yet tried by mankind. There is simply no reason why we cannot sustainably and abundantly feed all of humanity in the 21st century while protecting wild habitats and ecosystems.

Chapter 12:

Organic Farming Versus Wildlife Habitat

Organic Faithful Say:

"Whenever you buy organic products, [you are telling] farmers, producers, and retailers that you care about the earth, too, and that you want them to continue with their efforts to save the planet."

Organic Trade Association ($)[1]
http://www.openharvest.com/ohthearchives/ohnewsletters/99January/savetheplanet.html

"When you purchase organic food, you are using the power of your dollar to … help save our environment."

Pioneer Organics Company ($)
http://www.pioneerorganics.com/why.html
(Web address correct as of Nov. 6, 2003)

"When it comes to buying fruits and vegetables that go easy on the earth, it's hard to beat organic."

Newsletter "Earth Saving Tips From Earth Share," Spring 1998, Earth Share bills itself as "a federation of America's leading non-profit environmental and conservation charities."
http://www.earthshare.org/tips/spring98.doc
(Web address correct as of Nov. 6, 2003)

---

[1] ($) Indicates that the person quoted has a profit motive or other financial interest in promoting organic food.

"Good for you and good for the planet, because it is all 100% pure organic."
Eckhart Kiesel, president Rapunzel Pure Organic confection company ($)
News release, Monday, April 22, 2002
TimesUnion.com
http://www.rapunzel.com/company/company_press_042202.html
(Web address correct as of Nov. 6, 2003)

"We know that our current agricultural system is killing the planet and making us sick; we know that most of the foods available in the supermarket lack basic nutrition. Organic farming, biodynamics and other philosophies show how we can sustain both human life and planetary life through one process."
Eric Francis, astrologer and sex educator

Reality Says:

Question: "What do you think of organic farming? A lot of people claim it's better for human health and the environment."

Borlaug: "That's ridiculous. This shouldn't even be a debate. Even if you could use all the organic material that you have — the animal manures, the human waste, the plant residues — and get them back on the soil, you couldn't feed more than 4 billion people. In addition, if all agriculture were organic, you would have to increase cropland area dramatically, spreading out into marginal areas and cutting down millions of acres of forests. At the present time, approximately 80 million tons of nitrogen nutrients are utilized each year. If you tried to produce this nitrogen organically, you would require an additional 5 or 6 billion head of cattle to supply the manure. How much wild land would you have to sacrifice just to produce the forage for these cows? There's a lot of nonsense going on here."
Norman Borlaug, Ph.D.
1970 Nobel Peace Prize winner and "Father of the Green Revolution"
Interview from Reason Magazine

"There is a big confusion — I have always said use all the organic fertilizer that's available. But please don't have the extreme greenies come to the developing nations and tell their agriculture leaders that it's simple, all they have to do is use the organic fertilizer and they can change production. This is nonsense!

There's 83 million tons of [synthetic inorganic] nitrogen fertilizer used in the world today and the affluent nations are among the highest users. People who are carrying these extreme ideas have never been involved in production. They are looking at it very often — I'm talking about the extremists — they are talking about things from a theoretical standpoint, not from a realistic one. And by the use of the so-called [Green Revolution] technology, we have saved wildlife habitat and many endangered species. Had we tried to produce the food of the year 2000 with the technology of 1960 we would have had to have much more than doubled the area under cultivation, which would have meant cutting down forests, plowing up lands that were marginal because of rainfall and would never have had sustainable production. So what would have happened to wildlife? ... Remember, in my lifetime, when I was born 90 years ago, the world's population was about 1.3 billion people. Today we're 6.3 billion and we're adding 80 million more a year. And without the use of high-yield technology we would have chopped down all of our forests, destroyed our wildlife, much of the beauties of nature that people who have good incomes can use during vacations to see the wonders of nature. I'm a firm believer in that."

Dr. Norman Borlaug
National Public Radio's "All Things Considered," March 26, 2004

O rganic farming, on a large scale, poses the single greatest threat to natural ecosystems and biodiversity in human history. Why? An organic-only fertilizer mandate would force us to clear-cut, graze, and plow large areas of the earth's remaining wildlife habitat because of lower yields and the need to obtain enough organic nitrogen fertilizer. This fact alone makes organic farming, on even a moderately large scale, a serious threat to the planet's wildlife.

It is that simple and that important.

Without additional cropland taken from wildlife, we'd either have to eliminate more than half of the current world population or force all of humanity to eat barely adequate, subsistence diets with virtually no meat and dairy products. Malnutrition would become a vastly greater problem.

As long as organic farming remains a comparatively small segment of food and fiber production, it poses no threat to the planet. But organic advocates don't want to remain a small segment. As the opening quotes to this chapter amply demonstrate, they see organic as the way "to save the earth." The Rodale Institute, created by U.S. organic farming pioneer Jerome Rodale, states on its Web site: "'Actually, we'd like nothing more than to work ourselves completely out of the market,' [Rodale Institute farm manager Jeff Moyer] confides. That would mean that everybody's growing food organically. That's our whole goal." These organic groups are not alone. Virtually all of the large, mainstream environmental activist groups openly and strongly advocate organic farming. Greenpeace, the Sierra Club, Friends of the Earth, Environmental Defense, etc., all are lock-stepping in a crusade for organic farming as the way to farm.

These allied groups envision organic as the organizing paradigm for global agriculture in the 21st century. They vigorously push for government mandates that would allow only organic farming and for consumer boycotts of non-organic foods. While they haven't had tremendous success in achieving their goal yet, they have steadily chipped away at non-organic farming through negative public opinion and increasingly restrictive regulations. There is no mistaking that an all-organic world is the vision of a very vocal and well-funded movement.

If these environmental groups are serious about conserving wildlife habitat and preserving natural biodiversity, then they are seriously misguided in advocating only organic farming.

We must analyze the issue from the "think globally, act locally" perspective wisely advocated by these very same environmental organizations.

The first rule of organic farming is to use only so-called "organic" nitrogen fertilizers: animal manure, plant composts, fishmeal, kelp, dried animal blood from slaughter houses (bloodmeal), ground up animal bones (bonemeals), etc. No synthetic nitrogen fertilizers are allowed in organic farming.

The problem is that organic fertilizer requires land for its production. More importantly, it requires land that is suitable for farming — either for grazing or animal feed production or for crops. Land good enough for pasture or feed and crop production is in critically short supply globally. According to the latest estimates by the United Nations Food and Agriculture Organization, humanity has already converted 11% of the earth's land area to crops and another 26% is devoted to pasture and rangeland. This accounts for fully half of the land area not covered by glaciers and deserts.[2] What is left is critical wildlife habitat — the marginal land that harbors the most biodiversity. Globally, the land poorest for farming tends to naturally have the most species. For example, rain forests and wetlands are generally terrible for farming, but they harbor high densities of diverse species of insects, plants, and animals.

Fertilizer Review

All plants require three major nutrients for growth: Nitrogen (N), phosphorus (P), and potassium (K).[3] Nitrogen, however, is the most important plant nutri-

---

[2] United Nations Food and Agriculture Organization, Production Yearbook 1995.

ent, required in relatively large amounts in comparison to the other plant nutrients. Nitrogen is needed to make the most basic and essential ingredients of life — proteins, nucleic acids (DNA and RNA), and other key components of cells.

The nitrogen for both organic and non-organic fertilizers originates from the exact same source, the earth's atmosphere, which is nearly 80% nitrogen gas. Yet the nitrogen in the atmosphere (N_2, or di-nitrogen) is unavailable to and unusable by plants.[4] Before plants and other organisms can utilize atmospheric di-nitrogen, it must be chemically converted, or "fixed," into ammonia (NH_3) or nitrate (NO_3).

Bacteria are the only life forms on earth able to biologically "fix" atmospheric di-nitrogen into nitrate, so their role is critical in the production of organic fertilizer. Legume plants host nitrogen-fixing bacteria in special structures in their roots, called nodules. It is an ancient symbiotic relationship where the bacteria and plants have co-evolved as partners over millennia. The nitrogen-fixing bacteria in the roots of legumes make nitrate from the atmospheric di-nitrogen and trade it with the plants in exchange for sugars.

The nitrogen in virtually every other source of "organic" fertilizer — animal wastes (urine, feces), animal bloodmeal, plant composts, etc. — comes ultimately from legume plants. For example, the nitrogen in cattle manure and urine comes from legumes growing in the pasture on which the animals grazed or from legume feed crops fed to the animals on the farm, such as alfalfa, clover hay, soybean meals, etc.[5]

This legume-sourced "organic" nitrogen requires land. To produce any non-legume crop organically, such as corn, wheat, rice, or potatoes, legumes must be grown somewhere to fix enough organic nitrogen to fertilize the non-legume crop. The farmer can do this directly, in what is called "green manur-

---

[3] Plants actually require 26 other trace mineral nutrients in various amounts, but all of these 26 are needed at far lower levels than the "Big Three" of N, P, and K. Fertilizer is, in fact, labeled to indicate ratio of the Big Three, such as 10-10-10 or 10-20-10, describing the ratios of N-P-K.

[4] Without getting too technical, atmospheric nitrogen is in the di-nitrogen (N_2) form where two nitrogen atoms are strongly bonded to each other chemically. This strong self-bonding makes the nitrogen biologically unavailable to most organisms. Biologically available nitrogen is in ammonia (NH_3) or nitrate (NO_3).

[5] There are other, much smaller sources of "organic" nitrogen. The weathering of rock releases small amounts of plant-available nitrogen, as does the intense heat from lightning. But these sources of "organic" nitrogen are negligible compared to the volume that comes from bacteria.

ing," in which the farmer grows a legume crop and then plows it directly into the soil as fertilizer rather than harvesting it. Or it can be done indirectly, by growing legumes (either in pastures or as feed crops), feeding them to live-stock, and utilizing the resulting nitrogen-rich manure as the fertilizer for the non-legume crop.

Again, farmers could plant polycultures as the Native Americans did, mix-ing legume plants with non-legumes (i.e., corn/squash/beans), but the yields from these crops would be low compared to most modern cropping systems and would require that large amounts of additional cropland be planted to obtain the same amount of total food or fiber.

Thus, there is really only one source of organic nitrogen fertilizer — legumes — and it takes a comparatively large amount of land to produce it. That said, nearly all farmers use "organic" fertilizers whenever they are available, not only because they are often by-products of their farms, but because organ-ic fertilizers have additional benefits in maintaining good soil structure. Farmers of all kinds recycle animal wastes back onto cropland and plow crop residues back into the soil to recycle the nutrients in these materials as well as to improve and maintain soil structure. All of this adds some nitrogen back to farm fields. But this isn't nearly enough for humanity's current and future needs.

Few consumers realize that many organic farmers today rely heavily on nitrogen-rich farm wastes generated on non-organic farms to maintain the fer-tility of their fields. For example, manure from a non-organic livestock opera-tion is often used as crop fertilizer on nearby organic farms. However, the nitrogen in the wastes from these non-organic farms most often originates from synthetic fertilizer. In the all-organic world envisioned by the activists, there wouldn't be any non-organic farms from which to borrow, and no "sur-plus" nitrogen.

The USDA estimates that the United States produces less than 30% of the organic nitrogen necessary to support current crop production, even after including the human wastes and food scraps not currently being recycled back to cropland. Globally, the percentage is closer to 25%.

That means that globally we would have to make up for a 70% to 75% shortfall in nitrogen fertilizer needs by growing more green manure crops or increasing the amount of land in legume feed crops to feed to animals. Moreover, those animals would need to be kept in some sort of confinement system where we could collect their manure for application onto non-legume crops. Increasing the amount of grazing lands doesn't help because the manure is distributed throughout the pastures and rangelands — unless, of course, we devoted significant labor to manure collection. Yet even doing this would yield a paltry amount of manure.

An all-organic mandate would immediately require that huge areas of additional land (wildlife habitat) be converted to growing legume animal feed or green manure crops because of the current shortfall in organic fertilizer supplies. Worse, global food demand is expected to at least double over the next 50 years through a combination of a 50% larger human population (the United Nations and most respected demographers expect world population to peak at between 9 billion and 10 billion people) and increased demand for animal protein. These trends would require the destruction of even more wildlife habitat for organic fertilizer.

All for what reason? Why is it so important to not use synthetic nitrogen fertilizer?

Plants must wait until organic (as in biological) materials are degraded, releasing the nutrients in their inorganic chemical forms — ammonia, nitrates, calcium, phosphorus, etc. — before those nutrients can be physically taken up by a plant's roots in any appreciable quantities. Plants do not and cannot distinguish nitrate or ammonia ions released from compost or animal manure from the ammonia and nitrate ions from synthetic fertilizer. The ions are identical. In fact, one reason why organic farmers generally achieve lower crop yields (See Chapter 9 on yields) is the naturally slow degradation rate of organic matter in the soil and, thus, the slow release of chemical nitrogen forms available for uptake by the crop.

Therefore, there is no biological reason for insisting on "organic only" fertilizers in agriculture. This is a good thing, because otherwise a huge land area would be needed to feed and clothe humanity.

Dr. Vaclav Smil, professor of agriculture at the University of Manitoba in Canada and author of an excellent book on the history of synthetic fertilizers, gives the simplest measure: To replace all of the estimated 85 million tons of synthetic nitrogen fertilizer used by the world's farmers in 2004 would require that we apply the equivalent of four times more animal wastes onto cropland than we currently do — either with actual animal waste or with equivalent green manure legume crops. Where would we get four times more collectable and applicable animal waste? Remember, the animal waste generated by animals on pastures and other grazing lands is not available, and is actually needed to maintain the fertility and productivity of the pasture and rangeland.

Instead, either we would need to grow more harvestable legume animal feed to generate four times more animal manure to apply to cropland or we would need to grow the equivalent amount of legume green manure crops. Any way you go about it, far more land would be needed to produce the same amount of food that is produced using synthetic fertilizer.

Hypothetically, if we attempted to do it with just cattle manure, it would require the manure from an additional 5 billion to 7 billion cattle. How many is that? That is four to five times more cattle than the current total global cattle population! Where would we put all those extra animals? How much wildlife habitat would we destroy just to grow enough feed for those extra animals? What would happen to water quality?

The world's current cattle population of 1.3 billion animals is raised on pastures and rangeland that occupy roughly one-fifth of the earth's total land area. This does not include the corn and soybean acreage currently used to grow feed for some of them. There really isn't any room in existing pastures for extra animals, which means we would need to grow more animal feed to support animals raised in confinement. (Again, we need the manure in a collectable form so we can then apply it to cropland for human foods and fiber crops.) At a conservative estimate of two acres of feed/forage land to support each additional animal, that works out to roughly 20 million square miles of additional feed crop acreage needed. An easier way to put it is an additional one-third of the planet's entire land area would be needed!

The Bichel Committee Report

More proof of the huge land costs of organic farming is found in an obscure and little-noted report from a high-level technical committee of the Danish government. In the late 1990s, the Danes were contemplating a total ban on synthetic chemicals in agriculture and industry. The Danish politicians contemplated converting Denmark's entire farm sector to organic and assigned a group of experts to examine the costs and consequences.

The expert panel became known as the Bichel Committee, named after the committee's chairman Dr. Svend Bichel, the former president of the Danish Society for the Conservation of Nature. It was staffed by the most knowledgeable university and government scientists and organic farming academics, by all accounts a very expert and well-rounded group.

As Dr. Bichel stated upon the release of the committee's detailed report, "For the first time in history [politicians] have a sound basis for decision making in the pesticide and organic farming areas that will enable them to foresee by far the majority of the consequences of the decisions to be taken during the course of the next five to 10 years."

The committee calculated the impacts of six different scenarios. Three scenarios were based on existing organic crop yields, and three were based on a situation in which, as stated in the committee's report, "it is assumed that cereal production could be increased by 15% and clover grass production by 10%. This is based on a more goal-oriented effort to increase cereal production and better use of pastureland as a result of the lower yield of the individual dairy cow compared with present organic practice."

Setting aside this completely hypothetical assumption — as several long-term organic farming research projects have failed to increase organic cereal crop or clover grass yields by such amounts — let's examine the remaining three scenarios.

These three remaining scenarios are based on "three levels of feed imports to Denmark" from other countries:

1. No feed imports (complete self sufficiency in feed)

2. 15% of feed imported for ruminants (cows, goats, sheep) and 25% of feed imported for non-ruminants (pigs, chickens, etc.)

3. Unlimited import of feed and maintenance of pre-organic (1996) levels of livestock production

As the report states, "In a 100 percent organic Denmark, there would be no conventional farms from which to purchase manure or feed, although it would be possible to import both organic and conventional feed."

Seeing as we're considering the impacts of an all organic world, where no non-organic feed or manure is available to import from non-organic farms or non-organic foreign countries, the only scenario of these three that is relevant is the zero import scenario.

Under that scenario, Denmark's food production would be cut by half. (See Table 3). Most of this food production decline can be directly attributable to the need to devote land to animal forage and fertilizer crop area.

As the report states candidly, "The nitrogen cycle is significantly reduced in the organic scenarios, to a level corresponding to Danish agriculture in the 1950s, because nitrogen would not be imported in the form of artificial fertilizer. It would instead be obtained by symbiotic nitrogen fixation in clover grass fields and through importation of feed, but [cereal grain] production would be limited by nitrogen in all scenarios. The calculations show a 50 to 70 percent reduction of the net contribution of nitrogen to the soil in the organic scenarios compared with Danish agriculture in 1996."

Elsewhere in the report it states, "In organic farming, there are more limits to what can be grown in the way of different crops than there are in conventional farming. There must be a considerable proportion of nitrogen-fixing crops and the crop rotations must be diversified and include perennial crops. Land use in the scenarios differs considerably from present-day use."

As far as food production losses, grain production would drop 62%, potato production would plummet by 80%, total pork and poultry production would fall 70%, and sugar production would drop by 54%. In total, human-edible food production in Denmark would drop by 47%.

DANISH TOTAL HUMAN FOOD PRODUCTION *(Million kilograms)*		
	1996	**100% Organic**
Grain	9,850	3,678
Milk	4,690	4,650
Pork and Poultry	1,773	531
Potatoes	1,617	327
Sugar	493	225
Vegetables	291	291
Beef	198	202
Eggs	88	88
Fruits/Berries	61	61
Total	19,061	10,053

Table 3: Total Danish human food production under conventional agriculture (using 1996 average yields) and 100% organic methods.

Denmark would no longer annually export 2 million tons of grains, over a million tons of pork and poultry, and hundreds of thousands of tons of potatoes and sugar. Whichever countries were consuming those exports would have to grow or import more to make up for the losses, adding to the land costs.

Again, the main reason for the massive cut in food production is the need to replace synthetic nitrogen fertilizer. In the Bichel scenario, "organic fertilizer" production area displaces food production land area.

Examining the Bichel scenario in detail finds that milk and beef production were kept at 1996 levels, mainly to maintain the all-important manure production. (Denmark's beef production comes primarily from its retired dairy cows, so by keeping dairy production high, beef production remains high as well.) In fact, even under the no feed import scenario, the need to maintain manure production results in the continued net export of 2 million tons of milk and 100,000 tons of beef. While beef and dairy product exports remain at near their pre-organic levels, pork and poultry exports are cut by over 90% in the organic scenario.

Maintaining dairy, beef, and manure production levels organically requires a 160% increase in grass forage area. (See Figure 10). Pasture and grass forage areas combined would need to increase more than 50%, consuming nearly half of Denmark's total farmland. (See Figure 11). Legume crop area would need to increase 150%.

All of these increases in feed and forage crop area cut grain crop area by 30% and reduced potato crop area by 70%.

The Bichel Committee estimated the costs of shifting Denmark to 100% organic at between $1.6 billion and $3.7 billion U.S. dollars per year. A comparative figure for the United States for going "all organic" would be $85 billion to $200 billion per year — three to eight times more money than is currently spent by the USDA on all farm programs combined. The committee couldn't narrow

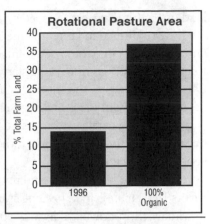

Fig. 10: Amount of farmland devoted to grass and hay in 1996 versus amount needed under 100% organic management.

the potential cost increases any further than this large range because no country has ever tried to grow all its food using only organic methods, so they simply couldn't say what the overall consequences would be — other than that they'd be pretty huge.

This is essentially a microcosm of the consequences of going organic globally, except we really can't afford to cut global food and fiber production by half and there will be 3 billion more mouths to feed by 2050.[6] Not only that, but we're already farming — defined as the totality of the land area in crops, pasture, and rangeland —nearly half of the

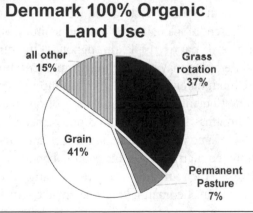

Fig. 11: Projected farmland use under 100% organic management.

---

[6] Thankfully, the World Bank, U.N., and others project that the world's population is expected to peak at between 9 billion and 10 billion by 2050 and then begin to shrink due to already declining birth rates in the developing world and sustained below-replacement birth rates in the developed world.

land on earth not covered in ice or deserts.

If we continued to farm only the 37% of earth's land area currently in farms and rangeland, we would see a huge drop in global food output and half of humanity would go hungry or starve. As the studies show, a significant portion of these costs — in money, land use changes, and lower productivity — are associated with the prohibition on using synthetic nitrogen fertilizer. There is no way for organic farming systems to overcome this inherent limitation because the foundation — indeed the origin —of organic is the prohibition on synthetic nitrogen fertilizer.

Realistically, humanity would not constrain itself to farming just 37% of the earth's land area. As food became scarcer, hungry peasants and societies would inevitably chop down wilderness and farm additional marginal land areas at the expense of nature in efforts to feed themselves and their children.

Organic agriculture is already causing expansion of farmlands into wildlife habitats in less developed countries to satisfy the organic food demands of wealthy consumers in Europe and the United States. In China, some conservationists are already lamenting the encroachment of organic farms into local forests and grasslands in Heilongjiang and Jilin provinces as well as Inner Mongolia.[7] The organic farms are growing foods for export to wealthy Western nations. This shows that even moderate increases in organic food demand will pressure the current system and lead to habitat destruction.

The entire global food and agricultural system is interconnected, and resource demands ripple throughout. Environmental impacts from organic food demands may not be directly apparent, but they are there nonetheless.

Unfortunately, many in the organic movement simply don't realize the inherent organic nitrogen limitation of organic farming and the implications that limit has for humanity and our planet if imposed globally. Worse, many in the organic movement realize these limits and consider that the problem is simply too many people. Instead of abandoning the organic religion or compromising their strict doctrine, they'd rather abandon billions of people.

Fred Kirschenmann, longtime organic farmer and recognized leader in the organic farming movement, writes the following in response to the question "Can organic feed the world.":

> *"Posed this way, the food/population issue appears to be a simple matter of producing enough food and inventing the technologies capable of producing it. I want to argue that production is not the prob-*

---

[7] Reuters (via CNN) http://wireless.cnn.com/pqa/cnn/en/NEWS/SCITECH/nature/5.1.html

lem. The problem is the imbalance of humans relative to the millions of other species with whom we co-evolved." *[Emphasis added.]*

Personally, I'd rather keep all of humanity and all the wildlife, rather than risk losing both to the "organic solution."

Chapter 13:

Biotechnology: Beyond Organic

Organic Believers Say:

"The Organic Consumers Association calls [for a] moratorium on all genetically engineered foods & crops. ..."

Organic Consumers Association

"Citing the adverse impact of genetically modified organisms (GMOs) on organic production, the Organic Trade Association (OTA) is calling for a moratorium on the use of GMOs in all agricultural production. ... At the very minimum, OTA said, there should be mandatory labeling of GMO foods, with the real goal of an outright, worldwide moratorium on GMO use in all agriculture."

Organic Trade Association ($)[1]
Press Release, January 17, 2000

"Tired of waging defensive battles, we've decided to focus on lobbying and passing a mandatory labeling law for genetically engineered (GE) foods in

---

[1] ($) Indicates that the person quoted has a profit motive or other financial interest in promoting organic food.

Congress, similar to the law in effect in the European Union, which has basically driven GE foods off the market."

Organic Bytes #85, June 21, 2006
http://www.organicconsumers.org/bytes/OrganicBytes85.pdf

"Labeling GE foods is the only way to ... drive GE foods and crops from our food system."

Organic Consumers Association
http://www.organicconsumers.org/ge-free.htm

As I've already stated several times in this book, I support organic farmers' right to grow and market their products. Live and let live, or more accurately, farm and let farm. But the organic activist community totally rejects this philosophy. It tries at nearly every turn to take away non-organic farmers' freedom and right to farm the way they choose.

Nowhere is this community's intolerant extremist philosophy more obvious than agricultural biotechnology. Rather than being content with barring their own farmers from growing biotech crops, organic activists would take this technology away from all farmers — organic or not. In addition to advocating bans, their compatriots in the eco-extremist fringe have literally burned down university research buildings where biotech crop research was being conducted in their efforts to stop this technology from being developed.

Why such extreme intolerance of agricultural biotechnology? They claim it is because biotech crops might "contaminate" organic crops and render them unacceptable to organically minded consumers. That perspective is at best selfish. But it is also hypocritical and deliberately unrealistic. If contamination with non-organic materials or inputs were sufficient to render a product unorganic, then fully 25% of organic fruits and vegetables would have to be tossed. They're not. In fact, no testing for unapproved inputs or materials is required or undertaken under any current organic rules in any country in the world.

So what is likely the real motivation behind the intense organic opposition to biotech crops? Competition.

Biotechnology offers a more cost effective way to achieve the lower pesticide use and more eco-friendly farming systems claimed by organic farmers and desired by consumers. In short, biotechnology represents a direct threat to organic agriculture's current monopoly on eco-conscious consumers and the illusions of super-safety.

Consider the following examples of biotechnology's environmental and food safety potential and ask yourself if it really makes sense to ban this technology.

Bt Insect-Resistant Crops

As discussed in Chapter 6, organic farmers have been using sprays of the natural soil-dwelling bacteria *Bacillus thuringiensis* (Bt) for more than 50 years to kill plant-eating caterpillars and other insect pests. This bacteria naturally makes a protein (called an endotoxin) that binds to and creates pores in the insect's intestinal lining. It causes internal bleeding and eventual gut paralysis that leads to the insect's death within a few days. The Bt endotoxin protein is harmless to birds, fish, people, and other mammals.

Bt sprays break down rapidly in sunlight and exposure to air, however, and must be reapplied many times over the course of a growing season. Every application requires more tractor fuel and/or farmer time and also contributes to compaction of the soil. Moreover, the rapid breakdown increases the likelihood that pests will develop resistance to the toxin due to their exposure to a less than lethal dose.

Crop scientists realized that with the tools of genetic engineering, the specific gene for the Bt endotoxin protein could be added to a plant's genome. Plants could then be genetically programmed to produce the endotoxin inside the portions eaten by insect pests. Not only would this reduce the number of pesticide sprays, saving fuel and reducing soil compaction, it would dramatically reduce the risk of pests developing resistance to Bt. Moreover, only those insects eating the crop would be affected.

Biotech Bt crops have been extremely successful. They have reduced pest damage in a number of crops, reduced fuel costs, saved farmers considerable time, and reduced overall pesticide applications by 50% to 75%. In South Africa, small farmers (often women) who have planted Bt corn have seen bigger harvests and less contamination of their corn with natural fungal toxins that can cause cancer and birth defects.

Currently, insect-resistant Bt varieties of cotton, corn, soybeans, and rice are being grown in more than a dozen countries and tens of millions of acres of cropland.

Bt crops are not a magic bullet, however, and farmers must continue to monitor for and deal with other pests that aren't controlled by Bt. For example, research in China has shown that in some years, sucking insects can become the dominant pests because Bt controls plant-eating insects so well. However, Bt cotton now accounts for more than 60% of Chinese cotton acreage and a rapidly growing percentage of acreage in India.

In the U.S., Bt cotton has cut annual insecticide use by more than 3 million pounds per year while increasing annual cotton production by over 360 million pounds through reduced pest damage. Bt cotton farmers continue to use roughly half as much pesticide as conventional cotton farmers. As of 2006, more than 90% of cotton acres in the U.S. are planted to biotech varieties. Bt corn has increased annual U.S. corn production by an estimated 5 million pounds while cutting insecticide use by more than 3.6 million pounds per year.

Herbicide-Tolerant Biotech Crops

The most widely planted biotech crops are herbicide-tolerant varieties, primarily soybeans, corn, and cotton. Put simply, scientists insert genes (usually from soil bacteria) that allow the plants to rapidly deactivate herbicides. This enables farmers to control weeds with one or two sprays of eco-friendly herbicides like glyphosate (most common branded name is Roundup™) rather than controlling weeds through erosion-causing methods such as tillage and plowing (or with less effective and more environmentally harmful herbicides).

Herbicides allow farmers to use "no-tillage" farming systems that cut soil erosion by 65% to 95%. Biotech herbicide-tolerant crops have allowed millions more acres of cropland to be managed with no-till practices than before biotechnology.

Biotechnology is not necessary to develop herbicide-tolerant crops, however, and conventional breeding methods have been used to create several varieties of herbicide-tolerant crops that are now grown around the world. Biotechnology does allow herbicide-tolerant crops to be developed far more rapidly.

No matter which way no-till farming is achieved, it confers significant environmental and long-term sustainability benefits. Not only does it reduce soil erosion, it also reduces fuel use (pulling plows and other tillage implements through the soil takes considerable horsepower) and increases soil organic matter levels. Raising the soil organic matter levels increases soil porosity and water holding capacity (and therefore drought resistance), and encourages earthworm and microbe populations.

No- and low-tillage cropping systems are so beneficial and sustainable that organic farmers have been working to develop their own no-till cropping systems for over a decade. But without any organic-acceptable herbicides, it is proving a difficult task, so organic farmers continue to rely largely upon tillage and plowing for weed control.

Virus-Resistant Crops

Plant viruses can be devastating to a large variety of crops. Until biotechnology, the only tools available to farmers were (a) frequent sprayings of insecticides to kill the insects that spread the virus to the plants, (b) destroying fields when outbreaks occurred, or (c) not planting susceptible crops at all. Biotechnology has now given farmers (and humanity) a far more effective and sustainable solution: virus-resistant crops.

To make virus-resistant crops, scientists insert the gene for a virus's coat protein, conferring immunity to the virus. Before a virus can infect a plant, it must unwrap its genetic material from the shell of coat proteins that protect it. In plants that are engineered to produce the viral coat protein, the viruses are unable to unwrap themselves and this blocks the infection from ever occurring.

This "coat-protein mediated immunity" can be used against nearly all varieties and types of plant viruses and in virtually every type of plant and crop. Already, virus-resistant potatoes, cucumbers, squash, melons, and papaya have been created in this way, and many are now being grown and sold to consumers. Some, however, have been created and approved but are not being grown by farmers because of consumer unease resulting from the anti-biotech fear mongering of organic activists.

The Eco-Potato

Perhaps the best example of a superior and environmentally friendly biotech crop that has been shelved due to organic activism is the NewLeaf-Plus™ Potato, aka the Eco-Potato. Potato crops are pesticide-intensive because potatoes are so susceptible to insects, viruses, and fungi. Organic potatoes usually get about half the yield of non-organic potatoes because these multiple different pests are so difficult to control and so prevalent.

To address nature's onslaught against potatoes, scientists with Monsanto first developed an insect-resistant Bt potato that could ward off the Colorado potato beetle, marketed under the name NewLeaf™ Potato. But growers discovered that when they didn't spray insecticides to control the potato beetles (which were now controlled by the Bt protein), sucking insects quickly spread viruses that also decimated the crop. So the scientists then added biotech virus resistance to the potato variety and marketed it under the name NewLeaf-Plus.

The combined Bt and anti-virus traits were a huge success. Instead of needing to spray insecticides 10 to 15 times per season, farmers could control insects and disease with just one or two sprays of insecticide and a fungicide treatment. Yields increased, pest damage decreased, and insecticide treatments dropped dramatically.

I was at one grower meeting where a pest control scientist and crop consultant showed pictures of pheasant tracks in the middle of a NewLeaf-Plus potato field. She said it was the first time in over 20 years of scouting potato fields for pests that she had seen pheasant tracks in a potato field. The reason for the pheasant's presence was the sudden abundance of pheasant food (insects, etc.) in the fields because they weren't constantly being sprayed with insecticides.

Yet within two years of the release of these potatoes to growers, activists convinced McDonald's and other large potato buyers that consumers would freak out if they found out that their french fries were "genetically engineered." In response, these companies told their growers to stop planting the superior eco-potato out of fear of an activist-led backlash. With no market for the potatoes, the biotech varieties are no longer grown, and farmers are now back to spraying their fields a dozen or more times per season with broad-spectrum insecticides. The losers are the birds, spiders, and other small wildlife.

Fungal Resistance

Scientists can also use biotechnology to create fungus-resistant crops. For example, scientists found a naturally fungus-resistant potato variety in Mexico in the 1950s. As you may recall from history class, a fungus called potato blight caused the Irish Potato Famine that killed millions in Ireland in the 1840s, so this is a serious problem.

Blight and fungal diseases are among the worst potato pests, and farmers must regularly spray fungicides to control them. Organic farmers can successfully grow potatoes only by spraying them with copper sulfate and other toxic, copper-based fungicides that are so eco-unfriendly that the European Union has scheduled a complete ban on their use.

But each time scientists tried to cross the bitter-tasting naturally blight-resistant potato found in Mexico with large, good-tasting varieties, they either didn't get the fungus resistance or got an inedible potato. Fifty years of conventional crossbreeding led nowhere. Then, starting in the late 1990s, scientists from three universities began using biotechnology to engineer the natural blight-resistance genes into modern potato varieties. They succeeded in 2005 with a potato that can ward off every fungal disease they've exposed it to without fungicide applications.

If scientists combined the insect resistance, virus resistance, and blight resistance traits into one variety, potatoes could be grown with 5% to 10% of the pesticide applications necessary in conventional or even organic potato production. Yet organic-led anti-biotech activism has poisoned the consumer market for these incredible breakthroughs. Consumers are convinced that biotech crops, or the companies that supply them, are a threat to the environment and human health.

And that leads us to the last area of biotechnology's incredible transformative power.

Consumer Benefits

Biotechnology has the power to bring unprecedented and massive consumer benefits, including improved nutrition, greater safety, and flavors never before tasted.

- *Biofortification:* Swiss researchers have inserted genes into rice from corn that lead to the production of beta-carotene. Rice is naturally deficient in this key vitamin precursor (beta-carotene is converted in our bodies into Vitamin A). Because rice lacks beta-carotene, poor children in rice-dependent developing countries often suffer from severe Vitamin A deficiency, leading to night blindness and increased susceptibility to lethal diseases such as measles. Through the distribution of biotech "golden rice" to poor farmers in remote areas, the vitamin A deficiency can be alleviated and a vast improvement in public health is made possible without the constant difficulty and expense of supplying vitamin supplements to remote areas. Researchers in several countries are now crossing golden rice with local rice varieties and conducting field trials in anticipation of distribution to farmers in 2007 or 2008. This "biofortification" strategy can be used to increase the nutritional value of any number of food crops with a variety of nutrients.

- *Allergy-free foods:* Scientists have used biotechnology and genetic engineering to remove the allergenic proteins from high-allergy foods such as soy and peanuts. For example, scientists at Alabama A&M University have successfully eliminated a major peanut allergy protein using RNA interference, which stops the allergenic protein from being made in the plant. The highly nutritious peanut is the most allergenic food in the world and causes more than two dozen deaths each year in the U.S. and perhaps hundreds of deaths per year worldwide. Soy is perhaps the second most-common food allergy and here, too, scientists are using biotechnology to alter or eliminate the allergenic proteins and improve soy's food safety.

- *Low-fat foods:* Scientists have created a potato that produces a denser starch, reducing the amount of oil absorbed during deep-frying.

- *Healthier cooking oils:* Scientists have altered oil-seed crops so that they produce healthier oils that are higher in unsaturated fats. Several groups are working on plants that can produce the heart-healthy omega-3 fatty acids normally found in abundance in fish. Not only would this increase the healthfulness of foods containing these oils (such as salad dressings), but biofortified animal feeds could also produce animal proteins and meats that are higher in omega-3s, such as eggs and farmed fish.

- *Healthier animal proteins:* Scientists have cloned transgenic pigs that when fed a normal diet produce three times more omega-3 fats than non-engineered pigs, making them more like fish in their healthy fat content. This means biotechnology has given humanity two routes to producing healthier meat and animal proteins — enhancing the feed or enhancing the animals.

The health benefits to consumers from genetic engineering have only just begun to be realized. So, too, the environmental benefits of biotech crops and animals.

Researchers recently added a gene to pigs for an enzyme called phytase that unlocks the phosphate in feed. Normally, pigs pass large amounts of phosphorus through their digestive tracts unutilized because they lack this enzyme. The unutilized phosphorus represents unnecessary feed costs because even more phosphorus must be added to the pig feed to make up for this inefficiency. It is also an environmental hazard because phosphorus in pig wastes represents a water pollution hazard. By adding the gene for phytase, the researchers enabled the pigs to grow healthily without costly dietary supplements and the phosphorus content of their manure was cut by 75%.

For the future, scientists are already working on crops that will be able to fertilize themselves with nitrogen from the air and produce even more food from less water. Drought resistance is one of the most promising untapped areas of agricultural biotechnology.

Conclusion

Biotechnology has the power to improve just about every aspect of farming and has already done so in major ways. Our food supply will be safer, more environmentally friendly, and healthier because of the power of biotechnology to make fundamental changes at the genetic level. With it, farmers are using far less pesticide and are producing more abundant crops and healthier foods.

This power has only begun to be tapped. Biotechnology is still in its relative infancy, comparable to the bi-plane era of aviation. Yet already biotechnology is transforming the way we view crops and farms. At some point, farms may produce not only food, but also vaccines, medicines, and raw materials for high-value specialty products in ways that are far more eco-friendly than traditional manufacturing methods.

Just why organic farmers and activists are so dead set against agricultural biotechnology given these proven and potential benefits remains a mystery to me. But there is simply no good reason why we should join them in their extremist, anti-technology stance. There is plenty of room for both organic farmers AND biotech farmers to live and farm peaceably on this planet — each group pursuing its own path to a brighter, more livable, healthier, and more eco-friendly future.

Live and let live, in peace, hope, and charity, so that all may be fed, clothed, and well cared for.

Appendix

Spiritual Manuring and Other Organic Voodoo

While no science has ever shown any benefits from Rudolf Steiner's ultra-organic farming techniques or from any of the "biodynamic preparations" he described in his lectures in 1924, a sizable group of farmers and consumers fervently believe that "biodynamic" farming and foods are superior and impart enhanced nutritional qualities to food. In some countries (Austria, Switzerland, New Zealand, etc.), biodynamic foods account for a surprising percentage of the food sold, especially in milk and dairy products. "Biodynamic" foods are certified by a global organization, Demeter, and there is even a research center in Switzerland devoted to studying biodynamic farming techniques.

Steiner's spiritual teachings are the basis for what eventually became the organic movement, and a quick examination shows just how odd (and unscientific) his beliefs really were.

Steiner claimed to know from his spiritual "studies" that the earth contained "forces which come not from the Earth but from the so-called distant planets, the planets beyond the Sun — Mars, Jupiter, and Saturn. That which proceeds from these distant planets influences the life of plants via the silicious and kindred substances into the plant and also into the animal life of the earth. ... The silicious nature opens the plant-being to the wide spaces of the universe and awakens the senses of the plant-being in such a way as to receive from all quarters of the Universe the forces which are molded by these distant planets.

"We must treat the whole agricultural life with the conviction that we need to pour vitality, nay even astrality, in all directions, so as to make it work as a totality. Taking our start from this, another thing will result. Have you ever thought why cows have horns, or why certain animals have antlers? It is a most important question, and what ordinary science tells us of it is a rule one-sided and superficial. Let us then try to answer the question, why do cows have horns? ... The cow has proper horns and hoofs. What happens at the places where the horns grow and the hoofs? A locality is formed which sends the currents inward with more than usual intensity. ... The cow has horns in order to send into itself the astral-ethereal formative powers, which, pressing inward, are meant to penetrate right into the digestive organism. Precisely through the radiation that proceeds from horns and hoofs, much work arises in the digestive organism itself. ... Thus in the horn you have something well adapted, by its inherent nature, to ray back the living and astral properties into the inner life. In the horn, you have something radiating life — nay, even radiating astrality. It is so indeed: If you could crawl about inside the living body of a cow — if you were there inside the belly of the cow — you would smell how the astral life and the living vitality pour inward from the horns. And so it is also with the hoofs."

According to Steiner, manure has special properties as well.

"What is farmyard-manure? It is what entered as outer food into the animal, and was received and assimilated by the organism up to a certain point. It gave occasion for the development of dynamic forces and influences in the organism, but it was not primarily used to enrich the organism with material substance. On the contrary, it was excreted. Nevertheless, it has been inside the organism and has thus been permeated with an astral and ethereal content. In the astral it has been permeated with nitrogen-carrying forces, and in the ethereal with oxygen-carrying forces. The mass that emerges as dung is permeated with all this. ... In the dung, therefore, we have before us something ethereal and astral. For this reason it has a life-giving and also astralising influence upon the soil, and, what is more, in the earth-element itself; not only in the watery; but notably in the earthy element. It has the force to overcome what is inorganic in the earthy element."

Steiner asks, "How can we adapt the soil of the earth, by its special consistency as it were, to densify the cosmic and thereby hold it back more in the root and leaf?

"Therefore, we need to treat our manure not only as I indicated yesterday; we should also subject it to a further treatment. And the point is not merely to add substances to it, with the idea that it needs such and such substances so as to give them to plants. No, the point is that we should add living forces to it. The living forces are far more important for the plant than the mere substance-forces or substances. Though we might gradually get our soil ever so rich in this or that substance, it would still be of no use for plant-growth, unless by a proper manuring process we endowed the plant itself with the power to receive into its body the influences which the soil contains. This is the point."

So how do you add "living forces" to the manure? Steiner says, "We take manure, such as we have available. We stuff it into the horn of a cow and bury the horn a certain depth into the earth — say about 18 in. to 2 ft. 6 in., provided the soil below is not too clayey or too sandy. (We can choose a good soil for the purpose. It should not be too sandy.) You see, by burying the horn with its filling of manure, we preserve in the horn the forces it was accustomed to exert within the cow itself, namely the property of raying back whatever is life-giving and astral. Through the fact that it is outwardly surrounded by the earth, all the radiations that tend to etherealize and astralise are poured into the inner hollow of the horn. And the manure inside the horn is inwardly quickened with these forces, which thus gather up and attract from the surrounding earth all that is ethereal and life-giving. … When it has spent winter in the earth, you take the stuff out of the horn and dilute it with ordinary water — only the water should perhaps be slightly warmed."

Steiner suggests using one hornful of this manure "diluted with about half a pail-full of water" to treat a quarter to a third of an acre of cropland. "You must, however, thoroughly combine the entire content of the horn with the water. That is to say, you must set to work and stir. Stir quickly, at the very edge of the pail, so that a crater is formed reaching very nearly the bottom of the pail, and the entire contents are rapidly rotating. Then quickly reverse direction, so that it now seethes round in the opposite direction. Do this for an hour and you will get a thorough penetration. Think, how little work it involves!"

Steiner calls the sprinkling of this dilute solution on the land "spiritual manuring" and says that farmers who do this "will soon see how great a fertility can result from such measures."

When asked by an audience member if the stirring needed to be done with the hands or if mechanical stirring would suffice, Steiner replied, "There can be no doubt, stirring by hand has quite another significance than mechanical stirring. A mechanist, of course, will not admit it. But you should consider well what a great difference it makes, whether you really stir with your hand or in a mere mechanical fashion. When you stir manually, all the delicate movements of your hand will come into the stirring. Even the feelings you have may then come into it. … With enthusiasm, great effects can be called forth. But if you begin to do it in an indifferent and mechanical fashion, the effects will soon evaporate. It makes a difference whether you do the thing with all that proceeds from the human hand — believe me, very much can issue from the hand — or whether you do it with a machine. By and by, however, it might prove to be great fun — this stirring; and you would no longer dream of a mechanical stirrer even when many cow-horns were needed. Eventually, I can imagine, you will do it on Sundays as an after-dinner entertainment. Simply by having many guests invited and doing it on Sundays, you will get the best results without machines!"

Steiner further advises that a cow's horn should be "as fresh as possible" and can only be used three to four times before it "will no longer work so well." Steiner also suggested that horns from different parts of the world would have different properties. "Possibly, horns from American cattle would have to be made effective in a rather different way. Thus it might prove necessary to tighten the manure rather more in these horns — to make it denser, hammer it more tightly." He concludes, "It is best to take horns from your own district." Why? "There is an exceedingly strong kinship between forces in the cow-horns of a certain district and the forces generally prevailing in that district. The forces of horns from abroad might come into conflict with what is there in the earth of your own country."

Ah, yes, cow horns were apparently nationalist partisans in the 1920s, as were most German intellectuals, including Steiner.

If the horn full of "astralised" manure must be stored for any period of time prior to its use, Steiner says that "you should make a box, upholster it well with a cushion of peat-moss on all sides, and put the cow-horns inside. Then the strong inner concentration will be preserved."

If you have no cow manure, which Steiner says is "undoubtedly best," you could use horse manure. "If you want to treat horse manure in this way, you will probably find that you need to wrap the horn up to some extent in horsehair taken from the horse's mane. You will thus make effective the forces which in the horse — as it has no horns — are situated in the mane."

For another "biodynamic preparation," Steiner suggests using "the same part of the yarrow which is medicinally used, namely the upper part. … Take one or two hollow handfuls of this yarrow-stuff pressed pretty strongly together, and sew it up in the bladder of a stag. Enclose the yarrow substance as best you can in the stag's bladder, and bind it up again. There, then, you have a fairly compact mass of yarrow in the stag's bladder. Now hang it up throughout the summer in a place exposed as far as possible to the sunshine. When autumn comes, take it down again and bury it not very deep in the Earth throughout the winter. So you will have the yarrow flower (it matters not if it be tending already towards fruit) enclosed in the bladder of the stag for a whole year and exposed — partly above the earth, partly below — to those influences to which it is susceptible. You will find that it assumes a peculiar consistency during the winter. In this form you can keep it as long as you wish. Add the substance which you take out of the bladder to a pile of manure — it may even be as big as a house! — and distribute it well. Nay, you need not even do much to distribute it: The radiation itself will do the work. The radiating power is so very strong that if you merely put it in — even if you do not distribute it much — it will influence the whole mass of manure or liquid manure or compost. … We re-endow the manure with the power, so to quicken the earth that the more distant cosmic substances — silicic acid, lead, etc., which come to the earth in homeopathic quantities — are caught up and received."

Why the bladder of the stag, you might ask? According to Steiner, "Here we must gain insight into the whole process that is connected with the bladder. The stag is an animal most intimately related, not so much to the earth but to the earth's environment, i.e., to the Cosmic in the Earth's environment. … Now that which is present in the yarrow is intensely preserved, both in the human and in the animal organism, by the process which takes place between the kidneys and the bladder. Moreover, this process itself is dependent on the substantial nature or consistence of the bladder. Thus, in the bladder of the stag — however thin it is in substance — we have the necessary forces. Unlike the former instance (the cow which is quite different), these forces are not connected with the interior. The bladder of the stag is connected rather with the forces of the Cosmos. Nay, it is almost an image of the Cosmos. We thereby give the yarrow the power quite essentially to enhance the forces it already possesses, to combine the sulphur with the other substances. In this yarrow treatment we have an absolutely fundamental method of improving the manure, while all the time we remain within the realm of living things. We never go out of the living realm into that of inorganic chemistry. This is important to observe.

"If we wish to get hold of the calcium influences ... this plant is chamomile. ... Pick the beautiful delicate little yellow-white heads of the flowers ... but now, instead of putting them in a bladder, stuff them into bovine intestines. You will not need very much. Here again, it is a charming operation. Instead of using these intestinal tubes as they are commonly used for making sausages, make them into another kind of sausage — fill them with the stuffing which you thus prepare from the chamomile flower. This preparation, once more, need only be rightly exposed to the influences of nature."

To combat plant diseases, Steiner suggests burying oak bark in an animal skull. "We collect oak-bark, such as we can get. We do not need much — no more than can easily be obtained. We collect it and chop it up a little, till it has a crumb-like consistency. Then we take a skull — the skull of any of our domestic animals will do, it makes little or no difference. We put the chopped-up oak-bark in the skull, close it up again as well as possible with bony material, and lower it into the earth, but not too deep. We cover it with peat-moss, and then introduce some kind of channel or water-pipe so as to let as much rain-water as possible flow into the place. ... This, once again, must hibernate ... it must pass through autumn and winter in this way. What you add to your manuring matter from the resulting mass will lend it the forces, prophylactically, to combat or to arrest any harmful plant diseases."

Steiner claims that adding composted stinging nettle to manure is important too. "The general effect will be such that the manure becomes inwardly sensitive — truly sensitive and sentient, we might almost say intelligent. ... This "condiment" will make the manure intelligent, nay, you will give it the faculty to make the earth itself intelligent — the earth into which the manure is worked. ... It is like a permeation of the soil with reason and intelligence, which you can bring about by this addition of [chamomile]."

If you have a problem with mice on your farm, Steiner suggests sprinkling burnt mouse skin. "You catch a young mouse and skin it, so as to get the skin. ... But you must obtain this skin of the field-mouse at a time when Venus is in the sign of Scorpio. ... At the time when Venus is in Scorpio, you obtain the skin of the mouse and burn it. Carefully collect the ash and the other constituents that remain over from the burning. It will not be much, but if you have a number of mice, it is enough. You can easily get enough. ... And there remains, in what is thus destroyed by the fire, the corresponding negative force as against the reproductive power of the field-mouse. Take the pepper you get in this way, and sprinkle it over your fields. … Provided it has been led through the fire at the high conjunction of Venus and Scorpio, you fill find this an excellent remedy. Henceforth, your mice will avoid the field. … So we begin really to reckon with the influences of the stars without becoming superstitious in the least. Many things afterwards became mere superstition, which were originally knowledge. You cannot warm-up the old superstitions. You must make a fresh start with genuine knowledge. This knowledge, however, must be gained in a spiritual way — not through the mere physical world-of-the-senses."